County Council

Libraries, books and more . . .

Millom 6/12 0 6 AUG 2013 1 6 NOV 2013		

Please return/renew this item by the last due date.
Library items may be renewed by phone on
030 33 33 1234 (24 hours) or via our website
www.cumbria.gov.uk/libraries

Cumbria Libraries
CLIC
Interactive Catalogue

Ask for a CLIC password

THE
talkSPORT
100 GREATEST
BRITISH SPORTING
LEGENDS

THE talkSPORT
100 GREATEST
BRITISH SPORTING
LEGENDS

BILL BORROWS with **TOM BAILEY**

SIMON &
SCHUSTER

London · New York · Sydney · Toronto · New Delhi

A CBS COMPANY

First published in Great Britain in 2011
by Simon & Schuster UK Ltd
A CBS COMPANY

Copyright © 2011 by Bill Borrows and Tom Bailey

Copyright © 2011 by talkSPORT

1 3 5 7 9 10 8 6 4 2

Simon & Schuster UK Ltd
1st Floor
222 Gray's Inn Road
London
WC1X 8HB

www.simonandschuster.co.uk

Simon & Schuster Australia, Sydney
Simon & Schuster India, New Delhi

A CIP catalogue copy for this book is available
from the British Library.

ISBN: 978-0-85720-093-8

Typeset and designed by Craig Stevens
and Julian Flanders

Printed and bound in Great Britain
by Butler Tanner & Dennis Ltd, Frome

Contents

FOR ELIZABETH LOUISE STEPHENSON

ACKNOWLEDGEMENTS
Keith Arthur, Eric and Judy Bailey, Alan Brazil, Adam Bullock,
Ian Chapman, Stan Collymore, Jonathan Conway @ MCA Associates,
Ian Danter, Moz Dee, Adrian Durham, Clint Emmins, Julian Flanders,
Andy Goldstein, Darren Gough, Andy Gray, Paul Hawksbee, Ronnie Irani,
Andy Jacobs, Danny Kelly, Richard Keys, John Mahood, Ian Marshall,
Mick Quinn, Mark Saggers, Rory Scarfe, Elizabeth Stephenson,
Craig Stevens, Scott Taunton, Lauren Webster.

Introduction

An Englishman, Scotsman and Irishman walk into a pub, and the Welshman behind the bar goes 'What is this? Some kind of joke.' But of course it isn't, and within five minutes they are talking and arguing about sport. It is, after all, the *lingua franca* of the British male.

Now let's get something straight from the start. This is a list of post-war British sporting 'legends', and nobody is going to come up with the same line-up that we have put together at talkSPORT Towers. Your response to the choices in this book will be partly down to your age, allegiance (in the case of football, in particular), nationality and how much you know about sport.

The first three, I can take. If you know nothing about sport, you have just picked up the wrong book.

This book was inspired by the tired, frustrating and inaccurate use by commentators and pundits of the term 'legend'. And fans are as guilty. It seems that everyone is a 'legend' these days. Last-minute goal in a derby match? – 'legend'. Bowl out an Aussie? – 'legend' (and probably an OBE down the line). Captain of your country once? – 'legend'.

This book is our attempt to put that right, and to define what it really takes to become a true 'legend'.

In terms of football, there are certain club 'legends' that have not made the cut – Steve Bull at Wolves, Norman Whiteside at Manchester United or Malcolm Macdonald at Newcastle United all spring to mind. There are many more – every club has at least one. We wanted our 'legends' to be those sportspeople whose achievements have received or deserve wider recognition than that.

The ubiquitous presence of the term in sport, and indeed in everyday life (there is now even a phone handset called 'Legend'), devalues the currency. It is a basis for judgment. Definitions vary but, for the purposes of this book, a 'legend' is defined as a sportsman or woman who not only transcends or has transcended their sport, and/or also has stories about them worth telling. And re-telling. We have also tried to cover a broader range of sports than just football, cricket and rugby – hence some notable omissions.

The people in our list became a 'legend' sometimes through one life-changing and astounding performance (for example, Archie Gemmill or Sir Geoff Hurst[*]), or by consistent excellence at the top level (such as Phil 'The Power' Taylor or Tony McCoy), or by providing the source for endless pub conversations about

[*] We have left out all the 'Sirs' and 'Dames' at the top of the profile pages, but there are 17 of them, so see if you can spot them all. A complete list (at the time of going to press) appears in one of the appendices at the back of the book.

their abilities and their antics (George Best and Alex Higgins perhaps). Many on our list tick all the boxes: Sir Ian Botham take a bow.

For that reason, every 'legend' in this book is given a rating not just for their sporting achievements but also for their hell-raising capabilities, both on and off the pitch. That said, ordering the 'legends' from a hundred down to one is not a purely mathematical exercise – the general rule of thumb is that these sports stars will be spoken about for many years to come. It's not just about what you won, it's how you won it and lived your life that counts, too.

As time passes, there are bound to be movements and shifts in this list, as new 'legends' arrive on the scene to replace those that appear in this inaugural top 100. Will Eric Bristow be there in ten years? Maybe not. Will Kevin Keegan? Almost certainly. Will Wayne Rooney still be at number 32? He could go up or down or drop off altogether as his career progresses. Will Paula Radcliffe be in the top 20? Let's see what happens in the 2012 Olympics.

To become a 'legend' one needs to have a kind of sporting half-life, an ability still to provoke debate and passion in the pub, even when one's achievements have long since disappeared into history. Think about the late Sir Henry Cooper – he became a 'national treasure' and merits inclusion in this book. People will still be talking about his 1963 fight with Muhammad Ali long after the centenary of the bout.

Selecting the candidates, and putting them in order, has been an enjoyable task, but also an incredibly demanding one. How do you compare and rate angler Bob Nudd with Paul Gascoigne, for example?

I am well aware that there are notable omissions that some may feel ought to have made the cut. Among those who just fell short is football manager Terry Venables, but can anyone say he should get in ahead of the other managers selected here?

Olympians Sir Chris Hoy and Dame Kelly Holmes miss out, too. Footballing mavericks Rodney Marsh and the other cult heroes of the 1970s were brilliant to watch, but their antics fell a long way short of Robin Friday's (and I don't think any of them featured on the front of a Super Furry Animals single).

Kauto Star, John Conteh, Tessa Sanderson and Fatima Whitbread, Willie John McBride, Nobby Stiles and many, many others that people will feel passionate about all failed to make the list. But then, who would you leave out to fit them in? That's the debate.

We thought it only fair to exclude any of the 'legends' that regularly grace the airwaves from talkSPORT Towers to avoid accusations of favouritism, but perhaps the two most surprising people not to make the list will, for many readers, be Don Revie, who built the extraordinary Leeds United team of the 1960s and early 1970s, and World Cup-winning rugby union captain Martin Johnson.

Undoubtedly an uber-legend in Leeds, Revie missed inclusion because of the way his team won things (or, more usually, just failed to) and the nature of his departure from the England job. Johnson was unlucky. Without a doubt, a leader on and off the pitch and one of the greatest lock forwards to grace the game but, if you don't follow rugby, have you heard any great stories about him?

As in those instances, this book is necessarily subjective and will provoke urgent disagreement, but isn't that one of the major reasons why we love sport? And if you disagree, you are wrong. BILL BORROWS

Geoff CAPES

BORN **23 AUGUST 1949**

Britain's greatest shot-putter and strongman could tear a phonebook in half and bend a metal bar with his bare hands.

It was the last time Capes put unleaded petrol in his flat-bed truck.

Budgerigar breeder Geoffrey Lewis Capes was the seventh of nine children. A gifted competitor from an early age, he joined Holbeach Athletic Club and competed in shot put, cross-country and – surprisingly – the 200m sprint, clocking 23.7 seconds.

In 1970 he joined the police force, despite a blossoming athletics career. That year he competed in the Commonwealth Games, finishing fourth in the shot. However, Capes had set his sights higher and his pursuit of Olympic gold began in Munich in 1972.

'There's only one prize worth talking

attention to the World's Strongest Man. Designed as a TV spectacle, it was nonetheless a gruelling, muscle-ripping test of brute force. Capes won it in 1983 and 1985, achieving worldwide fame in the process. He also found time for victory in six World Highland Games and set a string of Guinness World Records.

Given his diet, it's a mystery Capes had time to do anything: breakfast was three pints of milk, cereal, half a loaf, six eggs, half a pound of bacon, mushrooms, tomatoes and a can of beans; lunch was a 2lb steak, a pound

Capes never achieved the ultimate prize, but it's fair to say he's forgotten more about shot-putting than most garlanded Olympians will ever know.

TOM BAILEY

 AD NAUSEAM

Released at the height of his fame in 1985, the computer game *Geoff Capes Strongman* allowed players to emulate 'Big Shot's' achievements in truck pulling and tug-of-war.

> 'I used to think I was Tarzan, I used to read the comics like *Rover*, *Hotspur* and *Wizard*, and the stories of "Tough of the Track", "Morgan the Mighty" and "Wilson the Wonder Athlete".'
>
> Capes reveals his early inspirations.

about,' he said. The 21-year-old Capes didn't make it past qualifying, but gold at the 1974 and 1978 Commonwealth Games, plus European Indoor titles in 1974 and 1976 established him as world-class shot specialist.

In 1980, Capes smashed the British record with a throw of 71ft 3.5in, easily eclipsing anything his Olympic rivals had thrown that year. He was hot favourite but, under political pressure from Margaret Thatcher, who wanted British athletes to boycott Moscow, once again failed to produce, finishing fifth.

Numb with disappointment, Capes turned professional and switched his

of potatoes, three vegetables and a milk pudding; teatime would amount to a can of tuna; and supper a pound of cheese. As a midnight snack, he ate the fridge itself.

 HELL RAISING 2

 **SPORTING ACHIEVEMENTS** 6

BEFORE HE WAS FAMOUS
Capes honed his explosive physical power working up to eight hours a day as an agricultural labourer, and was capable of loading 20 tons of potatoes in 20 minutes.

 THE MOMENT HE BECAME A LEGEND
Winning gold at the 1974 Commonwealth Games in Christchurch with a throw of 69ft, setting a Commonwealth record.

99

Chris EUBANK

BORN **8 AUGUST 1966**

and Nigel BENN

BORN **22 JANUARY 1964**

A pair of opposites who definitely didn't attract but produced two of the most compelling and brutal grudge matches in British boxing history.

Both men were pugnacious fighters who came from troubled backgrounds and spoke with a lithp, but that's where the similarities ended…

Nigel Benn was anger incarnate, with an insatiable appetite for destruction. Conveniently enough, he earned the name The Dark Destroyer after sparking out his first

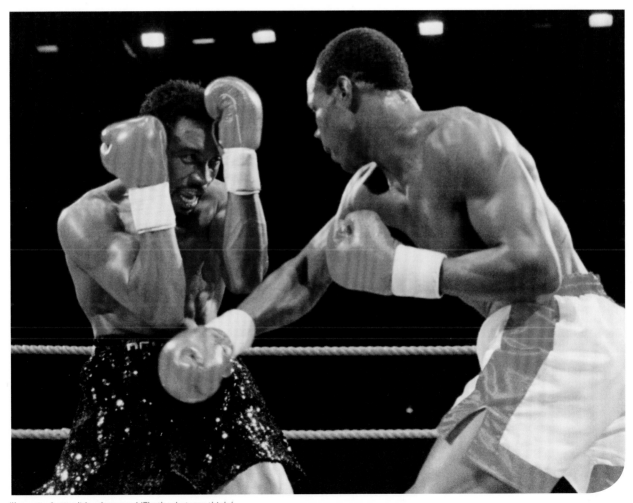

'I've got a better lithp than you.' 'Thath what you think.'

Chris EUBANK and Nigel BENN 99

'The British press hate a winner who's British. They don't like any British man to have balls as big as a cow like I have.'
Benn believing the media have a problem with his nationality and his unfeasibly large testicles.

22 professional opponents. Chris Eubank was an eccentric showman who modelled himself on the most unlikely of English country gentlemen and modestly called himself Simply The Best.

Their two worlds first collided to combustible effect in 1990 when Eubank challenged Benn for his WBO World Middleweight title (see picture p11). The fight was an all-time classic, but the Queensbury Rules seemed to go out the window. Benn's entourage sabotaged Eubank's entrance by silencing Tina Turner in mid-song, before the famous stare-out that captured Eubank's calm looking into the eye of Benn's storm.

'Savage…he was strong enough to kill me and I believe he desired to.'
Eubank after surviving his first fight with Benn.

Benn came out like a caged tiger on crack and spilt first claret by forcing Eubank to bite his tongue – not something the opinionated boxer has often been accustomed to doing. Eubank wound up Benn by posing and preening between rounds, while Benn answered by seeming to catch him below the belt and twice flooring his nemesis. Eubank was eventually crowned champion after cornering Benn with a flurry of blows before the referee put an end to the mayhem with seconds to spare in the ninth round.

It was three years before the pair resumed their feud, this time fighting for their respective World

Super Middleweight titles under the guidance of the electric-haired Don King. The bout was beamed to a worldwide audience of half a billion people. The sequel wasn't as ferocious: it was tenser, closer and a lot less like a bar-room brawl – until the final round when both boxers knew they had to do something to ensure a win. In the end, the judges settled for a draw – a decision Benn still refutes.

The two lords of the ring are now retired after sharing parallel careers tinged with tragedy. Eubank is the self-appointed Lord of the Manor of Brighton and still speaks in an affected upper-class accent while wearing jodhpurs sans horse. Benn has turned the tables, first as a celebrity DJ and now as an ordained minister – although it would take a brave man to count on him turning the other cheek if it came to a tear-up. RICHARD ARROWSMITH

 AD NAUSEAM
In 2000, Eubank endorsed coffee brand Nescafe with the immortal words 'Thimply the Betht'.

CHRIS EUBANK

 HELL **7** RAISING    SPORTING **8** ACHIEVEMENTS

NIGEL BENN

 HELL **8** RAISING    SPORTING **7** ACHIEVEMENTS

BEFORE HE WAS FAMOUS
Eubank was something of a problem child, getting suspended from school 18 times in one year before eventually getting expelled. He was taken into care and then lived on the streets before his father took him to New York where he first started boxing.

BEFORE HE WAS FAMOUS
Benn was also a young delinquent, who went off the rails after the death of his beloved older brother. It took the army to instil some direction in his life and that's where he started boxing – he was never beaten in an army bout.

 THE MOMENT THEY BECAME LEGENDS
The second the first bell rang for their fight in 1990 – Eubank actually ran out sideways before turning and striking Benn with a right cross, hoping for a surprise knockout – that would eventually come to define both of their careers.

98

Allan WELLS

BORN **3 MAY 1952**

Flying Scotsman who took up the 100m when most sprinters are hanging up their spikes – and claimed Olympic gold.

As Allan Wells waited, poised in his starting blocks for the crack of the pistol, he may have had time to reflect on the sheer unlikelihood of his being in Moscow at all, never mind having a chance of 100m Olympic gold.

As a youngster in Edinburgh, Wells had opted to specialise in the long jump and triple jump. Only at 24 did he make the switch to the track, surprising everyone with his lightning progress. Two years after quitting the sandpit, he gathered an armful of medals at the 1978

Imagine his disappointment when he discovered it had been a false start?

'If, at any time, I had thought that by boycotting the Olympics one child was not going to be killed, then I wouldn't have hesitated in staying behind.'
Wells assesses his presence in Moscow.

Commonwealth Games – gold in the 200m and 4 x 100m hurdles, and silver in the 100m. Further medals followed in the 1979 European Cup, making Wells a spiked shoe-in for the 1980 Moscow Olympics... until the Soviet tanks started to trundle into Afghanistan.

The USA immediately announced they would be boycotting the games. Margaret Thatcher wanted to back the US stance, and Wells received six letters from Downing Street, the last of which 'included a picture of a young girl sprawled dead on the ground with a doll lying six inches from the tips of her fingers.' That was the moment he decided to go.

Unfortunately, two weeks before the games, Wells woke up in agony to find that he was unable to move. Intensive treatment eased the pain of the slipped disc sufficiently for him to run, but his meticulous training schedule lay in ruins. Then, when he finally reached the USSR, Wells

discovered that starting blocks – something he'd never even learned to use – were compulsory.

Not surprisingly, Wells got off to a slow start in the final. It took him 60m to draw level with Cuban joint-favourite Silvio Leonard. After a nerve-jangling wait while the race was replayed on the giant screen, Wells saw himself finish inches ahead of Leonard (see picture left) and performed a joyous pirouette. He was the first Briton to win the 100m since Harold Abrahams in the 1924 Paris Olympics.

Two weeks after Moscow, Wells raced the top Americans Mel Lattany and Stanley Floyd in West Germany – and shocked the world by beating them both. To his credit, Lattany told the Scot: 'Allan, you would have been the Olympic champion no matter who you ran against in Moscow.' GARY SILKE

 AD NAUSEAM
Not actually an advert, but he did appear in the video for Belle and Sebastian's song 'I'm A Cuckoo'.

 HELL RAISING

 **SPORTING ACHIEVEMENTS**

BEFORE HE WAS FAMOUS
Worked as a marine engineer, quitting the day job six months before Moscow to concentrate on his training.

 THE MOMENT HE BECAME A LEGEND
The extreme lean at the finish line that gave Wells the precious inches needed for gold in Moscow.

Eddie 'The Eagle' EDWARDS

BORN **5 DECEMBER 1963**

Is it a bird? Is it a plane? No, it's a bespectacled Cheltenham plasterer! Raise your glasses to the ultimate British underdog…

Edwards smashes the British ski-jump record with an incredible leap of 3ft 7in.

As a boy, Michael Edwards dreamt of being a movie stuntman. However, a trip to the local snowdome aged 13 soon opened his eyes to opportunities for risking life and limb away from the big screen…

Young Michael proved a capable downhiller (nearly making the British Olympic team in 1984), but his real passion was for jumping and such was his commitment, he blew every penny he had on a training trip to Finland. During his stay, he scavenged his dinner from dustbins and lived

last in both, narrowly avoiding severe physical distress in the process. However, his hapless underdog charm won the crowd over, and they chanted his name continuously throughout the tournament.

The Olympic bigwigs felt he was making a mockery of the sport, but the people had spoken. Eddie 'The Eagle' became an overnight sensation. He had come to Calgary with little more than a £7,000 debt to his name. Within a week of his first jump, Eddie had set a British Olympic record (73.5m),

As failures go, Eddie 'The Eagle' Edwards was a roaring success. TOM ELLEN

> 'When I went bankrupt, I thought, "God, I should have spent it all on sex, drugs and rock 'n' roll." At least then I could have lost it but had a good time!'
> Edwards rues his missed opportunities.

rent-free in a mental hospital. In 1988 Edwards' bid to be the first man to represent Britain in the Olympic ski jump was accepted.

Edwards arrived in Calgary for the '88 Winter Games gloriously ill-equipped and under-funded. The Italian team had to lend him a helmet, and he borrowed his skis from the Austrians. With inch-thick Coke-bottle glasses and a chin upon which you could hang a coat, he looked more like a *Spitting Image* character than an all-conquering Olympian.

But, more than anything, Eddie was bad. In fact, scratch that: he was *bloody awful*. He entered two events – the 70m and 90m Hills – and finished

been interviewed by Johnny Carson and trousered a cool 87 grand. To this day, however, his name remains synonymous with underdog spirit, and there is even a film based on his life due to start shooting next year.

 AD NAUSEAM

Swapping woeful one-liners with a CGI hound in a recent Churchill car insurance ad was certainly not The Eagle's finest hour…

 **HELL RAISING** 2 / **SPORTING ACHIEVEMENTS** 1

THE MOMENT HE BECAME A LEGEND
When the Olympic President gave Eddie a personal nod in his closing speech at Calgary '88, claiming: 'Some competitors have won gold and broken records… One has flown like an eagle.'

96

Clive WOODWARD

BORN **6 JANUARY 1956**

Modernising, bald-topped boffin who guided England to Rugby World Cup glory in 2003, before spoiling it on the 2005 British Lions tour.

Very few men – or indeed women – will appear in this tome on the back of their exploits in balding middle age, but Woodward is one such animal.

A wiry centre who amassed 21 caps for England, the now 55-year-old laid the foundations for his eventual journey into folklore with a five-year spell in

And this, England football fans, is what a World Cup celebration looks like.

Australia. Woodward's experience of the southern hemisphere's more professional approach in an amateur era – and his astute mind – enabled him to make his 1990 return to English shores one of the most significant events behind the World Cup win of 2003.

Why? Woodward may have returned to coach at lowly Henley, but the mentality he brought with him – one advocating the merits of psychology, nutrition and technology to sporting preparation – were to revolutionise the national team he was to inherit.

And yet it very nearly never was. Woodward took the reins of the England team after Jack Rowell's retirement in 1997, but he almost hung a noose around his own neck with the insistence that he be judged solely on England's showing at the

'Many people in sport are scared of change. I'm not scared of change – I like it.'
Woodward looks to move on.

1999 Rugby World Cup. A dismal campaign ended against South Africa in the quarter-finals, but Woodward survived – and the rest is history.

Despite a succession of Grand Slam near-misses in the Five and then Six Nations, the team, so inspirationally led by Martin Johnson, and featuring giants such as Lawrence Dallaglio, Will Greenwood and, of course, Jonny Wilkinson (cf p62-3), cantered to a Grand Slam in early 2003 before, later that year, beating Australia in their own back yard to win a first World Cup.

Woodward received much of the credit and was knighted within months, but the glory was soon to fade. As the World Cup-winning side slowly disbanded, so England's results deteriorated; and what Woodward was to see as the crowning glory of his coaching career – leading the Lions on their 2005 tour of New Zealand – fell apart in the face of dreadful results.

But Sir Clive will always be the man who coached England to that historic World Cup victory – and, despite a brief and unsuccessful flirtation with football, Woodward has rebuilt his reputation as director of elite performance at the British Olympic Association. TONY HODSON

 **AD NAUSEAM**

Woodward's appearance in Carlsberg's 'best team talk in the world' advert ahead of 2010's World Cup may appeal only to those with fairly selective memories.

BEFORE HE WAS FAMOUS
As a student at HMS *Conway* Naval School, Woodward played rugby alongside future Conservative Party leader Iain Duncan Smith – one assumes they didn't form the polish-topped duo they so emphatically would today.

 THE MOMENT HE BECAME A LEGEND
When Martin Johnson lifted the Webb Ellis Trophy in 2003 in Australia after that dramatic Rugby World Cup final.

 HELL RAISING 1

SPORTING ACHIEVEMENTS 8

Sandy LYLE

BORN **9 FEBRUARY 1958**

Other than Sir Nick Faldo, only two British golfers since the War have won two Major championships. Sandy Lyle is one of them.

Sandy Lyle set one of the more difficult spot the ball competitions.

The late 1950s were a boom time for European golf. Not because of what was happening on the course, but because of what was happening in the bedrooms: Europe started to breed golfers.

During the 1980s, Sandy Lyle, Nick Faldo (cf p133-5), Seve Ballesteros, Bernhard Langer and Ian Woosnam were spanking the Yanks – proving that we could be every bit as ruthless. All were born in 1957 or 1958; all were Major winners.

Although Ballesteros and Faldo both won more big titles, it's acknowledged that at the top of his game, Lyle could leave the lot for dust. Ballesteros

'Never played there.'

In response to a media question about his thoughts on the then little-known amateur, Tiger Woods.

described Lyle as: 'The greatest God-given talent in history,' before adding: 'If everyone in the world was playing their best, Sandy would win and I'd come second.'

At the height of his powers, his golf swing was a thing of beauty. He should have won more Majors, but maybe his languid, self-effacing nature was his undoing. If he lacked anything, it was the killer instinct.

Having captured our own Open Championship in 1985, three years later Lyle etched his name in history by becoming the first Brit to win the US Masters, and it was the way he did it that was so special.

Leading by two with nine holes to play, he saw Mark Calcavecchia draw level with him until Lyle had just one to play. Needing a birdie to win, all hope seemed lost when his drive found the fairway bunker, 160 yards from the green. Unable even to see the flag, Lyle aimed instead at a cloud and hit a shot that he would not have been able to better had he kept trying until now (see picture left). Even so, he still had 18ft to go, but, pumped up by what he'd just done, he never looked like missing. SIMON CANEY

AD NAUSEAM

Never one to really 'get sponsorship', Lyle famously once thanked 'the Chinese' in a victory speech, as confused representatives of Japanese sponsors Suntory looked on.

BEFORE HE WAS FAMOUS
Before he was famous, he was waiting to be famous. He took up golf aged three and represented Scotland at schoolboy level, quickly getting a reputation as the brightest talent of his generation.

THE MOMENT HE BECAME A LEGEND
He already had one Major to his name when he stepped into a fairway bunker at the 72nd hole of the 1988 US Masters. His shot was so jaw-droppingly good that a whole generation packed up football and took up golf.

 HELL **4** RAISING

 SPORTING **7** ACHIEVEMENTS

talkSPORT LEGENDS

Frank BRUNO

BORN **16 NOVEMBER 1961**

The heavyweight champ who rocked Tyson and became the King of Panto – despite struggling with manic depression.

When Frank Bruno faced Mike Tyson for the second time, in 1996, he approached the executioner's block to collect what he later termed his 'pension'.

Back in the UK, chants of 'Broo-no, Broo-no!' rang out from wine bars, working-men's clubs and old ladies' nursing homes. Barrister or bin man, the British public adored Big Frank. Three rounds later and he was finished.

What the old ladies didn't appreciate was that, had Bruno not taken up the sport, he might have been out mugging them. Frustrated by his lack of academic success and the plight of his cancer-stricken father, he fell in with the wrong crowd.

At a school for 'problem children', Bruno surprised everyone by sculpting himself into a promising athlete and leaving the establishment as head boy.

The young man from South London immediately made an impact on the boxing scene. His repartee with BBC boxing commentator Harry Carpenter, usually punctuated with booming laughter and his rhetorical catchphrase, nurtured public affection.

But it was Britain's innate tendency to back the underdog that played a greater part in Bruno's popularity.

'Nah, I'm not that brave or clever. I wouldn't know how to tie a rope, know what I mean?'
On being asked if he had been suicidal.

Bruno took Tyson eight rounds. Shame it took him two fights to do it.

Despite leaving 38 of his opponents with stars in their eyes, it was his soap operatic struggles to win the world title that endeared him to all.

Often he would snatch defeat from the jaws of victory – leading on points against both an ageing Tim Witherspoon and a young Lennox Lewis before running out of steam.

But, good things come to those who wait. And, in front of a home crowd at Wembley in 1995, Bruno finally became the WBC World Heavyweight champion at the fourth time of asking – beating Oliver McCall. Bruno was so impressed, he bought the ring – and sometimes slept in it after the fight. Sadly, he suffered a rude awakening at the iron hands of Mike Tyson a year later – in what would be his first defence and final bout as a professional boxer.

After boxing, the breakdown of his marriage and death of his trainer led to him being sectioned and diagnosed with bipolar disorder in 2003. He's since recovered and is now back asking for more punishment, although this time it's usually from pantomime audiences. Let's be Frank, whether he's winning, losing or wearing tights, we all still love Bruno... know what I mean 'Arry? RA

 AD NAUSEAM

Harry Carpenter asks how to get on the wrong side of Frank Bruno, before serving him steak and chips sans Britain's favourite brown sauce. 'Frankly, I'm not HP' is Bruno's table beating response.

HELL **7** RAISING   SPORTING **7** ACHIEVEMENTS

BEFORE HE WAS FAMOUS
He was expelled from school for hitting a teacher at the tender age of 11 and started smoking dope at the age of 12.

 THE MOMENT HE BECAME A LEGEND
When a massive left hook rocked Tyson in their 1989 world title bout. It wasn't to be and the fight was stopped in the fifth.

Joe CALZAGHE

BORN **23 MARCH 1972**

Unloved Welsh southpaw proved he was no ordinary Joe by never being beaten.

Boxing isn't a sport usually associated with unblemished records. Even the greatest fighters in history – Muhammad Ali, Sugar Ray Robinson, Joe Louis and Roberto Duran – attended the occasional opening of a can of whup ass. Joe Calzaghe was the exception.

His professional record reads 46 wins and 0 losses – making him Britain's only undefeated world champion. He reigned for a decade, dominating his weight division with a flurry of fists and a cast-iron jaw forged in the Welsh valleys.

he would go on to successfully defend an incredible 20 times.

With such a stellar record, Calzaghe should have been a household name. Unfortunately it was not to be. The public thought he was a show-off; the critics thought he'd fought too many 'bums'.

Calzaghe finally swayed popular opinion late in his career by beating the highly rated Jeff Lacy to win the IBF Super Middleweight title. He followed this with his greatest victory, defeating tattooed Danish viking

thrashed the remnants of Roy Jones Jr. Finally, Calzaghe was officially The Pride of Wales. RA

 **AD NAUSEAM**

Calzaghe thrashes his son, Joe Jr, at the controls of Nintendo Wii's boxing game. *Nintendo – Punch Out!*

 HELL RAISING 7

SPORTING ACHIEVEMENTS 10

'When I was fourteen I told my careers adviser that I was going to be a world champion boxer. Of course she laughed.'

What she probably didn't know was that Calzaghe was already fighting for ABA titles.

Ah, the valleys. In fact, Calzaghe's Sardinian father Enzo had not intended to settle in Wales. But, on a trip to England, he ended up in a Wimpy in Cardiff, whereupon he was served by an attractive waitress named Jackie.

'My father was a cocky, long-haired musician, a song writer,' explains Calzaghe Jr. 'He upset my mum. He said, "I want this, I want that." Two weeks later they married.' Clearly, he didn't like to hang around. So, having watched his nine-year-old son punching the sofa cushions, Calzaghe Sr introduced him to a boxing gym.

After tearing up the amateurs, Calzaghe won his first world title by silencing Chris Eubank (cf p11-12) – no mean feat in itself – to win the WBO Super Middleweight belt that

Mikkel Kessler to unify the WBO, WBA, WBC titles and become *Ring* magazine's best pound-for-pound boxer.

Newly confident, Calzaghe then moved up to the light heavyweight division, taking on two American greats. He beat Bernard Hopkins – despite tasting canvas in the first round – and then, in his last fight, he

Calzaghe seems unperturbed that a big yellow glove is about to land in the middle of his face.

BEFORE HE WAS FAMOUS

His mum made him work in a cake factory for three days when he was 17. One suspects it may have cramped his style...

 THE MOMENT HE BECAME A LEGEND

Jeff Lacy was the overwhelming favourite before they contested the IBF Super Middleweight title in 2006. But Calzaghe dominated the fight, with British fans chanting 'Easy, Easy' during the last three rounds.

92

Shaun EDWARDS

BORN **18 OCTOBER 1966**

The rugby league great who turned into a rugby union coaching phenomenon, not to mention low-level celebrity paramour.

For anyone who grew up watching sport in the late 1980s, there were three things you could pretty much bet the mortgage on: one, that Liverpool would be league champions; two, that Steve Davis (cf p49-50) would be the world snooker champion; and three, that Wigan would win rugby league's Challenge Cup.

The Wigan team that emerged victorious from eight consecutive Wembley finals between 1988 and 1995 remains one of the genuinely iconic post-war sporting sides. Ellery Hanley, Martin 'Chariots' Offiah, Phil Clarke, Denis Betts, Jason Robinson (cf p25), Gary Connolly... the list of league legends who played a part in some of those wins could go on.

'The safest thing would have been to stay in rugby league... but sometimes you have to chase the adventure.'
Edwards shows his ambition.

But at the heart of it all, the only man to appear in all eight, the creative spark in the cherry and white shirt, was Shaun Edwards.

Born not far from the club's old Central Park ground in Wigan, Edwards had a face that belonged to the less glamorous days before Super League – but on the pitch he was all class, allying his undoubted northern grit to pace, skill and an unrivalled understanding of the game.

His commitment to developing both himself and the players around him is one that served him well after leaving Wigan in 1997, and rugby league itself three years later.

As a relentlessly determined and innovative rugby union coach, Edwards has won three Premiership titles and two Heineken Cups with Wasps, and a Six Nations Grand Slam with Wales in 2008. Mention 'Blitz Defence' to any rugby fan, and they will give you his name.

Off the pitch Edwards used his charms (and occasionally fearsome intensity) to woo former M People warbler Heather Small. Edwards and Ms Small may no longer be an item, but they remain one of the more interesting pop and sport interfaces.

In the news this year for receiving a one-week suspension after a spat with WRU performance analyst Fergus Connolly, he is due to step down from his role as Wales defence coach after the 2011 Rugby World Cup. TH

'We're never going to catch him if we keep lying about on the floor.'

AD NAUSEAM
Edwards does not have a profile you'd want to see in print too often, so his weekly column in the *Guardian* has long been bad news for middle-class rugby union fans who lean to the left. Both of them.

BEFORE HE WAS FAMOUS
Edwards was England schoolboy captain at both rugby league and rugby union – presumably leaving him very little time to do anything else.

THE MOMENT HE BECAME A LEGEND
His man-of-the-match performance for Wigan in their 1994 World Club Challenge victory over the Brisbane Broncos – on that day, he was the world's greatest league player.

HELL RAISING 5

SPORTING ACHIEVEMENTS 9

Brian JACKS

BORN **5 OCTOBER 1946**

Superfit, orange-fuelled, bronze medal-winning judoka who found true fame dipping and squat-thrusting on BBC's *Superstars*.

This could be Jacks on either his 385th dip on the parallel bars or just sitting on a bench.

Judo: 'The way of gentleness.' Try telling that to someone who's just been landed on the deck by a sweeping hip throw *harai goshi* and then been placed in a *shime-waza* strangulation hold.

Brian Jacks was taken to a judo club by his dad, a London cabbie, when he was eight. Jacks Sr had discovered the Japanese martial art when looking for a way simultaneously to lose weight and learn how to defend himself and was now an enthusiast. Jacks Jr soon saw the attraction: a Cabbies v Metropolitan Police event saw his 5ft 8in dad opposed by a 6ft 3in copper and his dad won. Easily.

'Judo gives you a hell of a lot of confidence, despite being a defensive sport. It's very good for warding off attacks, but not for attacking people.'
Jacks explains the benefits of judo but neglects to mention the variety of attractive coloured belts available.

Brian proved to be a natural and, within ten years, he was flying to Tokyo to compete in the 1964 Olympics. He didn't trouble the medals podium and was robbed of a second chance in Mexico 1968 when judo was dropped from the Olympics for the first and only time. But opportunity came knocking again in 1972 in Munich, when a gutsy display earned him a bronze medal.

This, however, was not enough to make him a household name. Martial arts hadn't quite become sexy. David Carradine had yet to wander round the Old West knocking out racist baddies; Karl Douglas had yet to release 'Kung Fu Fighting', and Bruce Lee hadn't yet died and been Blu-tacked to a million bedroom walls.

Judo didn't make Jacks famous – *Superstars* did.

The BBC programme that pitched the top names from different sports against each other had been running for five years when Jacks won the 1978 and 1979 UK and European titles, mainly thanks to his astonishing performances in the gym tests. The sight of this stockily built figure with tight blond curls doing parallel bar dips and squat thrusts at an impossible speed was usually enough to crush the spirits of fellow legends Daley Thompson (cf p165-8) and Geoff Hurst (cf p92-3). Jacks attributed his success to eating plenty of oranges, though the fact that he did 400 dips and 400 squat thrusts every day probably helped.

Jacks set up and sold a thriving bouncy castle business before retiring to Thailand. GS

Jimmy WHITE

BORN **2 MAY 1962**

Part genius, part Greek tragedy. The shy kid from Tooting who bunked off school and didn't stop until he reached the Crucible.

Buck-toothed, whiter than Colgate and prone to twitching like a wounded squirrel, White was no scholar. And it was while playing truant one day that he ducked into Zan's snooker hall in Tooting to hide under a table. Crawling through the cigarette ash and stubs, White took in the musty, beery, smoky air. Alice had fallen down the rabbit hole.

He quickly fell in love, playing a hundred hours a week. Despite breaking a foot aged 12, he continued to make century breaks with his walking stick, honing the flair shots that would see him dubbed 'the Whirlwind' – the natural heir to Alex 'the Hurricane' Higgins (cf p127-9).

Having cleaned up at the Amateur World Championship, White made his debut at the Crucible in Sheffield in 1981. He succumbed 8-10 to Steve Davis (cf p49-50), but such was his mastery of the game that winning the

'I was compulsive. In one day it would be dogs, then horses, then cards, then casinos. I was a binge gambler. I stopped because I went skint.'
White reveals how he sorted out his gambling problems.

Having just won his semi-final, White receives news that he will meet Hendry in the final.

World Championship, commentators agreed, was a mere formality.

White reached his first World Championship final in 1984, losing 16-18 to Davis. Snooker was booming and the Whirlwind was on his way to his first million. Not only did his BMW carry the number-plate CUE 80Y, but it had the ultimate yuppie toy – a car phone.

Despite winning a total of ten ranking events, by 1994 White had reached five previous world title finals, yet remained the sport's bridesmaid, having been denied by Stephen Hendry (cf p44) in 1990, 1992 and 1993, and John Parrott in 1991.

The 1994 final was a battle royale. Tied at 17 frames apiece, 37-29 in White's favour, Hendry missed, and the Holy Grail was there for the taking. Then White snatched at an elementary black – Hendry pounced and cleared. The People's Champion was typically gracious in defeat, famously declaring, 'He's beginning to annoy me.'

White is occasionally labelled a failure – by people who know nothing about the sport. But anyone who has been mesmerised by his performances at the table, signature 'banana' shots and fearless style of play will know he is, quite simply, a genius. TB

 AD NAUSEAM
Worked with Trump Technologies, who make automatic doors and help with disabled access.

 HELL RAISING 8

 SPORTING ACHIEVEMENTS 6

BEFORE HE WAS FAMOUS
White and his young pals enjoyed pretending to be orphans fleeing a cruel institution in order to trick shopkeepers into handing out free chocolate bars.

 THE MOMENT HE BECAME A LEGEND
Earning £147,000 for making a maximum break of 147 at the Crucible in Sheffield, the home of snooker, against Tony Drago in 1992.

89

Barry JOHN

BORN **6 JANUARY 1945**

He counted George Best and Richard Harris as drinking pals. Football had King Kenny, rugby union had King Barry.

Gareth Edwards (cf p151-3), Gavin Hastings and, more recently, Jonny Wilkinson (cf p62-3): names you're likely to hear the average sports fan reel off if asked to recall a rugby great. One name almost certain to be mentioned by those who know their stuff is Barry John, Wales' fabulous fly-half.

Richard Burton's missus, Sally, once chastised the number 10 because he was all her husband would talk about after a game. John could command the undivided attention of Burton's fellow thespian rugby fanatics – Harris, Peter O'Toole and Stanley Baker – who would hang on to his every word, listening to tales from the changing room.

All this attention, and he wasn't even a professional rugby player. The

> 'I never lost to England – it would have been rude, as a Welshman, to do so.'
> John was meticulous when it came to etiquette.

game still held amateur status and no matter what he did on the pitch, he would be in work the next day with the very men who had been singing his praises in pubs across Wales.

In 1971, on the Lions tour of New Zealand, he scored an incredible 188 points – a record that still stands – tearing the mighty All Blacks apart in the process. He lived in the space other players assumed they had covered. With ball-to-foot, at a time when the ball absorbed water and the pitches resembled the Somme, he was impeccable.

Such was the magnitude of his achievements in 1971 that the Irish centre Mike Gibson, who played with him in New Zealand has said, 'His control of the game and his composure influenced all the other players.'

A group of local evangelists are said to have walked through the streets asking locals what they would do if Jesus Christ came back to Earth. 'The Lions have already got him and he's playing fly-half,' was one reply.

However, the fame became too much. While on a business trip, a young clerk curtsied to him as he entered. 'If I needed something to show me it had all gone way over the top,' he said, 'that was it.' John retired at 27 with just 25 caps for Wales. DAMIAN MANNION

 AD NAUSEAM
During the mid-70s, Gola had their own 'Barry John Rugby' range – amazing considering rugby was an amateur sport.

🔥 **HELL**
4 RAISING

🏅 **SPORTING**
7 ACHIEVEMENTS

It was an odd place to find a Page Three girl, but Barry John had no complaints.

BEFORE HE WAS FAMOUS
At 18 years old he had a summer holiday spell at the Great Mountain colliery in Tumble, cleaning pipes and supplying the men with tools.

 THE MOMENT HE BECAME A LEGEND
John was hailed as 'The King' following his performances in the 2-1 1971 Lions series win, the first on Kiwi soil for three-quarters of a century.

88

Andrew STRAUSS

BORN **2 MARCH 1977**

Slightly balding, slightly rotund England cricket captain who became the first man to lead an Ashes-winning team in Australia for 24 years.

Little Urn: it may be small, but it's perfectly formed.

When Mike Gatting's England side returned home from Australia with the Ashes in 1987, few people spoke of the captain. They talked about prolific opener Chris Broad, dashing accumulator David Gower (cf p29), heroic all-rounder Ian Botham (cf p173-6) and a relentless bowling attack that had repeatedly torn an embattled Australian team to shreds.

Twenty-four years later, and echoes of that tour surrounded their successors. The vintage of 2011 featured run-machines Alastair Cook and Jonathan Trott, while an attack starring Jimmy Anderson, Chris Tremlett and Graeme Swann helped dish out three brutal innings victories. There was no heroic all-rounder, but Strauss's team didn't need one – the batsmen scored the runs and the bowlers took the wickets.

Therein lies the simple philosophy at the heart of a heavily nuanced sport, but only the very best captains can inspire it. Thankfully for England, Strauss is one such individual. A tidy left-hander reared on the public school fields of Radley College,

> 'I have always believed that if I do everything right, then no bowler will get me out. Ever.'
> As truisms go, it's unsurpassable.

his 6,000+ Test runs at an average of more than 43 qualifies him as a very decent batsman, albeit some way short of Sachin Tendulkar and Brian Lara.

Not an obvious athlete, Strauss has something quintessentially English about him – his face is ruddy, his demeanour reserved but gracious. But that tells only half a story.

Born in South Africa, Strauss's early cricketing education took place in Melbourne – no surprise, then, that behind the placid façade lie a fierce determination and quiet ruthlessness. In a crucial Champions Trophy match against the country of his birth in 2009, Strauss refused opposing captain Graeme Smith a runner when affected by cramp in a tense run-chase. 'My personal view is that you shouldn't get a runner, full stop,' said Strauss afterwards. 'I didn't feel he was cramping that badly – he was still able to run.'

Polite but as hard as nails, Strauss inherited the England captaincy in early 2009. Alongside coach Andy Flower, he transformed England into a formidable Test side, becoming the first captain since Mike Brearley to lead them to consecutive Ashes series wins. TH

 AD NAUSEAM

It's hardly Giorgio Armani, but a clothing deal with Austin Reed is about the extent of Strauss's commercial involvements.

 HELL
1 RAISING

 SPORTING
8 ACHIEVEMENTS

 BEFORE HE WAS FAMOUS
Strauss has a degree in economics from Hatfield College, Durham University – the same *alma mater* as fellow England captain Will Carling.

THE MOMENT HE BECAME A LEGEND
Captaining an Ashes-winning team on home soil was some achievement, but repeating the feat Down Under was Strauss's crowning glory.

87

Stuart PEARCE

BORN **24 APRIL 1962**

A psycho on the pitch and a nice bloke off it. Best remembered for his penalties and crunching tackles.

Not many footballers these days begin their career with five years at semi-professional level while working as an electrician and plumber, and later earn 78 England caps, manage in the Premiership and coach for England. But Stuart Pearce was not your average footballer.

'It can be a bit of a hindrance when you walk into a restaurant for a quiet meal and one or two launch into "Psycho, Psycho!"'
Pearce's search goes on.

Taken from his local West London non-league side Wealdstone to Coventry in 1983, two years later Pearce joined Nottingham Forest. Despite being transferred for £300,000, he doubted his livelihood as a footballer to the extent that he advertised his services as an electrician in Forest's match-day programme.

Pearce played at the City Ground for 12 years, making 401 league appearances, many as captain, and winning two League Cups. It was during his time at Forest that he gained his nickname 'Psycho', thankfully for his full-on commitment and tackling rather than for any unsavoury actions.

The left-back made his England debut against Brazil in 1987. Playing in the 1990 World Cup, Pearce is best remembered for missing a penalty in the semi-final shoot-out against, yes, West Germany, as England exited the competition.

Psycho redeemed his penalty miss by scoring in the shoot-out against Spain in the quarter-finals of Euro '96. His celebration was so psychotic that he looked as though he might have ripped someone's head off (see picture right). Naturally, this show of emotion endeared him to many an England fan. In the semi-final shoot-out against, yes, Germany, he scored another, but again England lost.

Following spells at Newcastle, West Ham and Manchester City, he became a manager for City where he survived for just over two years, almost a

'How many times do I have to tell you that I need a non-bio fabric softener?'

record in the blue half of Manchester. Some have suggested he may have lost his job following the humiliation brought to the club by Pearce using his daughter's soft toy horse as a mascot that he took into the technical area.

Pearce has coached England Under-21s since 2007. He is a massive punk fan, and it is thought that he is the only person known as Psycho ever to have received an OBE from the Queen.

JEREMY STUBBINGS

 AD NAUSEAM
Despite appearing in three adverts for the 2010 World Cup, the 1996 'penalty miss' Pizza Hut ad is Psycho's classic, mainly as he gets to mock Gareth Southgate.

BEFORE HE WAS FAMOUS
Appeared on the back of an album by punk band The Lurchers – he was, and still is, a big fan.

 THE MOMENT HE BECAME A LEGEND
Banishing the memory of his 1990 shoot-out miss by having the balls to take penalties at Euro '96 against Spain AND Germany.

HELL 4 RAISING

SPORTING 7 ACHIEVEMENTS

talkSPORT LEGENDS

Jason ROBINSON

BORN **30 JULY 1974**

God-fearing former alcoholic who fought his way out of poverty to become England's greatest cross-code rugby player.

'I want to be and live my life like Christ did. Now I'm a long way off, don't get me wrong, but I'm trying.'
Robinson aims high.

When Jason Robinson departed the field after 47 minutes of the 2007 Rugby World Cup final against South Africa, he did so to a standing ovation from the entire crowd. As he limped off with a hamstring injury, England fans knew they were bidding farewell to the jet-heeled winger for the final time.

England may have lost that final, but Robinson's place in the nation's affections had already been secured with the significant part he played in the World Cup win in Australia four years earlier – while everyone will always remember Jonny Wilkinson's (cf p62-3) extra-time dropped goal,

they shouldn't forget the Robinson try that gave England crucial momentum.

Such later glories were a world away from Robinson's early years as an ultra-talented but ill-disciplined rugby league professional. Nicknamed Billy Whizz after the *Beano* character, Robinson was part of a brilliant Wigan team featuring Shaun Edwards (cf p19), Gary Connolly, Martin Offiah, Kris Radlinski and a young Andy Farrell.

But the ghosts of a difficult childhood – Robinson never knew his father – were expressed through a hard-drinking and philandering approach to life that saw him lose form and endanger his career.

Under the influence of legendary team-mate Va'aiga Tuigamala, Robinson discovered the faith and temperance that would see him become not only a world-class league player, but also give him the belief to cross codes in 2000 and become one of England's greatest-ever exponents of the 15-man game.

Allying his pace with intelligent

angles of running, absolute reliability under the high ball and a surprisingly effective kicking game, Robinson could be used on the wing or at full-back and was a devastating finisher – the ideal cherry on top for Clive Woodward's (cf p15) all-conquering England team.

Aged 37, he has a new lease of life as a player at Fylde. Robinson retired from international rugby with 51 England caps and having been on two British Lions tours. In rugby league, he won 12 caps for Great Britain. Not bad for a lad with his head in the Bible most of the time. TH

 AD NAUSEAM
'Left a bit!' screams Robinson at a giraffe, as he sets two of them up to look like rugby posts in an 'amusing' short ad for HSBC's sponsorship of the 2009 British Lions tour of South Africa.

HELL RAISING 5

SPORTING ACHIEVEMENTS 9

And so he came to pass… but not when he had half a chance of diving over the line.

BEFORE HE WAS FAMOUS
One of the few high points of Robinson's troubled upbringing in the dodgy Chapeltown district of Leeds was the annual family holiday to Scarborough – often financed by the sale of pilfered fruit and veg.

THE MOMENT HE BECAME A LEGEND
Crossing the line to score England's only try in the 2003 World Cup final victory over Australia.

85

Pat JENNINGS

BORN **12 JUNE 1945**

You know what they say about a bloke with big hands: 'Look out, it's Pat Jennings!'

It wasn't that his hands were huge, more that he had a really small head.

'If Pat Jennings had been available on that memorable occasion when the Romans met the Etruscans, Horatius surely would have had to be satisfied with a seat on the substitutes' bench.'

So said Eric Todd of the *Guardian* in a report on an epic Leeds–Spurs clash in 1971 – referencing the commander who single-handedly defended a bridge into Rome against a horde of aggressive barbarians.

There's plenty more praise for the huge Irish keeper throughout *The Glory Game*, Hunter Davies's football classic penned behind the scenes during the 1971-72 season when Tottenham lifted the UEFA Cup.

'He's a genuine team man, shy and retiring, with no signs of flash. His fans are always on at him to put a bit of show into his game, make it look a bit harder, just to work up the crowd excitement and draw attention to himself.'

Paul Trevillion, early football agent and marketeer, earholed Jennings with the idea of a pair of signature goalie gloves. All Pat had to do was deny having giant hands, and put his shot-stopping ability down to the magic gloves. And while he was about it, why not make a habit of picking the ball up with one hand, to give himself a gimmick? From that point on, Pat self-consciously stopped picking shots and crosses out of the air with one giant hand –

and eventually rejected his own 'trademark' gloves.

After Gordon Banks' career-wrecking car crash, multiple contemporary sources confirm that the 1973 FWA and 1976 PFA Footballer of the Year was generally regarded as the best goalkeeper in the world. It was a subject the towering Irishman, capped a record 119 times for his country, always refused to discuss.

'… I think my positional sense kept me out of trouble.'
Jennings assesses his key attribute.

Now back within the fold, coaching at Tottenham, Jennings continues to prove his value with action rather than words, passing on his skills with all the quiet reliability with which he once read the game. DEREK HAMMOND

 AD NAUSEAM
Jennings merchandise included a collectable signature edition pencil sharpener, complete with inbuilt ball-bearing game, produced by Helix in 1981.

HELL RAISING 0

SPORTING ACHIEVEMENTS 8

BEFORE HE WAS FAMOUS
Jennings worked as a timber loader: 'I'll never forget how sometimes one of those big four-ton logs would slip the chains and come crashin' down…'

 THE MOMENT HE BECAME A LEGEND
Ditched by Spurs after 13 years and 591 games, Big Pat promptly switched to Arsenal and became a Gooners legend with another 327 appearances.

Colin McRAE

BORN **5 AUGUST 1968** ▨ DIED **15 SEPTEMBER 2007**

Cavalier Scotsman who lived life in the fast lane as Britain's greatest rally driver before meeting an untimely end.

For many, Colin McRae was the name behind the world's best-selling video driving game. Anyone who's owned a games console has probably spent time burning through a pixilated rally course while a computerised co-driver screams directions. In reality, the Scotsman was one of motorsport's fastest rally drivers and the first Brit to win the World Rally Championship, in 1995.

'If in doubt, flat out.'
McRae offers some insight into his cerebral driving technique.

With a father who was five times British champion himself, it's no surprise that the young McRae felt a need for speed. He started thrashing a Mini around old mines near his home, before borrowing a mate's car to enter his first rally, aged 17. He won his first outright event a few years later, with his wife-to-be as co-

driver – a lesson to any couple who've infuriated each other on a road trip.

British racing fans loved him for his fearless, uncompromising style, which wasn't always forgiving on cars – earning him the nickname 'McCrash'. Nonetheless, he was signed up by Subaru and became

It is rumoured that McRae occasionally raced with all four wheels on the ground.

the youngest British champion in 1991 – winning again in 1992, before graduating with the team to the World Rally Championship (WRC).

Three years later, McRae became the youngest ever WRC champion, after sealing victory at the season-ending Rally of Great Britain against twice former champion and team-mate, Carlos Sainz. He never won it again – although he went close with both Subaru and Ford, before being denied by either an unreliable car or his own fabled bravado.

McRae could have reclaimed the championship in 2001, but crashed out in the final race – effectively handing the title to an English rival he often taunted for being too cautious, Richard Burns. McRae eventually fell out of rally driving, turning his attention to endurance races like the Dakar, where he was once stranded in the desert for two days.

For someone who had defied death for a living, it's a cruel irony that he died when he crashed his helicopter in 2007 while with friends – tragically killing three people, including his young son. RA

BEFORE HE WAS FAMOUS
McRae joined the family heating and plumbing business – but spent most of his time in the garage maintaining company vans and working on his first rally car, a Talbot Sunbeam he bought for £850.

THE MOMENT HE BECAME A LEGEND
On the eve of the 1994 RAC Rally, his team-mate, Carlos Sainz, had a slim chance of winning the title. But Sainz crashed and McRae led all the way to become the first British driver to win on home soil for 18 years.

 AD NAUSEAM
Just before his death, McRae teamed up with UK Transplant to urge motorists to become donors saying, 'Organ donation is one of the greatest gifts of all.'

 HELL
2 RAISING

SPORTING
8 ACHIEVEMENTS

Robin FRIDAY

BORN 27 JULY 1952 ▪ DIED 22 DECEMBER 1990

The greatest British footballer you've never heard of. Read on…

If George Best (cf p192-6) was football's very own Beatle, then Robin Friday was surely Syd Barrett, the genius and founding member behind Pink Floyd. On second thoughts, perhaps Friday was more Sid Vicious.

Friday spent his years undermining his talent with enormous amounts of booze and drugs. Scouts watching the reported miracle worker at Fourth Division Reading in the early 1970s marvelled at his touch and vision, but recoiled in horror at his behaviour.

Fans who witnessed him in his pomp still dine out on his electrical banana shot against Doncaster Rovers in February 1974, and the chest trap and reverse 35-yard thunderbolt against Tranmere Rovers two years later – of the latter, international referee Clive Thomas said, 'Even up against the likes of Pelé and Cruyff, that rates as the best goal I have ever seen.'

Yes, he really did once kiss a policeman behind the goal when he

in Wales. On his debut, he grabbed Bobby Moore (cf p187-91) by the balls. In his final match for them, he kicked Brighton's Mark Lawrenson in the face, was sent off and then defecated in his holdall in the dressing room – and for that alone…

He died aged 38 of a heart attack caused by a suspected heroin overdose. DH

Famed for his sportsmanship, Friday gives the goalkeeper a score out of three for effort.

> 'If you'd just settle down for three or four years, you could play for England.'
> 'How old are you? I'm half your age and I've lived twice your life.'
> Reading boss Maurice Evans doesn't get far with his new career advisory service thanks to Robin Friday.

His story leaves nothing to celebrate except memories for the lucky few, and seven seconds of YouTube footage. This is a tragedy of wilful, wanton waste. All we're left to do is sort the myth from the legend, and wonder at what might have been.

Friday first surfaced in 1973, starring for Hayes in the FA Cup during a second-round local derby against Reading. Hayes lost, but Friday had arrived. Reading swooped.

scored, but Friday had a deserved reputation as a hard-man and there was a darker side to him. He would strip naked on the team bus and once, when tripping on acid in the team hotel, threw darts and snooker balls and somehow appropriated a swan.

After hoisting the Biscuitmen into Division Three, Friday was offloaded for £30,000 to second-tier Cardiff. He was arrested upon his arrival

 AD NAUSEAM

Robin Friday was arguably the best imaginable advert for taking dope, pills, coke and LSD in mind-bending quantities. Try it yourself, and die.

 BEFORE HE WAS FAMOUS
Born in Acton, London, Friday was in and out of the borstal system throughout his troubled youth.

THE MOMENT HE BECAME A LEGEND
Friday started just 20 league games for Cardiff before resigning, aged 25, from the game because he was 'Fed up of people telling [him] what to do'.

 HELL RAISING 10

 **SPORTING ACHIEVEMENTS 1**

82

David GOWER

BORN **1 APRIL 1957**

Duckling-haired, biplane buzzing, left-handed Cavalier who wielded the willow with poetic elegance, but didn't always get the runs.

'When you are out of form, every ball looks like a hand grenade.'
Gower recalls the bad days.

Gower strongly refuted any suggestions that he was a player born out of his time.

team-mate Phil, to comment: 'Difficult to be more laid back without being actually comatose.' And there was…

How about that first ball he faced in Test cricket, against Pakistan in 1978 at Edgbaston, audaciously pulled to the boundary? And his maiden Test century that soon followed against New Zealand? And that golden year of 1985 when he captained his country to a series victory in India and then regained the Ashes, scoring 732 runs at 81.33 in the campaign?

Between 1978 and 1992 Gower amassed 8,231 runs in 117 Tests, at an average of 44.25, hitting 18 centuries – and he didn't achieve that by being Bertie Wooster in a Harpo Marx wig. GS

There should be an abiding image of David Ivon Gower, perhaps in cartoon form, tootling off towards the pavilion with a 'Gone Fishing' sign hanging from his bat, having been caught angling for a ball outside the off stump that should have been left alone.

Gower delighted the purists but often infuriated those who simply wanted to see England win. He also suffered from lapses of concentration that too often saw his innings end just as it was warming up. The perception was that he didn't care enough, but he certainly did.

Maybe this son of an old-school colonial officer had been born too late, as the *Observer*'s Scyld Berry suggested: 'Gower might have been more at home in the 1920s, cracking a dashing hundred for MCC, the darling of the crowds, before speeding away in a Bugatti and cravat for a night on the town.'

This image was reinforced when Gower hired a Tiger Moth to buzz a warm-up game in Queensland before the 1991 Ashes series. He wisely decided against using the water-bombs he had prepared, otherwise his £1,000 fine might have been more substantial.

But there had to be more to Gower than the image that prompted writer Frances Edmonds, wife of England

 **AD NAUSEAM**
Gower, unveiling his dish: 'One golden duck?'
Botham, peering at burnt offering:
'More like the Ashes.'
The Sky Sports 2010 Cricketers as Chefs.

 HELL RAISING **SPORTING ACHIEVEMENTS**

BEFORE HE WAS FAMOUS
Got bored of studying for 'A' levels and played for Leicestershire seconds at £25 per week instead.

 THE MOMENT HE BECAME A LEGEND
Lifting the Ashes urn at The Oval in 1985 after skippering England to a 3-1 series win.

81

BIG DADDY

BORN **14 NOVEMBER 1930** ■ DIED **2 DECEMBER 1997**

Giant blond Yorkshireman from the age of big-time British wrestling, when Margaret Thatcher and the Queen were among his fans.

Shirley Crabtree was no lady. Boasting a British record 64in chest, he was the daddy of all the gimmick-toting wildmen of 1970s TV wrestling – bully Mick McManus with his whining 'Not the face' catchphrase; 6ft 11in caveman Giant Haystacks; Kendo Nagasaki with his mask – and his signature 26-stone belly-splash reverberated far beyond the sweaty canvas arena.

Big Daddy's gimmick? Well, he was large, of course. And he was 46 when he first made it Big, in his spangly Union Jack cape and top hat. Most memorably, he sported a terrifyingly immodest leotard, decorated with a large capital 'D'. Remember, wrestling was serious showbiz box-office back in the '70s, thanks largely to a Saturday afternoon TV slot before the *World of Sport* teleprinter, and Big Daddy claimed this primetime show as his own. But, God knows, he'd earned his ten years in the sun…

In 'A Boy Named Sue', Johnny Cash told of a kid who hated his long-absent dad, who then returned to explain that he'd christened his boy to help him survive alone in a tough world. In fact rather than fiction, pro wrestler Shirley Crabtree Sr went one worse. Not content with suffering ritual humiliation every day of his life, the Yorkshireman then chose to inflict the same fate on his son.

Little Shirley Jr hit back by training himself in the art of grip 'n' grapple, spending his weekends in swimming trunks entangled with men with hairy backs. Just as Dad hoped, it gave him a ticket out of the mills, but Shirl grew bored with the pantomime and retired to become a Blackpool lifeguard in the '60s. Only when his wrestling promoter brother Max suggested a comeback 15 years later – what, wrestling rigged? – was he rechristened and set on the road to legendary status.

Before long, Big Daddy had a legion of fans baying 'Easy! Easy!' at the box, hoping for a climactic Daddy Splash; but he blamed himself for Mal 'King Kong' Kirk's death in 1987, the victim of his grisly, suffocating finishing move. Daddy struggled on in increasingly poor health until 1993, receiving his own final tagout four years later, aged 67. DH

He bent down to tie his shoelaces and nobody saw the chair again.

'Ask a silly bloody question.'
To TV cameraman, in middle distance after enquiring how it felt to receive a Big Daddy belly-butt.

 AD NAUSEAM
In 1985, Shirley pronounced Daddies' tomato ketchup and sauce, in their new chunky bottles, to be 'knockout' with the kids…

 HELL RAISING 7

 **SPORTING ACHIEVEMENTS** 3

BEFORE HE WAS FAMOUS
Was working at 14 in a Halifax woollen mill before following his dad into the ring in the '50s – first as 'The Blond Adonis', then as 'Mr Universe'.

 THE MOMENT HE BECAME A LEGEND
A reported 18 million TV viewers watched the 1981 face-off between Big Daddy and Giant Haystacks; still nowt on the time they gut-barged each other and knocked out the ref in the first move of the match…

80

Jim LAKER

BORN **9 FEBRUARY 1922** ▨ DIED **23 APRIL 1986**

The spin bowler who answered his critics with the best bowling performance of all time, 'Lakering' ten Aussies in a single Test innings…

James Laker is a legend not for what he did in his whole career, impressive as it was, but for what he achieved in a single game.

Not only did he perform the phenomenal feat of taking ten wickets –

In 1956, most of the Australians assumed his full name was Bowled Laker.

ten very sweet Australian wickets – in a Test innings, he did so having already bagged nine in the previous innings. In the 55 years since, his achievement has not been bettered.

An off-spinner, Laker was a Yorkshireman, yet never played for the county. That can be put down to the war – having come back from the Middle East (where he played in a decent army team who were presumably having 'a good war'), he was given a desk job in the War Office in London. Before long, he was playing for Surrey and word soon spread about the extreme spin he imparted on the ball.

But his gruff demeanour did not endear himself to the post-war cricket authorities. He hated snobbery in all forms and, as such, refused to accept some of the Establishment's more eccentric habits.

Before his life-changing accomplishment he'd played just 27 times for England. The selectors had also dumped some of the blame

on him for England's defeat to Don Bradman's Aussies in 1948. Laker felt it was undeserved criticism, and exacted a fearful revenge on Australia.

Quite how anyone can take 19 wickets in a Test is hard to understand: less so when, at the other end, another perfectly competent spinner, Tony Lock, was bowling, and bowling well. The only explanation can be that the Australians at the time simply weren't used to playing off-spin (Lock was a left-armer with a natural leg break), and Laker simply bamboozled them.

> 'The aim of English cricket is, in fact, mainly to beat Australia.'
> Laker gets to the heart of the matter.

After that Test, the selectors looked on Laker in a different light, but it was too late. By 1959, suffering from arthritis in his finger, his powers were on the wane and he retired from county cricket.

The following year he wrote an autobiography, in which he savaged the Establishment. It led to him being banned from The Oval and the MCC revoking his membership. The honours were later restored when he became a BBC commentator. sc

---

BEFORE HE WAS FAMOUS
Laker was born illegitimately (while his mother was still married to another man) and his father left when he was barely a toddler.

THE MOMENT HE BECAME A LEGEND
No other bowler has ever taken more than 17 wickets in a first-class match, let alone a Test match. Laker's 19 in 1956 is a record that will surely never be beaten.

⊘ **AD NAUSEAM**
While never actually endorsing anything, Laker was one of the first sportsmen to cash in with a tell-all book, *Over To Me*, in 1960.

 HELL RAISING 5

 **SPORTING ACHIEVEMENTS** 8

Jim BAXTER

BORN **29 SEPTEMBER 1939** ■ DIED **14 APRIL 2001**

A swaggering magician with an eye for the ladies and a bottle of rum. Usually both at the same time…

Jim Baxter's words ruptured the roaring silence. 'That's the greatest goal in Wembley's history,' he cried, greeting his jubilant Scotland team-mates as they cavorted towards him.

In truth, the left-foot lash past Gordon Banks (cf p72-3) that earned the ten-man Scots a 2-1 victory over England in April 1963 was slightly more prosaic, but his hubris was merely a reflection of how others saw him.

Pelé claimed he should have been Brazilian, Sir Alex Ferguson (cf p110-11) referred to his 'wonderful aura' and Ferenc Puskas asked in his broken English, 'Where have you been hiding?' Baxter had just been introduced into a Rest of the World team for the second half of a game against England in 1963.

The then Rangers player took the imperious Real Madrid star for an alcohol-fuelled night on the pull. It was a successful night by all accounts and, as noted in *Hampden Babylon*: 'Had genealogy been kinder to Scotland, that night of illegitimate

'You'll hae to come with us, laddie, the Scottish FA have heard you're planning a party.'

sex should have produced two players around whom Jock Stein could have moulded a Scotland team.'

The story captures Baxter perfectly. Sufficiently revered to be a peer of Puskas, but a player for whom football was only one dish amid a banquet held in his honour.

Be it the drinking that caused him to undergo a liver transplant at the age of 55, the womanising that afflicted his relationships, or the gambling addiction that cost him around £500,000, the flamboyant Fifer was a prisoner to self-indulgence.

Not that he would agree. Life, insisted Baxter, was to be enjoyed. An elegant left-half with the strut of a peacock, he won ten major honours with Rangers, after arriving from

'Treat the ball like a woman. Give it a cuddle, caress it a wee bit, take your time, and you'll get the required response.'
Jim Baxter ignores the UEFA coaching manual.

Raith Rovers, but struggled to regain his swagger after a 1964 leg break. Though there was, of course, his matinee performance at Wembley in 1967, taunting England like a peely-wally* matador, playing keepie-uppie for several seconds.

Since pancreatic cancer claimed him in 2001, memories are all that remain – and, for Scotsmen of a certain vintage, there are none greater than that 1967 display at Wembley against the world champions (see picture left). RICHARD WINTON

 AD NAUSEAM
The only brand name associated with Baxter is a world-famous rum. He used to drink three bottles a day.

BEFORE HE WAS FAMOUS
Baxter served as an apprentice cabinet-maker and then worked as a coal miner.

 THE MOMENT HE BECAME A LEGEND
During Scotland's 1967 win at Wembley, Baxter placed a foot on the ball, glanced around with disdain at the opposition, and walked away to leave it for Denis Law (cf p88-9).

 **HELL RAISING** 9 | **SPORTING ACHIEVEMENTS** 6

* Scottish slang – 'pale' or 'pasty'.

Bob NUDD

BORN **24 SEPTEMBER 1944**

Four-time World Angling champion who should have been Sports Personality of the Year.

Bob Nudd may have won the World Angling Championships four times, but he's more famous for what he didn't win.

In 1991, Nudd received most votes in the annual BBC Sports Personality of the Year poll, but the Beeb threw them out. They claimed Nudd's 'victory' had been the result of a campaign by *Angling Times* magazine and as such couldn't count, infuriating the 100,000 fishermen who had dutifully posted in their votes. The eventual winner? Liz bloody McColgan.

Bob (in the white cap) did not become four-time World Angling champion without knowing that the secret to success was peace and quiet at all times.

Nudd was an angling sensation. Representing England for 24 years, he was virtually unbeatable in the 1990s. No matter where he sat in his trademark white cap – probably anywhere bar a nuclear puddle – he pulled out more fish than anyone else. Three of his world titles came in five years – in Yugoslavia (1990), Hungary (1991) and before an adoring home crowd of 30,000 at Holme Pierrepoint, Nottingham, in 1994.

 'I'm the man, King Maggot, the whip fish master, the blaster! The master caster!'
A line from Nudd's 'Maggots In Ya Catapult', his sadly underrated 1995 assault on the charts.

He managed the feat again in Spain in 1999 – with a jaw-dropping haul of more than 54kg – to go down as the father of modern-day match angling. Another Brit, Alan Scotthorne, has since gone on to take five world titles, but he would acknowledge that Nudd paved the way for him.

Nudd's skill lay in taking traditional continental tactics and adapting them to the modern era. British anglers had used rods and reels. But abroad, especially in France, the pole method – no reel, just line attached to the end of a longer-than-usual rod – was finding success.

Nudd was the first to realise just how effective this method could be.

In some matches, over a five-hour period, Nudd caught fish at an average of one every ten seconds. As much as any actual angling skill, he had the ability to concentrate on his job like nobody else.

Nudd also experimented with his bait and 'groundbait' – the mix thrown into the water to attract fish. A fishing equivalent of Colonel Sanders, he consistently found new recipes.

Nudd's fame has ensured he's long been in demand for public appearances and is a regular columnist in angling magazines. Now 67, he is still a fixture on the match angling circuit. sc

......

 AD NAUSEAM

Nudd has long been an ambassador for bait manufacturer Van Den Eynde. There aren't many people who can make money out of bait.

......

🔥 **HELL**
1 RAISING

W SPORTING
9 ACHIEVEMENTS

BEFORE HE WAS FAMOUS
In 1976, he bought a Commer van for £20, painted it bright yellow and started Pete and Bob's Hot Dogs, selling burgers and hot dogs at fishing matches.

 THE MOMENT HE BECAME A LEGEND
Surely the BBC scandal of 1991. As world angling champion he might have expected a few votes for Sports Personality of the Year, but not 100,000. The Beeb ruled him out. Outrageous!

Fred TRUEMAN

BORN **6 FEBRUARY 1931** ■ DIED **1 JULY 2006**

Straight-talking, quick-witted, fast-bowling, self-promoting, professional Yorkshireman.

When broadcasting doyen John Arlott said he was thinking of writing a biography of Fred Trueman, the man himself offered a title: *T' Greatest Fast Bowler Who Ever Drew Breath*.

Trueman was nothing if not sure of his own ability. With good reason too. A genuinely hostile bowler, he took wickets for fun – 307 in 67 Tests, at a remarkable average of 21.57, and with a strike rate of a wicket every 49.4 balls.

'My run-up lasted longer.'

Trueman's verdict on the bizarre and short-lived marriage between his daughter and the son of Hollywood beauty Raquel Welch.

A former miner, he didn't stand for any nonsense on the field of play, and often terrified batsmen into getting out: Trueman was one of the first sledgers. As one Test batsman came on to the pitch he closed the gate behind him. 'Don't bother, son,' said Trueman. 'You won't be out here long.'

He had a classical side-on action, which, as his career went on, enabled him to swing the ball at will. But it was his out-and-out pace that did for most of his victims, in the days of uncovered wickets. In his first Test in 1952, he helped reduce India in their second innings to 0-4 (which remains the worst start in Test history), and later that series took 8-31 at Old Trafford.

He was a showman. Like Shane Warne years later, he would relish setting his fields, and playing mind games with the batsmen as they waited nervously for him to swagger slowly back to his bowling mark before turning on his heel and racing back to the crease. It was cricket as theatre.

A typical Yorkshireman, he was never short of a quip. When fielder Raman Subba Row let a boundary go through his legs from Trueman's bowling, he said: 'Sorry Fred, I should have kept my legs together.'

'So should your mother,' Trueman fired back.

After retiring from cricket, he became a broadcaster – a celebrated grump in the commentary box, who once declared Ian Botham (cf p173-6) 'couldn't bowl a hoop downhill'.

On being told he had been invited to appear on Michael Parkinson's chatshow with Harold Pinter, Trueman said: 'Who's he play for?' Once a cricketer... SC

 AD NAUSEAM

Succeeded Denis Compton as a Brylcreem Boy – long before the days of David Beckham and Kevin Pietersen.

HELL RAISING 7   **SPORTING ACHIEVEMENTS** 7

'I've said it before and I'll say it again: I'd have looked faster in colour.'

BEFORE HE WAS FAMOUS
Coming from Yorkshire, he worked down t' pit – naturally. No wonder he had such broad shoulders.

 THE MOMENT HE BECAME A LEGEND
Like many cricketers, Fiery Fred's greatest moment is in the statistics. He was the first bowler to take 300 Test wickets.

talkSPORT LEGENDS

Graeme OBREE

BORN **11 SEPTEMBER 1965**

Maverick world record-breaking Scottish cyclist dubbed 'l'Incroyable Mister Obree' on the front page of the daily French sports paper *l'Equipe.*

After a meet in 1998, having swallowed 50 aspirins, Graeme Obree sucked up filthy water from a puddle. Luckily for his fans, the overdose did not have the desired effect. But it was not the only time he tried to kill himself.

Norway in July 1993 – a simple race-against-the-clock involving riding a bike round a velodrome for 60 minutes and measuring the distance travelled.

It is cycling's Blue Riband event and Obree rode a bike ('Old Faithful')

'If [the official] didn't move out of the way I would have smacked him. I didn't give a shit. This was about a kilometre and a half to go.'
Obree on his 'problematic' relationship with cycling's governing body.

Obree is a deeply complicated man and, despite being married with two children, publicly came out as gay in early 2011. He has subsequently blamed the suicide attempts on his confused sexuality.

This inspirational sportsman has said he 'would rather die than fail'. On the advice of his psychologist to write things down, he eventually penned his autobiography, *The Flying Scotsman*, which was made into a film of the same name.

It is not just the story of a cyclist, but of a man who 'came out of nowhere' to break the World Hour Record in

that he made himself from, among other things, a piece of scrap he found at the side of the A78, wheel-ends cut from old padlocks and part of a broken washing machine.

He failed at his first attempt, but insisted upon trying again the next day, despite his exhaustion. The record (51.151km), belonging to Francesco Moser, had stood since 1984. He pushed 'Old Faithful' and himself to 51.596km, riding in a right-angled crouch, elbows tucked in to the side as though he might be attempting a push-up – the 'Praying Mantis' or 'Obree Position'.

Chris Boardman, the Olympic champion and his great rival, broke the record in Bordeaux (52.270). So, on 27 April 1994, Obree won it back with 52.713. The 'Obree Position' was then outlawed by the cycling authorities. When he devised a new position, soon dubbed the 'Superman' style, it too was banned.

The 'Superman position' was banned due to his refusal to wear underpants over his lycra.

And it was all done without performance-enhancing drugs. As he put it, 'If you buy a signed poster now, it will not be tarnished later.' BB

BEFORE HE WAS FAMOUS
He ran a cycle shop and appeared on *Crimewatch UK* after an unsuccessful insurance scam.

THE MOMENT HE BECAME A LEGEND
Hearing the pistol shot as he surpassed Francesco Moser's nine-year-old record in the velodrome in Hamar, Norway.

 AD NAUSEAM
'Cyclist Graeme Obree's "The Hour" has been released this week – the watch maps twelve words to the hours of the day.'
For Mr Jones Watches 'Masters of Time' Collection.

🔥 **HELL RAISING** 9

W SPORTING ACHIEVEMENTS 8

Duncan GOODHEW

BORN **27 MAY 1957**

Hairless, dyslexic breast-stroker who overcame his misfortunes to claim gold at the Moscow Olympics…

As a child, Duncan Goodhew did not have troubles to seek. They found him. He suffered from dyslexia that went undiagnosed until his teenage years and was nicknamed Duncan the Dunce by his classmates. Things got worse when he was ten and he fell 20ft from a tree while on an assault course.

He landed on his face, damaging his teeth and jaw. But the true extent of the damage revealed itself some months later when his hair began to fall out. The accident had triggered alopecia universalis, which meant 100 per cent hair loss, even down to the eyelashes.

Goodhew was a gifted swimmer and was allowed to join in a training session with Welshman Nigel Johnson, who used the Millfield School swimming pool as he prepared for the 1972 Munich Olympics. That night an inspired Goodhew told anybody who would listen: 'I am going to the Olympics.'

Just four years later, after an intensive training regime at North Carolina State University, Goodhew

> 'I thought if I don't do something now then I'm not going to win it. And a voice in my head added… "And that's totally absurd!"'
>
> Goodhew reflects on his slightly unusual motivation.

Technically speaking, there was no law against sucking up the water in front of you.

honoured his promise, making the final of the 100m breast-stroke at the Montreal games. He broke the Olympic record in the heats but, wracked with self-doubt, finished seventh in the final.

As Goodhew prepared for Moscow, he finally solved his confidence problems with techniques that he now puts to use as a motivational speaker. But preparations were overshadowed by the USA refusing to send a team to Moscow in protest at the Soviet invasion of Afghanistan.

Team GB went to Moscow without the blessing of the government. Goodhew had been struggling with a shoulder injury and scraped through the qualifiers but found his form in the final, producing an immense finish to edge ahead of Russian Arsens Miskarovs to claim gold.

Goodhew stood on the medal podium with a flat cap covering his increasingly famous bald head. Duncan the Dunce. Duncan the baldy who didn't need a swimming cap. Duncan the gold medal winner. GS

BEFORE HE WAS FAMOUS
While on holiday in Corfu, Goodhew watched Mark Spitz's incredible seven-medal haul at Munich on a little black and white TV and had a poster of him on his wall.

THE MOMENT HE BECAME A LEGEND
When he reached the end of the swimming pool at the Olimpiysky Sports Complex before anyone else in the 100m breast-stroke final.

 AD NAUSEAM
Appeared alongside Gene Hunt in *Ashes to Ashes* for Sport Relief, with Sooty & Sweep and Emu. If that counts.

 HELL
2 RAISING

 **SPORTING**
8 ACHIEVEMENTS

74

Mary PETERS

BORN **6 JULY 1939**

Liverpool-born, Belfast-adopted secretary who bridged the Protestant-Catholic divide when she struck Olympic pentathlon gold.

As Peters waves, the crowd wonder what the lead singer of The Sweet is doing on the podium.

The year of 1972 was stained in blood and Mary Peters' incredible sporting achievement at Munich was book-ended by horrific acts of violence.

In January, 13 people were gunned down by British troops in Londonderry on 'Bloody Sunday', heightening The Troubles in Northern Ireland. Peters, an avowed atheist, had to negotiate barricades and security blocks to get to the gym for her fitness training to fulfil her burning ambition.

And in September, just two days after she had achieved an improbable gold in the pentathlon, 11 members of the Israeli team, athletes and coaches, were murdered by Palestinian terrorists in a gun battle with German sharpshooters.

'I desperately wanted to give [the people of Northern Ireland] a happy day.'
Peters sees the bigger picture.

Peters had moved to Ulster when she was 11 and knew this was her last chance of a medal – she finished fourth in Tokyo in 1964 and ninth in Mexico City in 1968. But she turned in a magnificent performance in a classic sporting confrontation with West German Heide Rosendahl.

Peters was inspired and set personal bests in the hurdles, shot put and high jump on the first day. The overnight leader, she had a sleepless night and didn't perform well in the long jump on the next day. Everything rested on the final event – the 200m.

As Denis Walsh put it in the *Sunday Times*: 'For Peters to win gold, she needed to run the 200m faster than she had ever done before. [At] 33 years of age… the clarity of her circumstances was piercing. One run would define her career. Absolutely.'

Rosendahl won and Peters finished fourth. Was it enough for gold? Not only had Peters won gold, but her 4,801 points represented a new world record. Gold round her neck, smiling broadly she waved from the top of the podium as, briefly, sport took the place of strife.

Dame Mary Peters has spent the rest of her life since that moment in the service of her twin loves, athletics and Northern Ireland, and is currently the Lord Lieutenant of Belfast. GS

....

 AD NAUSEAM
She now drives a Tigra sponsored by Saville's Auto Village with her name discreetly printed on the side.

....

 HELL RAISING    **SPORTING ACHIEVEMENTS**

BEFORE SHE WAS FAMOUS
Mary's father gave her two tons of sand to help her with her jumping. She also became adept at shorthand and filing documents as a secretary.

 THE MOMENT SHE BECAME A LEGEND
Setting a personal best in the 200m, which gave her a slender 10-point lead over Rosendahl.

John CHARLES

BORN **27 DECEMBER 1931** ■ DIED **21 FEBRUARY 2004**

The Welsh footballer who took Italy by storm and who was rated by Billy Wright as the greatest centre-forward he'd ever seen.

Which player do you think the Italian public voted for as the greatest-ever foreigner to play in Serie A? You might have thought Maradona and Zico would take a bit of beating, ditto Zidane and Van Basten.

No, it was John Charles. The Welsh 'Gentle Giant' topped the 1997 newspaper poll, having clearly made an unforgettable impression during his five years at Juventus – despite last kicking a ball in Italy in 1962 for AS Roma.

One of the first British players to be sold abroad, for a world-record £65,000 fee (which incidentally bought Leeds United a new stand at Elland Road, which now bears his name), Charles was a trailblazer as well as a wonderful ambassador.

'It was a complete culture shock…
The first time I was faced with a bowl of spaghetti it went everywhere but down my bloody throat.'
Charles on his transfer to Juventus.

Great in the air, agile and skilful with the ball at his feet, Charles was converted by Leeds boss Frank Buckley from a colossal young centre-half into a yet more devastating centre-forward. He ended his last year in Division One as top scorer, with 38 goals.

Juve followed Leeds' thinking, but added another tactical twist. In order to extract maximum value out of the asset that team-mate Jack Charlton

described as 'a team unto himself', Charles would play up front until he had secured a lead, then drop back to defend it. Three Scudettos and two Cups later, it was clear that Charlton had a point.

It's also a measure of his ability that during the 1958 World Cup, where Charles had helped Wales into the quarter-finals, pundits believed the Red Dragons could have beaten Brazil. Sadly, the Italian Player of the Year was injured and Wales fell to a goal by a 17-year-old kid called Pelé.

Il Buon Gigante netted 93 goals in 155 games against the reputedly impregnable Italian defences, and was never cautioned in a career that spanned four decades. DH

 **AD NAUSEAM**

As John Charles, Juventus' star player, put on Emidio Lazzarini's shoes for the first time, he exclaimed: 'This is not a shoe, it is a slipper. A golden slipper!' thus giving the brand its name – Pantofola d'Oro.

HELL RAISING 0

SPORTING ACHIEVEMENTS 9

The ball is in the box and the keeper does the only thing he can – pray.

BEFORE HE WAS FAMOUS
Moved from the groundstaff at Swansea's Vetch Field to join Leeds United as an amateur, aged just 15.

 THE MOMENT HE BECAME A LEGEND
When signing-on fees were capped at £10 for British players, Charles received £10,000 from his Juve transfer. 'The implications… are as yet hidden,' *The Times* reported. 'But it may one day prove a lever to greater incentives and rewards for the footballer at home.'

Danny BLANCHFLOWER

BORN **10 FEBRUARY 1926** ■ DIED **9 DECEMBER 1993**

Zen-like Irish right-half who destroyed the opposition with ideas, ideals and poetic beauty – a genuine original.

Spurs' great Double-winning side of 1961 was the last British team to play without compromise. Their game was beautiful, their aim simple: to score more goals than the opposition. The architect of the side was boss Bill Nicholson; its heart and soul was Danny Blanchflower.

The Tottenham team soon regretted getting the tube back to White Hart Lane.

When Nicholson took over the club's reins in 1958, he made full use of Blanchflower's ideas and leadership potential. All his previous bosses had been suspicious of the intellectual Irishman, but Nicholson had been a team-mate.

In an age of sergeant-major managers, Danny's views on artistry could easily be misinterpreted: 'The great fallacy is that the game is first and last about winning,' he said. 'It is

'Whether you're a player, manager, trainer, director, supporter, reporter, kit man or tea lady, football possesses the power to make the week ahead sparkle with a sense of joyous well-being.'
Blanchflower gives perfect expression to the term 'the people's game'.

nothing of the kind. The game is about glory, it is about doing things in style and with a flourish, about going out and beating the other lot, not waiting for them to die of boredom.'

Having outgrown Glentoran in his native Belfast and lower-league Barnsley, he had clashed with authority as skipper at Aston Villa,

only to be rescued by the £30,000 fee, a record for a half-back, that carried him to White Hart Lane.

Seeing him as a guru not a trouble-maker, Nicholson adopted Blanchflower's revolutionary ball-based training along with his astute tactical insights, employing the passing visionary to run matches not from the dugout but from the centre circle.

Pulling strings on the field and composing football's first haikus off it – 'We try to equalise before the other team have scored' – he helped Spurs romp to the 1960-61 championship with a record 31 league wins and 115 goals and then triumphed at Wembley to pull off the 'impossible' Double. They followed up with another FA Cup win in 1962, and capped their success with the UEFA Cup in 1963.

After football, Blanchflower sparkled as a journalist rather than as manager of Northern Ireland and Chelsea in the 1970s. Sadly, when he died in 1993, aged 67 and suffering from Parkinson's Disease, he was alone and all but penniless. DH

BEFORE HE WAS FAMOUS
Working as an apprentice electrician at a cigarette factory, Blanchflower lied about his age to join the wartime RAF.

THE MOMENT HE BECAME A LEGEND
Lifting the FA Cup at Wembley, skipper of the first Double winners of the 20th century.

Ø **AD NAUSEAM**
'Pass the hot milk, please!'
Shredded Wheat advert, circa 1960.

 HELL
3 RAISING

 **SPORTING**
9 ACHIEVEMENTS

Eric BRISTOW

BORN **25 APRIL 1957**

Charismatic cock-er-ney wideboy with a talent for throwing arrows.

'I have two bowls of confidence for breakfast every morning.'
Bristow reveals the secret of his self-assuredness.

Darts was still a sport played by fat blokes smoking fags and downing pints but, in the 1980s, the top players were household names. If anyone was responsible for turning a pub game into a mainstream sport it was Eric Bristow.

He couldn't have stepped up to the oche at a better time. The world championships were created in the late 1970s and he was a young player on the circuit when TV took an interest.

His Flash Harry style and cocksure charisma made him instant box office. Bristow was a geezer with glamour – personified by his infamous 'Crafty Cockney' nickname, which fittingly came from his favourite English pub… in Santa Monica.

He would swagger on stage and throw 'one-hundred-and-eightiiiies' with his signature raised pinky finger and a Cheshire Cat grin that was guaranteed to wind up opponents and crowds alike.

The only reason Bristow got away with it was because he was so bloody good. He dominated the sport for a decade, winning the first of five world championships in 1980, and reaching the final nine times in eleven years.

He didn't always get his own way, though. During the 1983 world championship, a TV audience of 10 million gasped when Bristow passed on the chance of a bullseye, in the belief that his unknown opponent Keith Deller didn't have the bottle to make a 138 checkout. Bristow was wrong.

In 1986, Bristow's confidence was shattered when he came down with a severe case of 'Dartitis' – a condition that meant he couldn't let go of the darts properly. Despite temporarily regaining the world No. 1 position in 1990, he was never the same player and retired from competing in 2000.

Without Eric Bristow, darts would never have gained such popularity – and dart-themed quiz show *Bullseye* would not have hit 17 million viewers. RA

Bristow steadies himself, focuses and… oh, and just look at what he could have won.

BEFORE HE WAS FAMOUS
He was part of a violent East London gang – he even admitted to keeping a claw hammer down his trousers for protection.

THE MOMENT HE BECAME A LEGEND
In 1982, he was jeered during a tournament in Scotland. In response, he hit a treble 20 and turned to face the abuse. After another treble 20, he turned to face an even more infuriated audience. Then, with his final dart he scored only a 20, but smiled and received an ovation.

 AD NAUSEAM
'Silver Arrow' darts 'styled on the tournament tungsten used by the Crafty Cockney' anyone?

 HELL RAISING 8

 **SPORTING ACHIEVEMENTS** 9

talkSPORT LEGENDS

Archie GEMMILL

BORN **24 MARCH 1947**

Diminutive era-defining World Cup goal-scoring midfield pocket battleship.

'Gemmill could go all the way on his own here…
Yes! Oh beautiful goal. Archie Gemmill.'

A slight, balding figure in an oversized Scotland[*] shirt is squinting into the sunlight, his arms snaked around the waists of two statuesque, scantily clad Brazilian dancers and a grin plastered across his weathered face.

Swigging a can of Irn Bru – the company having set up this bizarre photo shoot – Archie Gemmill wanders warily across to a group of journalists. The former Scotland dynamo has previous with the press, but here he is content to reflect on the summer of 1978, on Argentina, the World Cup. And *that* goal.

What the playmaker did in Mendoza has been immortalised in song, dance and film – the adroit control and shimmy to evade one defender, the jabbed pass to Kenny Dalglish (cf p76-7) and subsequent scuttle beyond another two Dutchmen to receive the reply, the way he righted his body shape, then the finish… clipped, classy and curling away from the grasp of Jan Jongbloed.

Football as art. Pure and simple.

That it counted for little, after a dreadful finals for the fancied Scots, made it more cherished and imbued the moment with an orgasmic potency.

That *Trainspotting* interpretation (after sex, one of the characters reflects, 'I haven't felt that good since Archie Gemmill scored against Holland in 1978'), insists Gemmill, is a source of some embarrassment ('[Watching it] I was slinking down in my seat'), but it has also helped right the persistent neglect of a wonderful career.

This, after all, is a man who captained his country on 22 occasions, won three English league titles under Brian Clough (cf p197-203) with Derby County and Nottingham Forest, and would have earned a European Cup medal had the revered Forest manager not surprisingly left him out of the side that beat Malmo 1-0.

Even as a coach, his efforts remain under-appreciated. Having assisted Clough, Gemmill led the Scotland Under-19 side to the final of the European Championships in 2006, where only the Spain of Gerard Pique and Juan Mata could halt them.

RICHARD WINTON

. . . .

 AD NAUSEAM
Overlooked for the Chrysler Avenger campaign, featuring the more telegenic members of the Scotland squad, he was nonetheless one of the 'faces' of Tennent's beer.

. . . .

 **HELL** **5** **RAISING**   **W** **SPORTING** **8** **ACHIEVEMENTS**

[*] Ever the patriot, Gemmill drove his heavily pregnant wife north from Derby to Scotland to ensure that his son wasn't born on enemy territory. He even called him Scot.

'I hated every minute of the ninety and I hated afterwards as well.'
Gemmill on being surprisingly dropped for the 1979 European Cup final.

BEFORE HE WAS FAMOUS
Having joined St Mirren after leaving school, Gemmill became the first player to be introduced as a substitute in a Scottish match in August 1966.

 THE MOMENT HE BECAME A LEGEND
Gemmill once scored a goal against the Netherlands in the World Cup finals. You might have heard about it…

Gary LINEKER

BORN **30 NOVEMBER 1960**

From the time he stood out at junior level in Leicester, the goal poacher *du jour* was always destined for great things.

It's a story upon which Gary Lineker's father, Barry, has dined out for years.

'Wayne [Lineker – his brother] was tremendous: he had so much skill – a lot more than Gary. He had more dribbling ability and that sort of thing, whereas Gary is more direct and probably thinks more quickly… Wayne has a lot of talent but he doesn't like the discipline.'

'Football is a simple game: twenty-two men chase a ball for ninety minutes and at the end, the Germans always win.'
Lineker delivers a sardonic and depressing truth.

So it was something of a surprise when the second-best prospect in the Lineker household, elder brother Gary, made his debut for Leicester City aged 18 in 1978. He ran around like an eager whippet on the wing, betrayed a nervy first touch but made steady progress and in 1982-83 scored 19 goals. Suddenly he couldn't stop scoring.

Earning his first England cap in 1984, the young goalscorer was exposed to a new class of team-mate. Before long, with his trademark opportunist timing and original ideas on the use of space in the box he began to look fully developed.

He went to Everton for £800,000 (38 goals in 52 games) and then secured a move to Barcelona in 1986,

where he helped lift the Copa del Rey and European Cup-Winners' Cup. Suddenly the once-gawky kid from the East Midlands was on track for all-time greatness.

Name: Gary Lineker. Chosen Specialised Subject: Annoying Germans.

Today, there will be younger fans who know Lineker only as the affable perma-tanned presenter on *Match of the Day*, but he was the highest scorer with three different clubs at the top level, including his last English club, Spurs. Despite receiving some criminal clogging, he was never booked in 16 years of glorious goal-banging.

At international level, it took Bobby Charlton (cf p118-20) 26 more games to get the one extra goal that makes him No. 1 in England's all-time scoring chart with 49.[*] Lineker travelled to the European Championships in Sweden in 1992 one behind Charlton. As England faced an early exit he was, infamously and to general disbelief, substituted by manager Graham Taylor against the hosts in the final group game. DH

 AD NAUSEAM
Has netted millions as the face of Walkers Crisps ever since 1995, wearing a muscle suit and dressing up as a nun, a baby and the Devil.

HELL
4 RAISING

SPORTING
9 ACHIEVEMENTS

[*] He has scored more goals in the World Cup finals tournaments (10) than any other England player.

BEFORE HE WAS FAMOUS
While with hometown club Leicester, he never gave up his part-time job on the family fruit 'n' veg market stall.

 THE MOMENT HE BECAME A LEGEND
Winning the World Cup Golden Boot in 1986 with six goals – the only English player ever to do so.[*]

Tony McCOY

BORN **4 MAY 1974**

The greatest jump jockey of all time, a winning machine who will put his body through hell to cross the finish line first.

Tony 'A.P.' McCoy is a jockey who, if he thought he would get there faster, would get off his horse and carry it over the finishing line. 'What is the point of taking part in a a race [the London Marathon],' he once asked his agent Gee Armytage. 'When you know you won't win the thing?'

He wasn't one for beauty treatments, but the mud facial seemed to work.

Physical strength is one thing, sheer horsemanship another. But somehow McCoy seems to be able to transfer his utter denial of the possibility of defeat to his mount.

In the pursuit of winning at all costs and in this most dangerous of sports, he has suffered numerous

'I'm a very talented digger driver. In fact, I'm better on a digger than a horse.'
Sitting in a JCB, planning a stable complex on his estate.

McCoy is the finest jump jockey of all time. The stats tell us that quite clearly – before him, nobody had got to 2,000 winners. McCoy now has well over 3,000. He has been champion jockey every year since 1995-96 (an astonishing 16 times). He has ridden more winners in a season than anyone, either on the Flat or over jumps, with 289 in 2001-02.

Ever since he started, nobody has galvanised a horse like he can. So how does he do it? Certainly success breeds success – the more wins you have, the better horses you are likely to ride.

injuries, but barely seems to notice as his focus is always on the next ride. Having suffered serious injuries prior to the Cheltenham Festival in 2009, he subjected his body to the torture of a cold chamber, and temperatures lower than -100°C.

That dedication has seen him win all the big races. However, a blot on his CV was his failure in the most famous race of all, the Grand National. But then along came a horse called Don't Push It in 2010, he won and finally McCoy was revered as a genius by more than just the racing fraternity,

becoming BBC Sports Personality of the Year.

For the record, it also looked as if the toughest man in the sport had a tear in his eye… SC

AD NAUSEAM

Better known for what he didn't endorse – McCoy refused to ride with the John Smith's logo on his breeches in the 2009 Grand National.

BEFORE HE WAS FAMOUS
McCoy was on a horse in his native Co Antrim as soon as he could sit up. He came to England aged 17 and immediately started winning races.

THE MOMENT HE BECAME A LEGEND
Despite being champion jockey for 15 seasons, it took the 2010 Grand National to confer legendary status as he won the world's greatest race.

 HELL **2 RAISING**

SPORTING **9 ACHIEVEMENTS**

Stephen HENDRY

BORN **13 JANUARY 1969**

Spotty kid with a cue who turned into a seven-time world snooker champion.

'Look closely at the lanky kid in jeans and a black T-shirt. He's the one with the soft-rock haircut, the one whose stone-dust pallor indicates that he's a daily phantom of this snooker hall.'

So began a *Sports Illustrated* article on the 21-year-old Stephen Hendry in October 1990. To be fair, it was an overly romantic view. The Scot was in fact a spotty young kid with crap hair, but it was telling that even an American magazine with little interest in snooker had identified him as something special.

> 'It would be good if I built myself up like something out of *Rocky*, but I pretty much just turned up.'
> Hendry de-romanticises his 1990s dominance at the Crucible.

And that he was. Given his first snooker table at the age of 12, Hendry destroyed his own father within an hour, made his first century break by 13 and turned professional at 16. It didn't all go to plan immediately – Hendry's 1986 World Championship debut ended with a 10-8 first-round defeat to Willie Thorne – but it was a matter of when, rather than if, he would come to dominate the sport.

As it was, Hendry – an unlikely hero with a tendency to look more miserable than any sporting great ever should – conveniently timed his rise to power for 1990, signalling the start of a new era of professionalism within the game. In many ways, he was the natural heir to Steve Davis (cf p49-50), the man who ruled the 1980s. Neither was truly appreciated in their own time, both too relentlessly dominant to sit comfortably in the nation's affections.

But, where Davis was a tactical magician, Hendry was pure talent – a potting machine who won so many frames at one visit he never really needed a safety game. He thrived under pressure and was at his most deadly when backed into a corner, invariably slotting in an aggressive long pot that would destroy his opponent's confidence. That style brought Hendry seven world titles (one, in 1994, with a fractured arm), 36 ranking titles and

Thinks: 'Maybe a Number Two round the sides and spikey on top. No, a bubble perm.'

over 750 competitive century breaks – all records that look unlikely to be surpassed.

Now into his 40s, Hendry last won the world title in 1999 but continues to compete at the highest level – though, with career earnings approaching £9 million, you'd think he'd sort his hair out... TH

BEFORE HE WAS FAMOUS
Hendry grew up in Fife, where he went to Inverkeithing High School at the same time as footballers Gordon 'Jukebox' Durie and Craig Levein, manager of Scotland.

THE MOMENT HE BECAME A LEGEND
His first Crucible final victory over Jimmy White, which made him the youngest-ever world snooker champion.

AD NAUSEAM
Appeared in a trailer for Eurosport. Er... that's about it.

 HELL RAISING 1

 **SPORTING ACHIEVEMENTS** 9

Tony JACKLIN

BORN **7 JULY 1944**

> When he was good he was very, very good –
> a golfer whose own website describes a career
> of 'brief but memorable brilliance'.

In 1969, the Ryder Cup match between America and Great Britain and Ireland went all the way to the final match on the final green at Royal Birkdale. With Tony Jacklin's ball just 2ft from the hole, American captain Jack Nicklaus stood for an age over his 5ft putt to prevent America losing the Cup. 'I was terrified,' he later admitted. 'I wasn't just putting for me, I was putting for my country.'

Tony Jacklin gulped as he watched Nicklaus's little ball fall into the middle of the big hole, and then he gulped again as he foresaw his own putt on the way to the hole, which suddenly looked small and distant.

Then, almost incredibly, Nicklaus picked up Jacklin's marker and conceded the putt. He took the half, or rather donated it, because Nicklaus knew what Jacklin feared and what everybody watching knew and feared.

'I know you wouldn't have missed that,' Jack said as the pair embraced. 'But, in these circumstances, I didn't want to give you the opportunity.'

Earlier in the summer of 1969, Jacklin had become the first home player since 1951 to lift the old claret jug when he won the Open. High on confidence, Tony could beat the world. In 1970, he proved his mettle to the Americans on their own patch, the first Brit to win the US Open since 1926 (and then until 2009). Yet still Jacklin's self-belief was incomplete.

In the 1972 Open at Muirfield, Jacklin had a 15ft birdie putt on the par five 15th, while Lee Trevino was bunkered in four. Trevino chipped in while Jacklin three-putted and then bogeyed the 18th, never again to challenge in a major. As he said later, 'Up to that point I had believed that with sheer determination and will, you could achieve anything…'

However, the man who single-handedly revitalised the British game went on to underline his power as a generational inspiration when, in the 1980s, he served as non-playing captain in four Ryder Cup contests, steering his boys to the first home victory for 28 years and then, in 1987, the first-ever win on US soil. DH

> 'I think I would have made [the putt]… I was at the top of my game – I'd won the British Open that year and I wasn't afraid to make it.'
> Jacklin on Royal Birkdale 1969.

Jacklin just could not believe he'd left his locker key at home. Again.

 AD NAUSEAM
'Confident co-ordination shows on a man… wear it at your leisure!'
Jacklin Jump Jets – co-ordinating polos and vee-necks, trousers and casual shoes, 1974.

 HELL RAISING 1

 **SPORTING ACHIEVEMENTS** 8

BEFORE HE WAS FAMOUS
From a working-class family in Scunthorpe, he followed almost every other school-leaver in town into an apprenticeship at the local steelworks.

 THE MOMENT HE BECAME A LEGEND
For a British player to win the Open after 18 years of hurt sparked a resurgence in the sport and gave the whole country a boost.

65

J.P.R.WILLIAMS
BORN **2 MARCH 1949**

Mutton-chopped Welsh full-back who alternated his time between breaking bones on the rugby field and mending them as a surgeon.

A selfish man, it was his ball and nobody else was getting their hands on it.

Using initials in place of names is a preference usually reserved for pop stars, authors or extra-terrestrials but, when contemplating the greatest British rugby full-back, three letters come to mind: J.P.R. With sideburns that would make Elvis envious, a mane of mouldy locks and his socks riding perpetually around his ankles – J.P.R.Williams was one of rugby union's most recognisable icons.

Williams was the ever-dependable last line of defence for the all-conquering Welsh team of the 1970s. Few people can remember him spilling

'No doctor has played rugby with such a wilful disregard for his own well-being since J.P.R.Williams was charging around the old Arms Park like a wounded bison.'
Tim Glover, the *Independent*, 1992.

a catch, while anyone on the wrong end of his thundering tackles probably still has the scars to prove it. And, he could also turn defence swiftly into attack – scoring the late dropped goal that secured the British Lions' first win over the All Blacks in 1971.

He took up egg-chasing as a means of studying to become a qualified orthopaedic surgeon – possibly working on the notion that he wouldn't be able to understand bone surgery without

exposing his own body to every possible type of fracture on the playing field. He is said to have treated his own injuries during half time and even cared for opposition players, despite the treatment they gave him.

Between 1969 and 1981, Williams fired the Welsh team to eight Five Nations, six Triple Crowns and three Grand Slams. He played like a man possessed, and on the ten occasions he faced England, not once did he finish on the losing side. And, as a member of the British Lions, he played a famous role in memorable victories over both New Zealand and South Africa.

J.P.R. retired from international rugby in 1981 to concentrate on his medical career but continued to play club rugby until he was well into his fifties – when most men that age would prefer to spend their Saturday afternoons avoiding their wives on the golf course. RA

AD NAUSEAM
Too busy being a doctor but promoted his own book, *Given the Breaks*.

 HELL RAISING 6    **SPORTING ACHIEVEMENTS 8**

BEFORE HE WAS FAMOUS
J.P.R. started his sporting life as a tennis player and won a junior event staged at Wimbledon in 1966 – beating fitness guru David Lloyd.

 THE MOMENT HE BECAME A LEGEND
J.P.R.'s almighty tackle on French winger Jean François Gourdon in the 1976 Grand Slam decider, turning a certain try into a traffic accident.

Bryan ROBSON

BORN **11 JANUARY 1957**

'He's here, he's there, he's every [expletive deleted] where,' they used to sing. And he was, except when he was injured, of course.

Unfortunately, the ball to the back of the head rendered Robson unconscious.

Clad in the tight red-white-and-blue garb of 'Captain Marvel', Bryan Robson was England's most influential and inspirational player of the 1980s, an all-action up-and-downer who popped up all over the park with last-ditch tackles, crosses, long-range shots and headers.

Not just our best midfielder by a country mile, but also one of our best defenders, and unquestionably in the top two attackers, scoring 26 goals and creating countless others in his 90 international outings between 1980 and 1991. If anything, his injury-prone style of play, and the countless ensuing absences from frontline duty, served only to underline the Geordie's warrior-like reputation and his profound importance to the national side.

There seemed something genuinely superhuman about a real-life hero who could break a metatarsal, an ankle and three legs, suffer three fractured noses, two hernias, a snapped Achilles' tendon and countless calves and hamstrings torn asunder. Not to mention *that* dislocated shoulder in the 1986 World Cup (see picture left).

If only he could have lined up against Maradona in 1986, he might have swayed events. And in 1990, the suspicion remains that Captain Marvel could have superpowered us further than the semis.

In 1981, Manchester United manager Ron Atkinson paid a British record £1.5 million to sign his former West Brom charge. He spent 12 of his 13 years with the club as their longest-serving captain, twice leading them to FA Cup wins under Big Ron. Under Alex Ferguson (cf p110-11) he added a further FA Cup triumph, two Premiership titles and European Cup-Winners' Cup honours. He not only led the way on the pitch, but also in training and in lively team-bonding sessions.

In the past 17 years, Robson came close to doing a famous job as Middlesbrough boss – three finals, three losses – but struggled in the hot seat at Bradford City, West Brom, Sheffield United and, most recently, Thailand – he resigned in June 2011. He has been diagnosed with throat cancer but those closest to him have no doubts he will beat it. As a player and a man, his legend remains intact. DH

'In a way, certain sections of the media always wanted to knock me because I had captained my country and been skipper at Old Trafford. It was all a bit odd really.'
Robson forgets that the media also christened him Captain Marvel.

BEFORE HE WAS FAMOUS
As a teenager he underwent trials with Burnley, Coventry City, Sheffield Wednesday and Newcastle United before finally accepting a £5-per-week apprenticeship with West Brom.

THE MOMENT HE BECAME A LEGEND
At Espana 82, Robson scored the then fastest-ever World Cup goal in 27 seconds, and followed up with a header as England beat France 3-1.

 AD NAUSEAM
'Bryan Robson, the new face of Seatone Green-Lipped Mussel Extract, is a strong advocate of joint care.'

🔥 **HELL** **8** **RAISING**   W **SPORTING** **9** **ACHIEVEMENTS**

63

John BARNES

BORN **7 NOVEMBER 1963**

Mercurial winger, accomplished rapper and scorer of the best goal ever seen in an England shirt.

It is the great tragedy of John Barnes' football career that he will be most remembered for one sublime goal against Brazil. It was June 1984, and a twisting, turning, dribbling masterpiece from him gave England an unlikely 1-0 victory at the Maracana stadium. It should have been the launchpad for the 20-year-old to embark on a sparkling international career.

But it was never to be, and although Barnes went on to win 79 caps across a 12-year period, he never reached the heights in an England shirt that his phenomenal talent had suggested.

There were mitigating factors – Barnes suffered greatly at the hands of a disgracefully racist Wembley minority who plagued his career. But, for all his travails at international level, the Barnes of Watford and then Liverpool was a force of nature.

Born in Jamaica in 1963, he moved to England as a 12-year-old and was eventually spotted playing non-league football in 1981. Watford were the

'You've got to hold and give, but do it at the right time, you can be slow or fast but you must get to the line.'
ENGLAND*neworder*'s World Cup song, ' World in Motion', 1990.

lucky club, and Graham Taylor the astute judge who signed the 17-year-old Barnes for the price of a set of kit.

It proved to be quite a bargain: Barnes would spend six years at the club, scoring 65 goals in 233 league appearances before Kenny Dalglish (cf p76-7) shelled out what now seems the unfeasibly small amount of £900,000 to take him to Liverpool.

So began a meeting of minds, with Dalglish the brains and Barnes the on-field inspiration behind the last truly great Liverpool side of the 1980s. Nominally a winger, Barnes was a rippling hulk of muscle who combined great strength with blistering pace and more skill than English football had seen since George Best (cf p192-6).

Barnes passed the trial and eventually became lead guitarist in New Order.

A lovely finisher, he scored 84 league goals in ten seasons at Liverpool – even more impressive considering he played the last three of those in a deep-lying midfield role.

Barnes eventually retired in 1999, his two league titles and two FA Cups with Liverpool the extent of his major honours. Now 47, he is concentrating on media work and cultivating a more expansive shape – which not even an eight-week appearance on *Strictly Come Dancing* in 2007 could decelerate. TH

Ø **AD NAUSEAM**
'This is isotonic Lucozade Sport – it gets to your thirst, fast.' You'd have to watch it many, many times before tiring of Barnes in the classic Lucozade advert – but it is possible.

BEFORE HE WAS FAMOUS
When Barnes first arrived in England, the thing he remembers most from his journey was the number of football pitches he could see from the plane as it flew in.

THE MOMENT HE BECAME A LEGEND
Dancing through the Brazilian defence in 1984 to score a goal worthy of the *selecao* in the Maracana.

 HELL 4 RAISING   **SPORTING 8 ACHIEVEMENTS**

62

Steve DAVIS
BORN **22 AUGUST 1957**

and Barry HEARN
BORN **19 JUNE 1948**

The shy ginger 'Nugget' with a killer instinct and the Essex deal-maker, Davis and Hearn ruled snooker in the 1980s…

Bravado, razzmatazz and a tan, Barry Hearn was not your average chartered accountant. But then, Steve Davis was not your average snooker player. Dedicated, obsessively technical

all four World Championship semi-finalists on its books.

While Alex Higgins (cf p127-9) and Jimmy White (cf p21) endured a punishing schedule of exhibition matches, Davis concentrated on winning titles, safe in the knowledge that Hearn was setting up deals to endorse everything from aftershave to computer games.

Snooker's popularity peaked in 1985, outstripping even football in the ratings thanks to the epic moment when Dennis Taylor snatched the world title on the final black. Davis recalls it as the 'best and worst moment' of his career – though he has obviously erased the moment the single 'Snooker Loopy' charted in the Top 10 from his memory.

When he was not winning 28 ranking tournaments (including the first televised 147 break at the Lada Classic in 1982) and 53 non-ranking tournaments, he was building up one

> 'A tall, skinny, long-haired ginger kid turned up and asked if he could play in one of my competitions… one of the luckiest moments of my life.'
> Hearn on the chance meeting that defined both their careers.

and devoted to the sport, his only vice appeared to be a penchant for Space Invaders.

'Chalk' met 'Cheese' in 1974 at the Romford Snooker Club, an establishment frequented by layabouts and – as it transpired – a future world champion. Hearn, the club's manager, was sitting in his cramped office crunching numbers when a punter burst in, 'Barry, you've got to see this kid.' So began one of the most lucrative and successful partnerships in British sport. The secret was simple: 'I have never tried to tell Steve how to pot balls and he has never tried to tell me how to do a deal.'

The results spoke for themselves: Davis amassed six world championships and became snooker's first millionaire. Hearn dominated snooker to such an extent that, in 1988, his Matchroom Sport operation had

As 'Whispering' Ted Lowe might have put it, 'There are five reds on the table now.'

Steve DAVIS and Barry HEARN ▬▬▬ 62

of the best collections of Northern Soul vinyl records in the world. Possessed of an extremely dry sense of humour, he has matured into a commentator and personality of renown.

Davis still calls Hearn his 'best mate' and is now a ceremonial figure within the game, while Hearn has successfully applied his talents to boxing, poker, fishing, pool, darts and, as chairman of Leyton Orient, football. More recently he's returned to snooker in an attempt to bring back the glory days when the game was a soap opera and the players were goldmines. As Davis might say: 'Interesting…' TB

'You know the rules: brandies are for management. Can I get you another fruit juice, son?'

⊘ AD NAUSEAM
When *Spitting Image* created Steve 'Interesting' Davis, Hearn exploited his client's 'boring' reputation to help sell Irish Life insurance and Heinz baked beans.

STEVE DAVIS

🔥 **HELL**
2 **RAISING**

🏆 **SPORTING**
9 **ACHIEVEMENTS**

BARRY HEARN

🔥 **HELL**
4 **RAISING**

🏆 **SPORTING**
7 **ACHIEVEMENTS**

BEFORE THEY WERE FAMOUS
Davis, a keen chess-player, failed to win the English Championship – the amateur game's premier title.

Hearn, the son of a bus driver, qualified as a chartered accountant and purchased an interest in a chain of derelict snooker clubs.

THE MOMENT THEY BECAME LEGENDS
When Davis won his first world title in 1981, Hearn lifted him off the ground in a bear-hug and pumped his fists at the TV cameras.

61

John SURTEES
BORN **11 FEBRUARY 1934**

The only man to have won world titles on both two and four wheels, a feat that will never be repeated.

'Now where are my goggles, I definitely had them a minute ago.'

John Surtees had to pay tribute to his teenage son Henry in 2009 after he died in a freak accident in a Formula 2 race at Brands Hatch. He could hardly have denied Henry the chance to follow a dangerous dream.

Born in Surrey in 1934, Surtees was the son of Jack, a motorcycle dealer and sidecar champion. In 1948 they won a sidecar race at Cockfosters, but 'Team Surtees' were disqualified when it was discovered that the one in the sidecar was just 14.

Leaving school at 16, he went to work at Vincent Motorcycles. On a bike, as in a car, Surtees was a fearless, tough but fair competitor, as quick as the best without being wild. But where most of his rivals contented

'I was a bit nuts, really.'
Surtees loved understatement.

themselves with riding or driving, he had a deep interest in the workings of his machines.

Surtees' big breakthrough came in 1956 when he joined MV Augusta. He dominated the sport during his time with the Italian manufacturers, winning seven world championships on 350cc and 500cc bikes between 1956 and 1960.

Having lifted the 1959 BBC Sports Personality of the Year award, Surtees decided to take up Formula 1 racing. After a false start with Yeoman, he then joined Ferrari where he was already adored by Italian motor-racing fans from his time with MV Augusta.

They had even more reason to love the man they called 'Son of the Wind' when he won the F1 title in 1964. Wins in Germany and Monza, plus second place in the USA and Mexico Grands Prix, were enough to clinch the championship for Ferrari and give Surtees his unique achievement of world titles on two and four wheels.

Surtees suffered a serious crash in Ontario in 1965, fell out with Ferrari in 1966 and joined Honda. In 1970 he formed the Surtees Racing Organisation, retired from competitive racing two years later and enjoyed nine years as a constructor in Formula 500, Formula 2 and Formula 1. GS

 BEFORE HE WAS FAMOUS
Surtees earned the nickname 'Bullet' at school for his speed on the athletics track.

 THE MOMENT HE BECAME A LEGEND
Victories at the Isle of Man, Dutch TT and Belgian Grand Prix earned Surtees the 500cc world motorbike title in 1956. Legendary status came with the F1 title in 1964.

 **HELL RAISING** 2

SPORTING ACHIEVEMENTS 9

talkSPORT LEGENDS

60

Bob PAISLEY

BORN **23 JANUARY 1919** ■ DIED **14 FEBRUARY 1996**

Masterminded Liverpool's conquest and subsequent domination of Europe in his cardigan and slippers.

The plain facts are impressive enough. Over a period of nine years (1974-83) Bob Paisley won 20 trophies as Liverpool manager: six league titles, three European Cups, one European Super Cup, one UEFA Cup, three League Cups and six FA Charity Shields. That all this was achieved by such a shy man makes it all the more astonishing.

Bill Shankly (cf p177-81) made his shock decision to retire, Paisley moved reluctantly into the limelight. Three years later he became the first English manager to win the European Cup.

His strength was simplicity founded upon attention to detail, not least an appreciation of each player's physical limitations. Training was geared towards building stamina and

'There'll be hell to pay when the Kop find out I'm only at Number Sixty.'

> 'I knew there was no way that I could establish the rapport with the Liverpool fans that Bill Shankly had done. So I simply said, "I'll let the team do the talking for me."'
> Paisley demonstrates the acuity that was the key to his success.

Paisley served Liverpool as a player and manager for 44 years. Born in the Durham pit village of Hetton-le-Hole, he joined Liverpool in 1939 but did not make his first-team debut till after the war, as wing-half for the Championship-winning side of 1946-47.

The Rory Delap of his day with a turmoil-inducing long throw, he made 250 appearances before retiring in 1954 to join Liverpool's soon-to-be-fabled 'Boot Room' staff. In 1974, when

preventing injury – getting players fit and keeping them that way. In season 1978-79, Liverpool romped to the title using only 15 players, one of whom, Sammy Lee, played just twice.

Paisley was nicknamed 'Dougie Doins' (pronounced Do-ins) by those same adoring players because he described everything from bootlaces to shin pads to substitutes as 'Doins'. Michael Robinson, a player under Paisley, recalls, 'It was all "Wye-aye-

aye laddie". Bob never said a word that anybody could understand, but everyone knew what he meant.'

Graeme Souness put it best: 'After the final in Paris all the lads went out to celebrate [winning the 1981 European Cup]. Alan Hansen and I decided we'd stay in the hotel, and we went up to Bob's room. He's sitting there in a cardigan with soup stains on it. He's got his slippers on because he always had problems with his ankles. And it's like a night in watching *Coronation Street*.' DAVID COTTRELL

 AD NAUSEAM

The nearest he ever got was posing on the training pitch with Bill Shankly in matching, shrink-wrapped Gola T-shirts some time in the 1960s.

BEFORE HE WAS FAMOUS
An apprentice bricklayer, then a tank gunner during the Second World War who helped to liberate Rome from the Nazis.

THE MOMENT HE BECAME A LEGEND
Guiding Liverpool to their first European Cup triumph in 1977, having already won the league and narrowly missed out on the FA Cup.

 HELL RAISING*

 SPORTING ACHIEVEMENTS

* Waging war in Italy not included.

59

Glenn HODDLE

BORN **27 OCTOBER 1957**

Sublimely talented midfielder with Tottenham, Monaco, Chelsea and England. And Swindon. With some unconventional beliefs.

'You and I have been physically given two hands and two legs and half-decent brains. Some people have not been born like that for a reason. The karma is working from another lifetime.'
Hoddle delivers his resignation speech.

It was as though the ball had been blessed by a higher power – Eileen Drewery.

Hoddle found God and, as somebody once noted, 'That must have been one hell of a pass.' However, if any player in the last 50 years could make it, Hoddle would have been the man.

His captain at Spurs, Steve Perryman, compared him to a top-flight golfer. 'Glenn swerves the ball,' he said. 'Fades it, flips it, spins it, drives it, chips it and uses backspin to make it stop.'

Hoddle announced himself to the football world in February 1976, firing a long-range effort on his full debut past Stoke keeper Peter Shilton. It was the first of many wonderful goals in a Tottenham career that spanned 12 years and 478 appearances.

It soon became clear that he was one of the most gifted players in the game, and he had White Hart Lane gasping with his 40-yard ball-to-feet passes and graceful goals. He was the fulcrum of the Spurs team as they won the FA Cup in 1981 and 1982.

Hoddle also played a big part in the Spurs 1984 UEFA Cup win, but missed both legs of the final due to injury – a theme that would run through his last few seasons in England.

In 1987 Hoddle moved to Monaco, enjoying a successful career in France under Arsene Wenger, away from the muck and bullets of English football. Hoddle was always happier creating rather than getting stuck in. This also, perhaps, explains why he won only 53 England caps – Michel Platini claimed that, had he been born in France, he would have got 150.

Hoddle was a very successful player-manager at Swindon and Chelsea before England came knocking… He left Paul Gascoigne (cf p169-72) out of the 1998 World Cup squad and took middle-aged faith-healer Eileen Drewery to help deal with injuries, but England failed to progress beyond the quarter-final stage.

Hoddle hadn't been forgiven the following year. He gave an interview to a national broadsheet newspaper where he discussed his thoughts on reincarnation. The knives were out and Hoddle was sacked in February 1999. GS

....

 AD NAUSEAM
Shredded Wheat dropped a TV advertisement as 'inappropriate' in 1997. It featured his family, but his marriage was reported to be in trouble.

....

HELL RAISING 3 | **SPORTING ACHIEVEMENTS** 7

BEFORE HE WAS FAMOUS
Schoolboy football but, let's face it, he must have done something pretty spectacular in a previous life to be graced with that kind of ability.

 THE MOMENT HE BECAME A LEGEND
His inspirational performances through the 1977-78 season, as he hauled Spurs out of Division Two. Definitely not releasing 'Diamond Lights'.

talkSPORT LEGENDS

58

Steve REDGRAVE

BORN **23 MARCH 1962**

Arguably the greatest Olympian of all time, London Marathon charity hero, best-selling author and Chelsea fan. Well, nobody's perfect...

Blimey, look out – we've got competition. And if there's anyone in the world you'd rather avoid in toe-to-toe combat, it's Britain's greatest-ever Olympic athlete. Not content with the feat of winning five gold medals at five successive games, Steve Redgrave has only gone and written a book profiling some of the world's greatest sportsmen and women.

'Winning was great and everything, but can we try powerboat racing next?'

It's enough to make you turn to drink, the prospect of being pitched in at the deep end against a bloke who also won nine rowing World Championships and three Commonwealth Championships before bowing out of the water after that ultimate 2000 Olympic triumph (see picture above).

It isn't as if there's any room to rubbish the man. He's a sporting

'If anyone sees me anywhere near a boat, they have permission to shoot me.'
Redgrave, post gold number four, in 1996.

giant, who took motivation from his heroes and peers along the way as he summoned the mental and physical strength required to triumph against staggering odds. He's personally raised £5 million for charity. He's not just a Sir, he's 6ft 5in. He was even a founding member of London's successful 2012 Olympic bid.

Every sports fan knows how Redgrave began accruing gold in 1984 in the Coxed Four, before switching to the Coxless Pair to make it four in four. But did you know he was also a member of the national bobsleigh team, and national champion in 1989-90? Did you know about the ulcerative colitis he suffered post 1992 – or the trauma of being diagnosed with diabetes in 1997, faced with the scientifically proven fact that 38-year-old diabetics don't win Olympic gold at the Coxless Four?

Perhaps best of all, as an insight into Redgrave's endlessly ambitious, ever-challenging character, can you guess the quintuple superman's favourite sporting memory? 'To win the Commonwealth Games in 1986 in the single scull. I always wanted to be a single sculler. I won three golds in Edinburgh and it was one of the most fun weeks of my life.'

We're not legally required to tell you which book that quote came from. DH

 AD NAUSEAM

There's a parrot with an 18th-century admiral's hat, and an actor in admiral's garb racing Redgrave on a rowing machine.
Steve: 'Hi, I'm Steve Redgrave, and Admiral want to help you find cheaper car insurance.'
Parrot to admiral, as Steve pulls away: 'You're a disgrace.'

 **HELL RAISING**

 SPORTING ACHIEVEMENTS

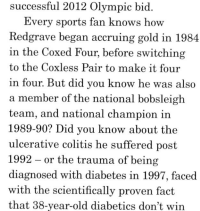

BEFORE HE WAS FAMOUS
'She was my first love, a demanding mistress who dominated my youth,' admits Redgrave. Turns out he's talking about the River Thames.

 THE MOMENT HE BECAME A LEGEND
Slumped over his oar after winning his fifth gold in Sydney, triple gold-winning partner Matthew Pinsent crawled back along the boat to give Redgrave a hug.

Lennox LEWIS

BORN **2 SEPTEMBER 1965**

The Canadian… erm… British Heavyweight Champion of the World. A man who kept at it until he beat the lot of them.

In June 2002 Lewis knocked out Mike Tyson in Memphis, Tennessee (see picture right). And that was when he earned his place in boxing history.

Simply destroying Evander Holyfield in 1999 wasn't enough, he had to beat Tyson: 'If I hadn't, no matter how many other fights I won, there would have always been people who said, "He never could have beaten Tyson."' He didn't just beat him. He took him to pieces, his devastating right-hook leaving Tyson lying on the canvas in the eighth round.

Born in East London, Lennox was taken to Ontario, Canada, when he was 12 to keep him out of trouble. As he recalls it: 'All the kids made fun of my accent and I punched the lot out.' A teacher advised him to take up boxing.

His 1983 Junior World Championship win was the first of many titles that culminated in a heavyweight boxing gold medal for Canada at the 1988 Olympics, beating Riddick Bowe. A career in pugilism

'I have been in there with all of them and there is nothing left for me to prove.'
Lewis tells it like it is.

'This is the last time I'm going to tell you, Mike: stop looking up my shorts.'

beckoned and, a year later, he turned pro and came back to England.

In 1993, Bowe was stripped of the WBC heavyweight belt for refusing to fight Lewis and with that Britain had a world heavyweight champion, our first since 1897.

Thereafter, Lewis dominated his division. And if he didn't always have the full support of every fight fan on these shores, then he gained respect in 1999 when, despite out-boxing Evander Holyfield (Lewis landed 348 punches to Holyfield's 130) in a title unification bout, the fight was called a draw. It didn't matter. Eight months later the promised rematch was on and it brought a new undisputed heavyweight champion of the world: Lennox Lewis.

Since calling it a day in 2004, Lewis has had to quell rumours of a comeback on numerous occasions. And why would he consider a return? When people talk of the sport's true greats, they mention him in the same breath as Gene Tunney and Rocky Marciano – he retired at the top. He had beaten every opponent he had faced. His legacy is secure. DM

AD NAUSEAM
'If I was called to a home [and a man had been] using his fists on a woman over something called a "domestic row", I don't know whether I could keep my cool with that man.'
Hard-talking ad for the Metropolitan police.

BEFORE HE WAS FAMOUS
He was a talented all-round sportsman in his schooldays, doing well in football, basketball and athletics.

THE MOMENT HE BECAME A LEGEND:
Having been told by 'Iron' Mike Tyson he was going to eat his children, Lewis left him on the floor. To bleed.

 HELL RAISING

 SPORTING ACHIEVEMENTS

Virginia WADE

BORN **10 JULY 1945**

British tennis player in Grand Slam victory shock. The eternal tennis bridesmaid who timed her big day to perfection.

In 1977, Britain was at a miserably low ebb, suffering from rising unemployment and double-digit inflation. Labour were just about clinging on to power and the country was assailed by the revolutionary stirrings of punk rock.

Against this grim backdrop, the nation prepared for summer and a street party to celebrate the Queen's Silver Jubilee... but first the traditional annual humiliation of Wimbledon.

In 1968, 23-year-old Virginia Wade had broken through to win the US Open, following up with the Australian Open in 1972. But having reached at least the quarter-finals for the previous five years, Wimbledon had eluded her. Seeded an optimistic and generous three, she looked staid and

She had very powerful legs for a woman. It was a back-handed compliment. Geddit?

stiff behind the slick new threat of Chris Evert and Czech powerhouse Martina Navratilova.

When Ginny walked out on to Centre Court everyone felt a stirring. It was in the jut of her jaw, in the unisex flutter caused by the tilt of her big frilly pants. It was time for

resilience, for calculated risk and aggression – for reinvention.

Having played the best tennis of her career to beat Evert in the semi, Ginny faced Dutch baseline-hugger Betty Stove – destroyer of Navratilova and new Brit hopeful Sue Barker – in the centenary final.

Wade lost the first set 6-4, recovered to win the second 6-3 and then cruised to victory with 6-1 in the third. There was a little skip as she went to meet a disconsolate Betty Stove at the net and then she brushed her hair.

'The atmosphere was phenomenal,' she said of the moment the Queen presented her with the winner's Venus Rosewater Dish. 'I've never experienced anything like that in England other than football's 1966 World Cup. The place went crazy.'

She went on to win the 1977 BBC Sports Personality of the Year and continued to play singles at Wimbledon until 1985, a record 24 years in all, and the grand dame still returns every year as BBC commentator. She remains number four on the all-time victory list with 839 match wins. Gawd bless her. DH

'It was my sixteenth attempt... Now I'm in the final for the first time. The Queen is watching. Everybody is watching. I'm going to win this thing if I have to kill myself to do it.'

Wade reveals her pre-match strategy.

 AD NAUSEAM

'Discover Pain Ease, the patch that relieves pain – I did and it really works!' Unfortunately, in 2009 the advertising watchdog banned it for 'discouraging people from seeking help for serious medical problems'.

 HELL
2 RAISING

 SPORTING
8 ACHIEVEMENTS

Roy RACE

BORN **SEPTEMBER 1954**

Melchester No. 9 who spawned the 'Roy of the Rovers Moment' – a byword for unlikely on-field moments.

In the 1950s, when every lad's idea of true romance was a football team that continually trounced the opposition 6-0, young Roy Race was a dream come true. He signed up for mighty Melchester Rovers along with his schoolmate Blackie Gray.

They did not just force their way into the first team – voice from the crowd: 'The big Hardcastle stopper is warning Racey not to nutmeg him again' – but embarked upon a 40-year silverware spree that would eventually include nine league titles, eight FA Cups, three League Cups and sundry European trophies played out against cynical/tinpot/cheating foreign players.

Favourite food(s): Trifle and smoked salmon (not together).
Favourite drink: Hot strong tea (I'm tea total!).
A Q&A reveals his 'sense of humour'.

It was during football's post-'66 marketing boom when Roy really came of age – 23 again – not as a long-haired troublemaker like Georgie Best (cf p192-6), but as a combination of every positive element of the legendary Two Bobs, Moore and Charlton (cf p187-91 and p118-20).

The goal-banging goodie was blond and clean-cut, a spunky rock up front when all looked lost with five minutes to go, before turning underhand defeat – 'Look! The ref is getting mirror signals from the Dynamo dugout!' – into improbable last-minute glory.

In every sense, 'Roy of the Rovers' had come to exemplify the British idea of the true sportsman. And, as such, he was all set for a fall in the 1970s, when he teased his hair into a centre parting. Now, merely winning was becoming oddly unsatisfying, and attempts were made to handicap Roy, to make him seem more human, possibly even a bit of an underdog.

As a nod to his age, he became Rovers' player-manager and took the club secretary as his lady wife – which most fans considered beneath him, even if she did look a bit like Suzi Quatro. They even had kids. Yurgh!

In the 1980s, Penny Race upped and left, triggering a nationwide Mexican wave of twentysomething 'Told you so's'. The plot long lost, a mulleted Roy signed up Spandau Ballet and suffered a foot amputation after a chopper crash, luckily escaping with light bruising when Middle Eastern terrorists assassinated eight team-mates. The three limping survivors won in the last minute, Race breaking the net with a pile-driver from his right stump. DH

 AD NAUSEAM
In the 1980s, Melchester Rovers wore red-and-yellow hooped tops with a Gola ad prominently placed.

Incredibly, this shot was miscued and the opposition broke and scored the winner. Not really.

BEFORE HE WAS FAMOUS
Before signing for Rovers in 1954, Roy was just a glint at the end of *Tiger* artist Joe Colquhoun's pencil.

 THE MOMENT HE BECAME A LEGEND
In 1977, Roy hit the headlines when he was shot by a mystery gunman – just a bit like *Dallas*'s J.R.Ewing.

54

Graham HILL

BORN **15 FEBRUARY 1929** ■ DIED **29 NOVEMBER 1975**

Motor racing's only 'Triple Crown' champion: winner of the F1 Drivers' Championship, the Indianapolis 500 and the Le Mans 24-hour.

'The chief qualities of a racing driver are concentration, determination and anticipation. A 1929 Austin without brakes develops all three – anticipation rather more than the first two, perhaps.' Hill on his humble first car.

'What? A helmet? Pah! I don't even wear a seatbelt, dear boy.'

In the early 1970s, you were nobody if your name wasn't Hill. There was Dave 'Superyob' Hill out of Slade. TV comedian Benny Hill, chasing scantily clad ladies in fast motion. And Graham Hill the racing driver, ditto.

With his pugnacious, jutting chin, 'Mr Monaco' had the look of another Hill – *Match of the Day* presenter Jimmy – but that caddish moustache and slicked-back hair left an impression of a speed demon who was equal parts Terry-Thomas and Dick Dastardly.

Always a larger-than-life figure, his celebrated high-jinks, his roving 'eye for the ladies' and more private black moods made him tough to live with, for his family and racing teams alike; but harder still to live without after his death in November 1975 – on a foggy Hertfordshire golf course, in the burning wreck of his Aztec aircraft.

Ironically, the end came four months after Hill's racing retirement. But his career had always been contradictory: he didn't even have a driving licence when, aged 23, he paid a quid for four laps around Brands Hatch, and decided to become a racing driver.

Part of his popularity was because he wasn't as cool as Jackie Stewart or a driving genius like Jim Clark, but Hill simply tried harder. This in the day when racing cars were little more than thin aluminium shells full of petrol, with rock-hard tyres, negligible brakes and no seatbelts.

Hill became a winner by sheer force of will. He was world champion in 1962 with BRM, and in 1968 with Lotus, winning the Monaco GP five times. In 1972, having taken up sports car racing, he added the Le Mans 24-hour race to his F1 and Indy 500 wins, showing a unique talent across the different racing disciplines.

Hill's racing attributes would re-emerge as his son Damon, F1 World Champion in 1996, completed a unique father-son double. DH

 AD NAUSEAM

'Grand Prix drivers know they can rely on Shell Oils. So can you.' Graham Hill is the poster boy for Shell Super Oil.

HELL RAISING 8

SPORTING ACHIEVEMENTS 9

BEFORE HE WAS FAMOUS
First grew that Dastardly moustache as the result of a rule outlawing facial hair during his national service in the Navy.

 THE MOMENT HE BECAME A LEGEND
Winning the Indy 500, at the first attempt, in 1966. He blew some of his £55,000 prize money on the Aztec aircraft in which he would meet his death.

53

DESERT ORCHID

BORN **11 APRIL 1979** ■ DIED **13 NOVEMBER 2006**

The big-hearted grey with a banzai approach to racing that saw him lead from the front...

In the cold world of statistics, *Timeform* places Desert Orchid as the fifth greatest National Hunt runner of all time. In the hearts of many racegoers, casual followers and animal lovers alike, the grey will always be No 1. His post-retirement public appearances went on for longer than his racing career, and never failed to draw an adoring crowd.

Foaled at Goadby in Leicestershire in the spring of 1979, sired by Grey Mirage out of Flower Child, you wouldn't have recognised Desert Orchid in his early days, as he was yet to start the greying process. There was nothing that singled Dessie out as special for trainer David Elsworth in those early days and his first race, a novice hurdle

Thinks: 'If that little git whips me again he's coming off at the next fence'.

at Kempton in 1983, was almost his last as he suffered a heavy fall.

He made gradual progress from that faltering start and won six of his eight starts in the 1983-84 season, but struggled again when stepping up from novice level. Dessie was then switched to the fences and improved rapidly as a two-mile steeplechaser. The first places piled up and he came

to virtually own the King George VI Chase at Kempton, winning it four times between 1986 and 1990.

His finest moment came at a sleet-blown Prestbury in the Cheltenham Gold Cup in 1989. Dessie was in irresistible form, having won his previous seven races, but the 3m 2f course was considered too long for him. The heavy conditions weren't suited to Dessie, and neither was the left-handed track, as he had a tendency to jump to the right when tired.

Despite having all this stacked against him, Desert Orchid ran himself into the ground, overhauling the mudlark Yahoo, and a crowd of almost 60,000 roared him home to a glorious one-and-a-half length victory.

'He was a great jumper, who had guts like a lion. You could ride him like you were driving a car, and just ask him to go faster or slower.'
Jockey Colin Brown was, however, less confident when reverse parking the famous grey.

Dessie won 34 of his 70 races, and after a fall at Kempton on Boxing Day 1991 he was allowed to retire. The magnificent sight of Dessie taking a hurdle would never be seen again.

After a long and happy retirement the beloved, handsome grey died in 2006, aged 27, having amassed career earnings of £654,066. His ashes were buried next to his statue at Kempton Park. GS

BEFORE HE WAS FAMOUS
Was a bay foal called Fred by his stable lads, gradually began to turn grey but not an instant success on the track. That would come later.

THE MOMENT HE BECAME A LEGEND
His magnificent Cheltenham Gold Cup win in 1989 when he defeated the conditions, the course and all the opposition.

⊘ AD NAUSEAM
Would never have lowered himself.

HELL RAISING   SPORTING ACHIEVEMENTS

talkSPORT LEGENDS

52

Ryan GIGGS

BORN **29 NOVEMBER 1973**

Welsh wizard who has cast a spell against the effects of ageing to become the most decorated player in English football history.

In the beginning, God created Giggs. Ever since the Premier League conceived football as we know it, Ryan Joseph Giggs has been twisting the blood of defenders and scoring wonder goals wearing a Manchester United shirt. That's a period spanning over two decades…and counting.

In that time Giggs has won an unprecedented 12 Premier League titles as well as four FA Cups and two Champions Leagues, and set more records than Norris McWhirter could count. It could all have been so different had a young Giggs decided to stay on as an apprentice with Manchester City, instead of selling his soul to a red-faced devil who came knocking on his 14th birthday.

United manager Alex Ferguson (cf p110-11) was persuasive, and it wasn't long before Giggs was scoring the winner against his former club on his full debut during the 1990-91 season.

Fergie took the first of his fledglings under his protective wing,

shielding Giggs from the media glare and temptations of fame – famously stopping a party at Lee Sharpe's house. Consequently, and despite some personal problems off the pitch, he has remained a model professional on it.

It's this dedication that has ensured the never-ending story of Giggsy's success. He'll soon be 38 years old, and while he may have lost some pace, his speed of thought remains undiminished – longevity that earned him the 2009 BBC Sports Personality of the Year Award.

The only regret is that he never played in a major international tournament. Despite representing England at schoolboy level, his Welsh roots prevented him from joining the international squad.

'Roy Keane is Damien, the devil incarnate off the film *The Omen*. He's evil. Even in training.'
Giggs reflects on his polar opposite.

Unfortunately, for legal reasons, we cannot reveal the identity of this player.

Somewhere in an attic there is probably a portrait of him getting older – but on the pitch there is still no finer sight in football than that of an elastic-limbed Ryan Giggs gliding past defenders. When the curtain is finally drawn on his glittering career his name will be etched above all others in the annals of United's illustrious history – maybe even better than Best. RA

AD NAUSEAM
What might have been. Giggs reminisces: 'I was about fifteen, I think. My mum gave me some money to buy some new Reebok football boots, but I decided to buy a cheaper pair so I could take a girl to the pictures. Jill Evans it was; she was gorgeous. I waited ages but she never turned up.'
Reebok, 1997.

BEFORE HE WAS FAMOUS
A young Giggs was probably counting sheep in the Cardiff valleys before fate intervened, forcing his rugby playing father to move to Salford, Manchester.

THE MOMENT HE BECAME A LEGEND
The FA Cup semi-final goal in extra-time in 1999 that saw Giggs slalom between five Arsenal players before scoring the winner and so helping United on to the Treble (see picture above).

 HELL **6** **RAISING**

 **SPORTING** **9** **ACHIEVEMENTS**

51

Carl FOGARTY

BORN **1 JULY 1965**

A death-defying, crowd-pleasing Superbiker with a controversial reputation, Foggy didn't so much race his opponents as declare war on them…

With his ferret-faced looks and two glowing lumps of coal where one might expect to find eyeballs, Carl Fogarty was not what you would call loveable.

But to the fans who worshipped him, the prickly Blackburn lad was the undisputed king of World Superbikes. During his eight years in the seat, Fogarty won no less than four championships and a record 59 races, making him the most successful Superbike rider ever.

'Nearly killing myself 50,000 times on that one lap.'
Fogarty's response when asked what made him decide never to race the Isle of Man TT again – where he had posted the then fastest-ever lap in 1992.

He was introduced to motorbikes by his father, a panel beater who raced in his spare time. Fogarty was soon burning up the countryside around Blackburn. It wasn't long before he progressed to road-racing bikes where he immediately made a name for himself.

What marked him out from his rivals was his undying dedication to winning races: he would rather crash than lose, and often did. It was a series of accidents that led Fogarty to exchange Formula 1 TT racing – where he was world champion, winning the Isle of Man TT three times – for Superbikes in 1991.

Forget about Jack Nicholson in *The Shining*, 'Heeere's Foggy!'

He won his first WSB title in 1994 and repeated the feat the following year before a brief but unsuccessful flirtation with Honda. Fogarty then returned to Ducati and claimed two more titles.

His career ended in 2000 when he narrowly cheated death. Foggy slammed into Robert Ulm at 140mph – a massive impact that left him in a seemingly lifeless heap. When paramedics arrived, they assumed he was either dead or that his spine had snapped.

In actual fact, the only thing broken was his arm: fractured in three places, it required a titanium plate and seven pins to hold together the shards of bone that brutally shredded his muscles, weakening them to the extent that he could no longer ride at the highest level.

Fogarty's short fuse earned him a few enemies on the racing circuit, but to his fans he was living proof that an ordinary boy could realise his dreams, especially if he was prepared to push it to the limit. TB/RA

 AD NAUSEAM
Fogarty was part of the TV ad for Carlsberg, the official beer of the England football team, in the build-up to the 2010 World Cup. It was all part of 'Probably the best team talk in the world…' It didn't work.

HELL RAISING 6

SPORTING ACHIEVEMENTS 9

BEFORE HE WAS FAMOUS
The shy teenager entered his first motocross race at the age of 14, and began teaching himself how to overcome the fear of failure…

 THE MOMENT HE BECAME A LEGEND
Beating his arch-rival Scott Russell in the final race of the 1994 World Superbike Championship to take the title – despite having broken his wrist earlier in the season.

talkSPORT LEGENDS

Jonny WILKINSON

BORN **25 MAY 1979**

He's rugby's starriest player; corporate gold dust with a crease in his jeans. But hey, who cares – this *Boy's Own* hero provided one historic moment of sporting poetry…

You can picture it now. Just 20 seconds of the 2003 Rugby World Cup final with Australia remained, Matt Dawson threw it back to Wilkinson, who'd positioned himself for the kick (see picture right) and, in the immortal words of commentator Ian Robertson: 'Jonny Wilkinson, he's done it! It's over.'

A decade of practising alone under the floodlights had spawned one iconic dropped goal, thus snatching the trophy from the holders in their back yard. Jonathan Wilkinson was a world champion – aged 24.

If his mum had been watching she would have been proud, but as it happened she was in Tesco doing a big shop. Not because she didn't care, mind, but because she couldn't bear to watch.

The rest of the country, however, was enthralled and 2003 became Wilko's year. Though, bizarrely, it wasn't for the man himself. Measured against his own painfully high standards, he actually judged it a failure, finding himself disappointed that he'd missed several earlier chances.

A series of demoralising injuries followed, meaning it was 1,169 days after the triumph Down Under before he could pull on the famous No. 10 shirt again. Though, instead of moping, he read up on quantum physics, specifically Schrödinger's

Cat (a thought experiment), which he put down to helping his obsession with perfection.

Cerebral and intense, there was no question he would overcome his injury

problems, and Wilko returned to the national squad in the 2007 Six Nations Championship and for the 2007 World Cup. The 'no-hopers' made the final – but lost, tempting the committed teetotaller out on the lash with Prince Harry, whereupon he poured vodka down the royal gullet till 6am.

It had all started for Wilkinson up in Newcastle, where he played for the

Falcons during the 1997-98 season. By the end of the campaign, his performances had been noted by the England selectors and he came on for Mike Catt in the final game of the Five Nations.

By the following season, he was a regular pick, though in the centre, not yet at fly-half, and scored 62 points in the Five Nations, after which he moved up to No. 10 and continued to kick goals.

Suddenly the fresh-faced star from Surrey was the poster boy of English

'At the age of eight, all I wanted to do was drop the goal that won the World Cup.'

Wilkinson reveals that he can also see into the future.

rugby. Ahead of that famous final in 2003, he received a good luck message from David Beckham (cf p154-6), with whom he had starred in a TV advert. One of his team-mates was chuffed to get a message from Shaun Goater.

Now often used by England from the bench, he broke Ronan O'Gara's record for most points in the Six Nations tournament in March 2010.

BEFORE HE WAS FAMOUS
Wilkinson's earliest memory is 'being three years old and having a tiny green jacket and wellington boots on the side of the rugby field, with my dad passing a little orange plastic ball around…'

THE MOMENT HE BECAME A LEGEND
It's now impossible, possibly illegal, to write about him at length without referring to how the mother of all kicks sealed his place in history.

Beating the Aussies? It's like takin' a Choo Choo bar off a baby, mate.

He joined Toulon at the start of the 2009-10 season after 12 years at Newcastle, and has recently signed a contract to stay there until 2013. He will hope to form a part of the 2011 World Cup squad (it will be his fourth tournament) and continue to add to his world record total of points.

So, to be clear: England international at 18, Grand Slam winner at 23, two World Cup finals (a tournament where he is the record points scorer), two Lions tours, an MBE and an OBE. He's intelligent, can play the guitar, speaks fluent French, studies Buddhism and, in case you'd forgotten, is one of England's greatest ever fly-halves. The swine. DM

⌀ **AD NAUSEAM**
Having attended the Cuprinol school of wooden acting, Wilkinson appeared in a 2004 Boots ad warning of the dangers of high cholesterol.

 HELL
2 RAISING

 **SPORTING**
10 ACHIEVEMENTS

 talkSPORT
LEGENDS

Tom FINNEY

BORN **5 APRIL 1922**

Wing wizard for Preston North End and England with a deadly eye for goal and a wicked way with a burst pipe.

Back in 2001, Tom Finney unveiled 'The Splash', a water feature sculpted in his honour at Deepdale. Inspired by the 1956 Sports Photograph of the Year (see picture below), it features the winger churning up jets of spray at a waterlogged Stamford Bridge.

But the watery theme was no coincidence. Back when Sir Tom was just plain Young Tom, his father had insisted he take a trade, even though he was offered part-time terms by

his local club, Preston North End. He chose plumbing, and it proved a useful asset in topping up his meagre maximum wage later in his career, also earning him the nickname – wait for it – 'The Preston Plumber'.

There's no better illustration of how things have changed for footballers: the modern-day equivalent would be Frank Lampard coming round to mend your boiler, while playing for Chelsea and England.

Although it isn't easy to prove – he was of the last generation of players whose exploits weren't televised and he has no winners' medals – Finney was one of the greatest players England ever produced.

We have to go on the opinions of those who knew an outstanding player when they saw one. One-time Preston team-mate Bill Shankly (cf p177-81) was asked to compare the up-and-coming Trevor Francis with Finney: 'Aye, he's as good as Tommy,' Shanks smiled at the memories, 'but then Tommy's nearly sixty now.'

Finney was a slight boy, at 14 he was just 4ft 9in and 5st, and was initially rejected by Preston on the

Accusations that the groundsman had over-watered the pitch were refuted by Chelsea.

talkSPORT LEGENDS

grounds that there was nothing of him. But he worked incessantly on building up his strength and focused on using his weaker right foot until it felt as natural as his left. This gave him a versatility that saw him play in each of the five contemporary forward positions for Preston, as well as left-wing, right-wing and centre-forward for England.

He had a fierce shot with either foot, the pace and skill to beat any full-back, the strength and balance to withstand challenges, was a highly accurate passer and was good in the air. Not surprisingly for a player with so much in his locker, he played 76 times for England between 1946 and 1958, scoring 30 goals.

Finney played in the 1950, 1954 and 1958 World Cup finals, but probably his finest moment for England came in a 5-3 victory over Portugal in Lisbon in 1950 when he scored four goals.

This is even more impressive when you consider that young Tom's career was interrupted by World War II. When the teenager should have been learning the game and working his way through the ranks to the first team, he found himself fighting with Montgomery's Eighth Army in Egypt.

By the time league football resumed,

Finney was 24 and went straight into the Preston first team. Born and raised a goal-kick away from Deepdale, Finney's first trip to a game came at the age of five; and he was to spend his whole career at the club, clocking up 473 appearances and 210 goals.

Choosing to serve his home town throughout his career probably cost Finney the chance to grab some winners' medals. There were near

did well. The Finney mantelpiece had to make do with the 'Footballer of the Year' trophy, which he was awarded in 1954 and 1957.

A persistent groin injury forced Tom to retire in 1960, and although 38 years old he was still on top of his game, scoring 21 goals in his final season. Preston were relegated as soon as he left and have never returned to the top flight.

'Pelé was a great player. He must rank one of the best of all time. I've said that Tommy Finney was the best I've seen and I'd bracket Pelé, Eusebio, Cruyff, Di Stefano and Puskas up there with him.'

Bill Shankly delivers his considered opinion.

misses – in 1952-53 and 1957-58 the Lillywhites finished as League Championship runners-up, and in 1954 they were beaten 3-2 by West Brom in the FA Cup final.

This remained Finney's greatest disappointment. Not fully fit, he failed to perform at Wembley – and when Finney wasn't firing, Preston rarely

Even today the concepts of Preston North End and Tom Finney are inseparably intertwined. There is 'the Splash' sculpture; Deepdale stands on Sir Tom Finney Way; his giant likeness is picked out in coloured seats in the Tom Finney Stand, and he is Life President of the club. GS

BEFORE HE WAS FAMOUS
Finney served his 'apprenticeship' in wartime football in the Middle East and Italy, where pitches had to be swept for enemy mines.

THE MOMENT HE BECAME A LEGEND
After a 7-4 win over Derby in 1947, the *Lancashire Evening Post* reported: 'Finney's dazzling runs were sheer artistry and it was fitting that the wingman should end it all by making a goal in a million.'

 AD NAUSEAM
Shredded Wheat with the wife and kids – where the family estimated they must have eaten 50-odd Shredded Wheats and a gallon of milk during a day's filming.

 HELL
RAISING
2

 **SPORTING**
ACHIEVEMENTS
7

Jimmy GREAVES

BORN **20 FEBRUARY 1940**

'It's a funny old game,' winks the lovable Cockney jester – the consummate, unparalleled English centre-forward.

It might seem wrong to base an appreciation of such a colourful character, arguably England's greatest ever goalscorer, around an armful of mindblowing stats; but Jimmy Greaves' successful role as a chirpy media Cockney over the past 30 years has blinded many modern fans to the self-deprecating, natural comic's primary incarnation as a lethal weapon.

Whether it's due to the historical distraction of the events of 1966, a decade-long crash into alcohol problems, or his current cherished status as a stand-up comedian, England's finest is now in danger of being very underrated.

Bobby Charlton (cf p118-20) is England's highest-ever scorer with 49 goals in a sedate 106 games (an average of 0.46 goals a game). More recently, Gary Lineker (cf p42) shot up to second with 48, collecting his total in just 80 matches (0.6 goals per game). Greaves, meanwhile, amassed his 44 international goals in just 57 games –

a whopping average of 0.77 goals per game. He is also the only player to have scored six hat-tricks for England.

The rapacious rapidity with which the pipe-smoking East Hammer banged the back of the net was bordering on the impolite. Fast and direct, he would embark on mazy runs – you could just tell what he was thinking: 'Aht ver fackin way!'

His speed of thought and deed was capped with a poacher's calm, and a cool preference for what Bill

'I've always said the person on the football field wasn't me. George Best felt that, too. I'm a very poor example of a footballer, really. I don't even know why I was a footballer. I'm not sure I even wanted to be one as a kid. I just liked playing.'

Greaves as existential philosopher. Who knew?

When Jimmy was hot – right from the day of his goalscoring Chelsea debut at 17 in 1957, throughout an England career that was sadly curtailed in 1967, and up until the time he moved on from Spurs after nine years, aged 30 in 1970 – he was on fire.

Nicholson famously called 'passing to the stanchions'. Greavsie himself was less poetic, claiming: 'I don't 'ave a funderous shot and I don't spend hours working out shooting angles. I just get in as close as I can and let rip.'

In 1960, when Greaves was still only 20, he became the youngest player ever to score 100 league goals – and three years later he had 200, including a post-war record six hat-tricks in season 1960-61.

With a phenomenal record of 132 goals in 169 games for the Blues, a brief spell following the lure of the lira with AC Milan was, in retrospect, a misjudgement, even a failure – but Greaves still scored nine goals in 12 Serie A games.

BEFORE HE WAS FAMOUS
Even when he was playing for Chelsea in the early '60s, Greaves ran his own removals business.

THE MOMENT HE BECAME A LEGEND
The 1962 World Cup match against Brazil when Greavsie got down on all fours to catch an elusive dog on the pitch – and it peed all over him! Garrincha enjoyed the spectacle so much, he took the dog home as a pet.

Safely installed at Spurs by manager Bill Nicholson's brave investment in the first £100,000 footballer (minus a single blush-saving quid), he went on to notch a club record 268 goals in 381 matches. He finished top Division One scorer on no less than six occasions: 1959 (32), 1961 (41), 1963 (37), 1964 (35), 1965 (29) and 1969 (27).

Having hung up his boots in 1971, after playing a season and a bit for West Ham, with a grand total of 357 goals in 516 league games, it's hard to say in which colours Greavsie played his best. 'If you ask Chelsea fans they'll say it was when I was at Chelsea,' he deadpans. 'If you ask Spurs fans they'll say it was when I was at Spurs. And if you ask West Ham fans they'll say it when I was at Chelsea or Spurs.'

You might have thought he'd mention England, but even now it's a sore point. The ultimate marksman's unenforced absence from the 1966 World Cup-winning side really was a turning point in his life. 'I felt sorry for myself and sick that I was out. But I was not, and have never been, in any way bitter against Alf. He did his job and England won the trophy.'

Greavsie played only three more matches for England. A year after his international swansong he hit the bottle, and looked as if he was heading for a Bestian fate for ten years until he swore off the booze in 1978.

The beginning of his long, happy ending came at non-league Barnet – and rest assured you can still find fans at Underhill who argue Greavsie's peak came in yellow, aged 38, when he scored 25 goals from midfield to be named Bees Player of the Season. DH

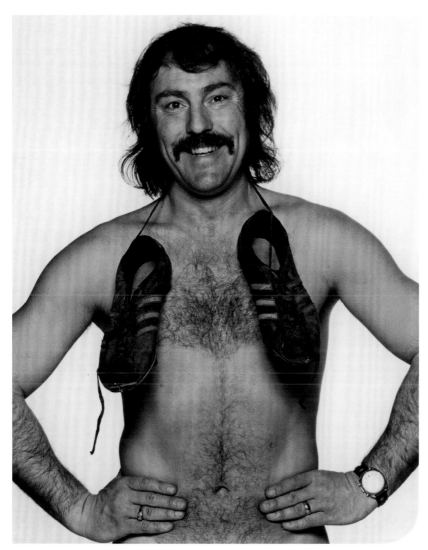

It's a naked Jimmy Greaves with a pair of Adidas boots round his neck. The stud.

⊘ AD NAUSEAM

The signature *Football Gone Crazy* video from 1991 includes glimpses of comic material from the groundbreaking 'Saint and Greavsie' double act.

 HELL
9 RAISING

 **SPORTING**
8 ACHIEVEMENTS

Linford CHRISTIE

BORN **2 APRIL 1960**

Lycra-filling Jamaican-born powerhouse, famous for being the only Brit to win 100m gold at all four major events.

It was less than 100th of a second later when he realised somebody had glued his left foot to the blocks.

Known for his speed out of the blocks, Linford Christie didn't announce himself on the world stage until he won the 100m title at the 1986 European Championships in Stuttgart. And yet his final tally of 18 podium appearances at the four most prestigious events (Olympics, World Championships, European Championships, Commonwealth Games) has never been matched by a fellow British athlete.

A robust 170lb of pure muscle in his prime, he demonstrated signs of athletic promise at primary school in West London. A year after emigrating from Jamaica as a seven-year-old, he took part in his first-ever 100m race at the White City Stadium – the same venue that hosted the London Olympics in 1908.

A self-confessed party animal in his youth, Christie's early sprinting career played second fiddle to his passion for blackcurrant and rum. In his wildest days, he often stumbled home at the same time as the milk arrived. And it wasn't until he was 24 that he responded to criticism from his coach, Ron Roddan, ditching the booze for extra training sessions.

Two years later, in 1986, his career finally took off when he shocked the sprinting world to become European champion over 100m in Stuttgart, having failed even to qualify for Britain's relay team at the Los Angeles Olympics two years earlier.

But it was on the Olympic stage where Christie enjoyed his finest moment at 32 – eyes bulging, the veins in his neck like co-axial cable, his face a picture of concentration as he crossed the line with his arms raised to the skies.

The moment he became the 100m Olympic champion would forever be etched into the minds of the millions tuning in at home, and the 70,000 spectators in Barcelona.

On the same evening, more than 72,000 Michael Jackson fans crammed into Wembley Stadium for a night of Jacko's 'Dangerous' tour – only for the gig to be pulled at the last minute. Such was Christie's popularity in the UK, when news broke of his victory, the crowd erupted as if the King of Pop himself was moon walking in mid-air.

despite setting a new European record of 9.92 seconds.

His perseverance proved to be the turning point in his career: a year after realising his Olympic dream, he clocked a new world record of 9.87 seconds in Stuttgart, and less than a mile from where he first raced as a child, the West London Stadium was renamed the Linford Christie Stadium.

His relationship with the press and the public nose-dived in controversial fashion when he tested positive for the performance-enhancing drug Nandrolone in 1999. A two-year ban

have envisaged a packed courtroom as the venue for his last headline-grabbing victory, but when a journalist suggested his earlier achievements could be attributed to doping, he sued for libel damages and won.

During the case, he made a point of referring to the embarrassment caused by the term 'Linford's Lunchbox' – a phrase earlier coined by the *Sun* newspaper. This created for many what turned out to be the highlight of the entire case, when Mr Justice Popplewell turned to Christie, who was under oath, and asked, 'What is Linford's Lunchbox?'

CHRIS MENDES

'At what point do you begin to run at the start of a race?'

'On the B of the Bang.'

A commemorative £1.4 million 'B of the Bang' sculpture was erected in Manchester in 2005.

At the games in Barcelona, Christie endured living conditions more commonly found in over-subscribed hostels: he was forced to share a box room with Colin Jackson that was so small he had to leave his suitcase in the corridor. The bathroom was shared by up to nine people.

They went on to become two of Britain's finest athletes, with Christie arguably the most celebrated of all time: three consecutive gold medals at European level, two at Commonwealth level, Olympic champion in '92 (see picture left) and world champion in '93.

Remarkably, he contemplated retirement the year before his crowning glory in Barcelona, following a soul-destroying fourth-placed finish at the World Championships in Tokyo –

followed, putting a sour end to an otherwise remarkable career. Sadly, despite continuing to protest his innocence, Christie never regained the same rapport and hero-like status he enjoyed with the British public in his prime.

But there was one thing that he had not lost, and that was his knack of winning. Christie may not

 AD NAUSEAM
Endorsed milk for schools in the 'Wake up to milk' TV ad of 1987, in which he loses a race against a milk float, despite a healthy head-start.

 HELL
6 RAISING   **SPORTING**
9 ACHIEVEMENTS

BEFORE HE WAS FAMOUS
Joined the Air Cadets in West London aged 18 before taking up sprinting full-time a year later.

 THE MOMENT HE BECAME A LEGEND
Becoming the oldest Olympic champion by four years to win the 100m, taking gold at the 1992 games in Barcelona as a 32-year-old.

Barry McGUIGAN

BORN **28 FEBRUARY 1961**

Some say the only good thing to come out of Clones is the road to Rosslea. But anyone who witnessed Barry McGuigan in the 1980s would almost certainly disagree...

Unlike many great boxers, teetotal Finbar Patrick McGuigan (as he was christened) – better known as Barry – has managed to hold onto both his money and faculties.

He has, however, endured other tragedies. His brother Dermot committed suicide in 1994 and there is no question that the night in 1982 when he knocked out Young Ali at the World Sporting Club will stay with him for life. His Nigerian opponent slipped into a coma and later died.

Understandably, the tough little Irishman was rocked. He later mused, 'I thought boxing was supposed to be a sport.' He even considered quitting the game, having turned pro only a year before. That tells you much about the man.

Just one year earlier, McGuigan (Catholic) had married childhood sweetheart Sandra Mealiff (Protestant). This – at the height of The Troubles – was a brave statement. But then nobody ever questioned the bravery of the 'Clones Cyclone'.

McGuigan had grown up surrounded by casual sectarian violence. Zig-zagging like a commando to reach the Immaculata Amateur Boxing Club, he had discovered his talent for 'handling' bigger kids after spotting a pair of boxing gloves in a derelict building. He slipped his hands inside, clenched his fists and found a vocation. By the age of 17, he would be a gold medal winner at the 1978 Commonwealth Games in Edmonton.

'It is not the size of the dog in the fight that counts, but the size of the fight in the dog.'

McGuigan, in reference to his diminutive stature.

The chance find led to a glittering career that would see him capture the WBA World Featherweight title, the British public's imagination and later earn him UN recognition (McGuigan boxed with the dove of peace on his trunks). The line was: 'Let McGuigan do the fighting.'

The moment McGuigan transcended boxing is easily pinpointed. In 1985, he earned a shot at the big one. After a rheumy-eyed (but slightly out of tune) rendition of 'Danny Boy' by father Pat, 24-year-old McGuigan took on 29-year-old Eusebio Pedroza, then the longest-reigning champion in boxing.

It was a battle between youth and experience, with McGuigan bobbing and weaving and moving forward with relentless determination. After 14 rounds, McGuigan's cuts man informed him, 'You have three minutes to beat the best featherweight champion this century. In three minutes you will be champion of the world.' No pressure, then.

A TV audience of nearly 20 million watched McGuigan take a unanimous points decision and tearfully dedicate his victory to Young Ali. Despite defending the title twice, he relinquished it to Steve Cruz in Las Vegas in June 1986 (see picture, right).

It has been argued that the fight should never have gone ahead in the

BEFORE HE WAS FAMOUS
Represented Northern Ireland at the 1978 Commonwealth Games and Ireland at the 1980 Moscow Olympics.

THE MOMENT HE BECAME A LEGEND
Beating Eusebio Pedroza in an emotionally charged fight at Loftus Road, which led to him being crowned the 1985 BBC Sports Personality of the Year.

baking Nevada sun at that time of the day, and McGuigan was hospitalised after suffering from dehydration. He retired, made a comeback and won a handful of inconsequential bouts, but finally called it a day after losing to Jim McDonnell in Manchester in 1989; it was just the third defeat in his 35-fight career.

McGuigan helped set up the Professional Boxing Association and enjoys a successful career in the media.

He was awarded an MBE in 1994 and honoured with a United Nations Inspiration Award for peace in 2010. More impressively, perhaps, he also won reality TV cooking show *Hell's Kitchen* in 2007 with 'McGuigan's Mash', having survived not only Marco Pierre White but also Jim Davidson.

TB/JEREMY STUBBINGS

 AD NAUSEAM

'Barry McGuigan World Championship Boxing' – an addictive 1985 computer game released by Activision that allowed the player to work his/her way through the featherweight division before meeting the 'Clones Cyclone' in a world title fight.

 HELL RAISING    **SPORTING ACHIEVEMENTS**

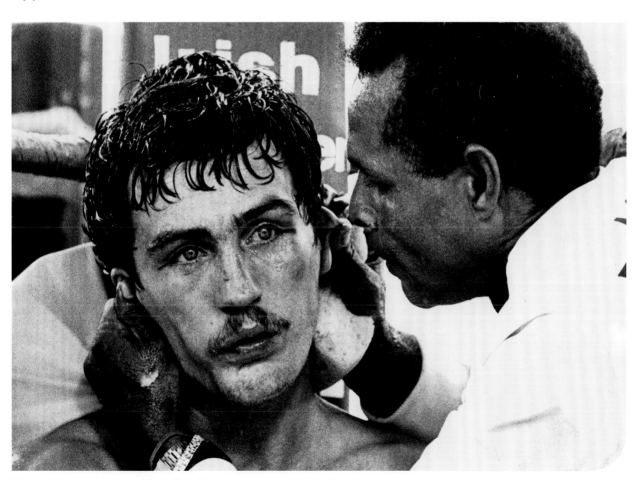

'It's bad news son, your ears are falling off. Let's hope you never need to wear glasses.'

Gordon BANKS

BORN **30 DECEMBER 1937**

Britain's greatest goalie, who won a World Cup winner's medal and pulled off the greatest save ever… before disaster struck.

A 1998 Worthington Cup second-round tie between Leicester City and Chesterfield was remarkable for the away fans' raucous barrage of booing throughout the match. It was only deep in the second half when the majority of home fans worked out the source of their anger.

Almost 30 years previously, the Filbert Street outfit had come in flashing £7,000 to rob the Spireites of their greatest prospect of all time – a skinny kid from Sheffield who had played only 23 games in Division Three for the Derbyshire club.

Gordon Banks was special. A goalkeeper whose legend lives long in the memories of all who saw him play – or even heard tales passed down of his lithe athleticism, his flycatcher reactions and his elevation of the humble shot-stopper's lot into a new sporting science.

He had first come to the attention of scouts for the bigger clubs in 1956,

Salmon now refer to a particularly lively jump up a waterfall as 'leaping like a Banks'.

when he had propped up Chesterfield's run to the FA Youth Cup final against Manchester United. As soon as he broke into the first team, he was clearly ready for a big step up.

Asked about the specialist goalkeeper training and coaching in the 1960s he recalled, 'No, there was none of that. I had to run the laps, do all the exercises, and then [play] five-a-side. But because we didn't have an actual training ground, we had to play on the car park. I couldn't dive about on that surface so I didn't go in goal, I played outfield.'

When Leicester eventually developed a training ground, Banks stayed behind after training to practise and work on angles and fitness like no other goalkeeper before him – and soon Banks, two-time FA Cup finalist and League Cup winner, became 'Banks of England'.

'[Winning the World Cup] was a fantastic feeling,' he has said. 'I knew I had lots of years left in the game, as I had trained well and worked hard, so at the time I didn't see it as the pinnacle of my career. I thought really that it was just the beginning.'

It was, but not at Leicester. Banks' goalkeeping revolution was about to be unexpectedly furthered by his understudy at Leicester, a 17-year-old called Peter Shilton.

'I'd seen this report in the paper where Peter was supposed to have said to the board, "I either want first-team football, or I want to leave." When I saw that I laughed. I thought, "I've played for England and won a World Cup, does he honestly think they're going to drop me and put him in?"'

'I wish I'd been a better driver!'

When a post-retirement Banks was asked if he had any regrets.

Stoke boss Tony Waddington – recognising the value of winning games via the new science of goal prevention – stepped in to match Leicester's previously unfeasible asking price for a mere goalie.

Banks was England's keeper at the Mexico 70 World Cup, where he famously pulled off his impossible save against Pelé (see picture left), who described the slim figure diving 'like a salmon leaping up a waterfall'.

However, a stomach upset ruled him out against West Germany in the quarter-finals, with Peter Bonetti deputising.

Banks watched the game on TV in his room and drifted off to sleep with England two goals ahead. He was awoken by third-choice keeper, Alex Stepney, coming in to his room and holding up three fingers on one hand and two on the other. Banks' double World Cup dream was all over. And tragically, his top-class career was soon to follow.

On Sunday 22 October 1972, Banks left the Victoria Ground after receiving treatment, but never made it home for tea. TV programmes nationwide were interrupted JFK-style to bring the sickening news of his car crash. When Banks regained consciousness, he was told that he had lost the sight of his right eye.

Playing on in America's NASL Soccer Circus, Gordon Banks OBE picked up the further honour of 1977 NASL Goalkeeper of the Year. But, without the crash, he could have continued to keep Shilton and Clemence out of the England side for many years. DH

BEFORE HE WAS FAMOUS
Was training to be a bricklayer, but during National Service in Germany his regiment football team won the Rhine Cup.

 THE MOMENT HE BECAME A LEGEND
Pelé shouted 'goal!' as he headed Jairzinho's cross downward just inside Gordon Banks' right post. But Banks flung himself yards, half-backwards through the air, and somehow clawed the ball off the line.

 HELL RAISING 3

 SPORTING ACHIEVEMENTS 7

Ricky HATTON

BORN **6 OCTOBER 1978**

A working-class hero is something to be, apparently, and just to prove it the 'Hitman' became a world champion on his own terms.

There are two sides to Ricky Hatton. When he was getting ready to rumble, he was a dedicated professional with a thirst for training. When not winning world boxing titles, Hatton could sometimes be found 35lb over his fighting weight with a bacon butty in one hand and a pint of Guinness in the other. Heaven, some might say.

While he played up to his 'Ricky Fatton' alter ego, even wearing a fat suit before fights, critics claim the extra-curricular calories stopped him from becoming an all-time great. They are wrong. Aside from his world titles, at light welterweight and welterweight (IBF and WBA), he became the 2005 *Ring* Magazine Fighter of the Year – the first British boxer to receive the award from the 'Bible of Boxing' since its inception in 1922.

Hatton remains the same lad who grew up in Stockport, Greater Manchester, and, despite his glittering career, still lives in the same area, sinks pints with the same mates and plays darts for the local pub team.

Hatton is one of Manchester's favourite sons – they say he doesn't have an entourage but an entire city. Thousands of Mancunians swaggered to Vegas for the fights with Jose Luis Castillo, Floyd Mayweather Jr and Paul Malignaggi singing, 'Walking in a Hatton Wonderland'.

A passionate Manchester City supporter who entered the ring to the club's 'Blue Moon' anthem, Hatton claimed to treat derby games as seriously as world title fights – when asked which sportsman he would most like to smack, he opted for the former Manchester United striker Cristiano Ronaldo.

As a child, Ricky Hatton wanted to be a footballer – both his father and grandfather played professionally. He had trials, but had already joined Hyde boxing club at the age of ten. He was immediately given his nickname, 'The Hitman', after a trainer watched him attack a punch bag with calculated and aggressive aplomb.

While he is a polite, charming and humorous chat show guest and after-dinner speaker, he's been described as 'cold, merciless...an awful man' (and more besides) when the gloves go on. Which is precisely how it should be

'I've got a lot on my plate at the moment.'

Hatton's excuse for putting on weight between fights.

for a boxer. His liver punches were a signature dish.

Hatton's first professional bout was in 1997 and he spent years tearing through a succession of fighters using his ferocious attitude and brutal body punching to wear them down. However, he wasn't really rated until he faced Kostya Tszyu for the IBF Light Welterweight title in 2005 (see picture right).

It was a fight that announced Hatton's arrival as a world-class boxer with a performance that left the highly rated Tszyu unable to rise from his corner at the beginning of the final round.

Hatton was unbeaten in 43 contests until he came up against a fighter with

BEFORE HE WAS FAMOUS
Hatton left school and entered the family carpet business but, after slicing his fingers with a Stanley knife, his dad made him a salesman to save his hands – although he was terrible at that too and often sold carpets at a loss.

THE MOMENT HE BECAME A LEGEND
Hatton was a massive underdog when he faced Kostya Tszyu at the MEN Arena in 2005. Tszyu was then considered one of the best pound-for-pound fighters in the world but, in front of a home crowd, Hatton roughed him up and then won.

44

It was an unorthodox way to administer collagen, but Hatton swore by it.

an even bigger reputation (and mouth) in December 2007: the undisputed world welterweight champion Floyd Mayweather Jr. Referring to the records of both fighters, the posters just said, 'Undefeated'. Something had to give.

The contrast between the two couldn't have been greater – with Hatton, the feral street fighter, taking on 'Pretty Boy's' counter-attacking technique. When the dust had settled, it was Mayweather who was still standing after an onslaught that forced Hatton's corner to call it a day in the tenth round.

Hatton came back successfully to retain his IBO Light Welterweight title twice before meeting Manny Pacquiao in May 2009. He was floored twice in the first round before an almighty hook finished it in the second.

That remains his last fight to date and there are doubts whether Hatton, now a successful promoter with his own company and several other business interests, will ever return to the ring.

There will always be questions whether Hatton's unorthodox conditioning – he used to eat a full English breakfast before a fight – was to blame for his two significant losses. And, to be fair, sinking pints on nights out with kindred spirits like Freddie Flintoff (cf p102-03) and the Gallagher brothers is not advised in any boxing manual known to man.

But, the man himself has no regrets and what's more, what's more than this, he became a legend and he did it his way. RA

....

 AD NAUSEAM

Churchill Insurance – The wagging dog who likes to say 'Oh Yes' apparently goes on holiday with Ricky Hatton. The two are seen in a hotel foyer where Hatton messes around shadow boxing while claiming, 'There's still life in the old dog yet, hey Churchy.'

....

 **HELL RAISING**   **SPORTING ACHIEVEMENTS**

Kenny DALGLISH

BORN **4 MARCH 1951**

Revered and record-breaking striker known for his 'Midas Touch' and almost incomprehensible accent. King of the Kop, and a man among men…

It's often argued (by Liverpool and Celtic fans) that there should be two lists when considering the game's greats – one for Kenny Dalglish and another for everyone else.

While Cruyff invented his famous turn and Maradona bamboozled opposition defences, 'King Kenny' concentrated on goals. Important ones too, including the winner in Liverpool's 1978 European Cup victory against Bruges.

He was the first player to net over 100 goals in both the English and Scottish leagues and, as a manager, is among the select few to have won the league title with two different clubs – Liverpool and Blackburn Rovers – not to mention the 'Double' in 1986, his first season in charge at Anfield.

Young Kenneth Mathieson Dalglish idolised Denis Law (cf p88-9), and spent many a happy evening honing his exquisite skills on a less-than-exquisite dog-shit-strewn concrete pitch. The team was modestly known as Milton Milan (Milton being an area in the north of Glasgow where he was brought up).

With Glasgow Schools he won the Scottish Cup and as a 16-year-old was snapped up by Celtic, who at the time were not only the best team in Scotland but, having beaten Inter Milan to win the European Cup in 1967, also the best in Europe – the first British side to win the premier continental competition.

'Call for reinforcements, there are only four of us and Dalglish has got the ball.'

That he grew up a fan of Celtic's fiercest rivals certainly didn't mean anything to the club's hierarchy – young Kenny ran to his bedroom to tear down the posters of the Rangers heroes adorning his wall when Celtic assistant manager Sean Fallon came calling.

The reserve team, known as the 'Quality Street Gang' due to the sheer class of their youngsters, was always going to be hard to break into.

appearances at club level, and a record – shared with his idol Denis Law – of 30 for Scotland), he soon became the focus of a quite brilliant Liverpool team. And to think he played his first ever game of football in goal.

His dry sense of humour, completely at odds with the public perception of him, is renowned throughout football – to quote one former team-mate who wishes to remain anonymous, 'He loves

funerals as he could – four in one day – and if he couldn't make one he made sure there was a club presence at others.

Eventually, he decided to step down as manager of the club, and thereafter moved to Second Division Blackburn Rovers in October 1991; by May 1995 they were Premier League champions. He had brief spells at Newcastle United (again replacing Keegan) and Celtic.

His list of honours as a player is too long to list here, but he has proved himself as a top-flight manager. He returned to Liverpool in that capacity in early 2011, initially on a temporary basis, but such was the impact he had that he was given a three-year contract before the season was over. Very few great players make great managers but he is, and always has been, an exception. DM

'One of the greatest disappointments of my life is that I never stood on the Kop.'

Kenny Dalglish explains how much he admired the supporters on the famous terrace.

He counted Danny McGrain, Lou Macari and David Hay among his young team-mates, but he persevered and medals came thick and fast from the moment he made his first team debut in 1969.

Yes, he spent his childhood supporting Rangers, but it was the fans assembled at Parkhead who worshipped him, and there were a few newborns christened Kenneth during those eight trophy-laden years in Glasgow.

Hard to believe now, but his move to Merseyside in 1977 caused some fans to question his ability to replace Kevin Keegan (cf p115-17), especially since it was for a then British transfer record of £440,000, but he defied the doubters. And how.

Back to goal, bent over the ball like he was walking into a wind, impossible to dispossess and, even at 5ft 8in, blessed with a preternatural ability to score goals (230 in 559 league

a prank and it can be quite harsh if you are on the receiving end but [expletive deleted] if you're not, well, you'd end up crying laughing.'

He took over from Joe Fagan as Liverpool manager in 1985, and four years later had to deal with the horrors of the 1989 Hillsborough tragedy where 96 Liverpool fans died.

He won not just the eternal admiration of the club's fans for the way he handled the situation but that of the country too. Despite the toll it had on him personally, he attended as many

 AD NAUSEAM
While Newcastle boss he appeared in an advert for BT with daughter Kelly phoning each fan to thank them for their support. Whether they could understand him is another matter.

 HELL RAISING 2   **SPORTING ACHIEVEMENTS** 9

BEFORE HE WAS FAMOUS
He was an apprentice joiner. After leaving the workshop at 4.30pm every day in full working gear, he would catch two buses to Celtic Park.

 THE MOMENT HE BECAME A LEGEND
His handling of the Hillsborough disaster revealed the essence of the man beyond the footballer.

Will CARLING

BORN **12 DECEMBER 1965**

Youngest-ever England rugby captain who called the RFU 'a bunch of old farts', but also picked up three Grand Slams.

In his 45 years on this earth, Will Carling has enjoyed a number of different identities: youngest man ever to captain the England rugby union team? Check. Outspoken critic who dared insult the entire board of an institution he represented? Check. Alleged romancer of the nation's most adored married lady? Check. And election correspondent for Chris Evans' breakfast show? God almighty man, but check.

that. Yes, they played a pretty dull, under-the-shirt brand of rugby that entertained few, but they knew how to win matches – and Carling was their young, dashing captain, with a glint in his eye and a bum for a chin.

Some would argue that the former public schoolboy got lucky – that he was a competent but limited player whose face fitted with the conservative rugby establishment, but who profited from breaking through in a period

stand outside the reliable fly-half Rob Andrew.

Furthermore, in a rare show of foresight from an RFU aware of the need to have the right captain for the 1991 World Cup, Carling was made skipper in only his eighth international. It was November 1988 and he was 22 – the youngest man ever to lead the team.

By 1991, Carling had overseen a vast turnaround in the national side's fortunes. His centre partnership with the elegant and elusive Jeremy Guscott was at the heart of this, together with an organised brute of a pack led by the raging Brian Moore, and jet-heeled finisher Rory Underwood on the wing.

England went into the World Cup

'If the game is run properly as a professional game, you do not need fifty-seven old farts running English rugby.'

Carling suggests that the 1995 RFU committee was not the right body to take the game into a professional era.

To the more sane-minded among us, however, Carling will always be the man who led England out on to the Twickenham pitch to contest their first Rugby World Cup final in 1991. That his side lost to one of the great Australia teams – Nick Farr-Jones, Michael Lynagh and David Campese – almost doesn't matter.

England's journey to reach that final, seeing off bitter rivals France and Scotland along the way, was a pivotal moment for a sport that, until then, had struggled to compete with football for the nation's affections.

But Carling's England changed

when the sport was gaining popularity and creeping towards professionalism.

But that is to underplay Carling as both sportsman and intellect. A human battering ram of a centre, he was quickly noted as the ideal candidate to

on the back of a first Five Nations Grand Slam since 1980 – and, although they fell at the final hurdle, Carling's work was done. The nation loved rugby, and he was the man who took the credit for it.

BEFORE HE WAS FAMOUS
Carling went to private school at Sedburgh and then joined the Army, before jacking it in to play for Harlequins.

THE MOMENT HE BECAME A LEGEND
Captaining England to consecutive victories against France and Scotland that saw them reach the World Cup final on home soil.

In reality, everything else Carling achieved acts as a mere postscript to 1991 – but what a postscript. On the field, he led England to two further Grand Slams (1992 and 1995) and set a then world record of 59 Tests as captain.

Off the field, he marked the dawn of the professional era with an amusing-as-it-was-accurate description of the RFU board as 'fifty-seven old farts' – an outburst that saw him sacked as England captain, but reinstated on a wave of public support before the 1995 World Cup.

And then there's the field where Carling seemed to apply the true Corinthian ideal of sport: his complicated love life. Even discarding those alleged trysts with Princess Diana – 'No, no, no, how many times do I have to say it?' he raged at the *Sunday Mirror* in 2004. 'We were just friends.' – he still made his mark.

Divorced from first wife Julia, a TV presenter, he later split from girlfriend Ali Cockayne (the mother of his baby son) to shack up with the estranged wife of a team-mate – something Ali said she had discovered when reading a half-prepared press statement Carling had written on his computer.

Still only 45, Carling is now merely a legend on the rugby dinners circuit. He may no longer have the dash of old, but the glint remains. TH

....

 **AD NAUSEAM**

Carling's image was used unofficially in an advertising campaign for the now defunct satellite channel Live TV, entitled 'Who knows what the future holds?' which portrayed him marrying Princess Diana.

....

 HELL RAISING 7

SPORTING ACHIEVEMENTS 8

Of his running style, he noted: 'Imagine there is a naked woman in front of you, but keep your eyes open for others.' He didn't really.

Vinnie JONES

BORN **5 JANUARY 1965**

Tough-tackling hardman on the football field turned method-acting mean machine in Hollywood films – he's a geezer!

Before he started portraying intimidating villains in Hollywood, Vinnie Jones spent most of his life preparing for the role – as a real-life hatchetman, both on and off the field. Typecast? You betcha.

Somewhere in between, football's most formidable midfield rottweiler became a national treasure – although his fame was based more on notoriety than sporting success. Jones' somewhat agricultural style was accompanied by an uncompromising determination, which allowed the former hod-carrier to scale greater heights as a player than many imagined possible.

He fought his way (sometimes literally) into the Football League, and

'I say ref, that was an excellent decision. You're having a great game.'

talkSPORT LEGENDS

became a cult hero at clubs including Leeds, Sheffield United and Chelsea. He even realised his international ambitions by discovering distant Welsh heritage (surely the clue was in the name?) and represented Wales on nine occasions, once as captain.

But, undoubtedly, his greatest sporting achievement came in the 1988 FA Cup final. Liverpool were the

Surprisingly, Jones was sent off just 12 times in his career and still holds the record for the fastest-ever caution – a mere three seconds into the game. He was suspended by the FA on several occasions for crimes ranging from career-endangering challenges to starring in an ill-advised video glamorising the game's dark arts.

people's champion – a geezer done good who came from the building site to become a sporting icon and Hollywood actor. His home in LA is decorated with an enormous Union Jack flag, which is said to irritate his neighbour, John Travolta.

He made his break into his second career, in film, when he appeared as Big Chris in Guy Ritchie's picture *Lock, Stock and Two Smoking Barrels*. It was the first of dozens of movies, including *Snatch*, *Gone in 60 Seconds* and *X-Men: The Last Stand*. He even found time to appear in 2010's *Celebrity Big Brother*.

You can take the boy out of Watford… RA

> 'The FA have given me a pat on the back. I've taken violence off the terraces… and onto the pitch!'

Jones accentuates a positive aspect of yet another brush with the Football Association disciplinary authorities. Wimbledon chairman Sam Hammam said he had a 'mosquito brain'.

aristocrats, Wimbledon the peasants – and boy were they revolting. Allegedly, in the tunnel before the game, Jones eloquently advised Alan Hansen, 'I'm going to rip off your leg and hit you over the head with the soggy end.'

The 33/1 outsiders triumphed 1-0 and the meanest, maddest member of the Crazy Gang celebrated in style by getting a tattoo of the Cup on his leg.

Jones has also struggled with authority figures armed with more than a whistle, getting arrested for several alcohol-fuelled scraps – involving the odd head-butt or a bout of nose-biting. No wonder his Hertfordshire house had a sign outside it: 'Never mind the dog. Beware of the owner.'

Despite his misdemeanours, Vinnie Jones is still regarded as a

 AD NAUSEAM

Jones is pruning flowers in his garden when he notices a robin crying because the birdfeeder is empty. Jones refills the feeder and places it on the windowsill of his kitchen. The robin flies towards the feeder, collides with the glass and slides down the pane while Vinnie laughs. Result? 390 complaints.

Red Devil power drink.

BEFORE HE WAS FAMOUS
After inexplicably being dismissed from the Watford schoolboys team because he was too small, Jones worked as a gardener and hod-carrier.

 THE MOMENT HE BECAME A LEGEND
Thanks to a *Daily Mirror* photographer, the time Jones grabbed a young Paul Gascoigne by the testicles will never fade from our memories. Nor will the look on a shocked Gazza's face (see picture p8).

HELL RAISING 9   **SPORTING ACHIEVEMENTS** 5

Stirling MOSS

BORN **17 SEPTEMBER 1929**

Pioneering race car driver and a true gent who never won the World Championship but will always be a legend 'Made in Britain'.

'Who do you think you are, Stirling Moss?' was usually the first line of police questioning if you were pulled over in your car during the 1960s – with reference to a name that was and still is synonymous with speedometer-troubling automobile action.

Stirling Craufurd Moss could have cast the mould for the archetypal British sporting legend – a gentleman renowned as much for his conduct as his competitiveness, despite missing out on the main event.

During his career, Moss won 212 out of 529 races but was always denied an elusive World Championship title. He did finish in second place for four consecutive years between 1955 and 1958, and would have undoubtedly taken the tallest place on the podium had he not been such a bloody nice bloke.

Moss believed that the manner in which battle was fought was more important than the outcome.

And it was his sporting grace that memorably cost him the Formula One Championship in 1958, but cemented his legendary status.

By defending his fellow Brit, Mike Hawthorn, at the Portuguese Grand Prix, Moss prevented him from losing points and that act ultimately saw his rival become Britain's first world driving champion. Can you imagine Michael Schumacher doing the same thing?

'Better to lose honourably in a British car than win in a foreign one.'

Stirling Moss gives his vote to the British cause. Before leaving the track in a Sopwith Camel.

Another reason for Moss being regarded as 'the greatest driver never to win the World Championship' was his loyal patriotism, which largely kept him in the clutches of British engineered vehicles – even if they lagged behind the German and Italian superpowers.

Moss's love affair with British machinery began early, fuelled by his parents' enthusiasm for motor racing. It's hard to imagine, but his first car was a three-wheeled Morgan.

By his 18th birthday, Moss had convinced his father to help fund the cost of his first competitive car, a Cooper 500. Post-war racing in Britain was a small-time affair, featuring numerous events every weekend and Moss entered as many as he could.

Moss was equally comfortable racing at Le Mans as he was behind the wheel of a Formula One car at Monaco. He was a jack of all events, including circuit racing, rallies, hill climbs, sprints and endurance tests, and a master at most of them, marking him as one of the greatest all-round drivers in motorsport history.

After limited success racing Formula One for British teams HWM and Jaguar, Moss briefly flirted with foreign manufacturers such as Maserati and Mercedes Benz – although he would never forget being unceremoniously dumped by Ferrari.

Teamed with the legendary Juan Manuel Fangio racing in Mercedes'

BEFORE HE WAS FAMOUS
When his indifferent school record ruled out following in the family footsteps as a dentist, he entered the hotel trade as a waiter and late night porter.

THE MOMENT HE BECAME A LEGEND
Moss won the 1958 Portuguese Grand Prix and then defended his countryman, Mike Hawthorn, who had been accused of illegally reversing on the track. His sportsmanship cost him the world title.

'So the basic strategy is to go out and finish first… is that right?'

famed 'Silver Arrows', Moss won his first British Grand Prix at Aintree in 1955.

Later that year, Moss gave the term 'speed demon' a new meaning. Partnered by sports journalist Denis Jenkinson, and using revolutionary navigation techniques, they became the first British team to win the Mille Miglia, the Italian endurance race, managing an average speed of 97mph across 1,000 miles of public roads.

Moss eventually returned to British teams and his ability to win races in inferior cars had its greatest expression at the 1961 Monaco Grand Prix. Despite driving an uncompetitive privateer Lotus 18, Moss staved off increasing

pressure from three state-of-the-art factory Ferrari 'Sharknose' 156s to become the first driver to win a treble at the spiritual home of motor racing.

The chequered flag unexpectedly came down on his career after a near fatal accident at Goodwood in 1962. The crash left Moss in a coma for a month and paralysed him for a further six months. And, after attempting to get back into the saddle of his car too soon, Moss retired with regret shortly after.

Today, Moss is involved in property management, including designing his own revolutionary remote-controlled home in Mayfair – although he might want to test the electrics after falling down an open lift shaft in 2010.

He still races historic cars at the ripe old age of 82 – and, doubtless, endures a tough time convincing clichéd policemen whenever he exceeds the speed limit. RA

....

AD NAUSEAM
'The person who made the greatest impression on my life was the doctor who sorted my erection difficulties in ten minutes,' Moss follows Pelé into hard-selling erectile dysfunction drugs.

....

 HELL
2 RAISING

 **SPORTING**
8 ACHIEVEMENTS

talkSPORT
LEGENDS

Malcolm ALLISON

BORN **5 SEPTEMBER 1927** ▨ DIED **14 OCTOBER 2010**

Bon viveur, radical free-thinker, innovator, coach nonpareil, bunny girl bothering, cigar-chomping, champagne-swilling charmer with a glint in his eye and a Fedora on his head…

'Drink up ladies, the lads will be back in for half-time in ten minutes.'

Let's get the clubs out of the way first: Bath City, Toronto City, Plymouth Argyle (twice), Manchester City (twice), Crystal Palace (twice), Galatasaray, Yeovil Town, Sporting Lisbon (and not many managers have gone from Yeovil to Sporting), Middlesbrough, Willington FC, Kuwait (and not many managers…), Vitoria de Setubal, SC Farense, Fisher Athletic, Bristol Rovers.

Where do you start? Allison was born walking tall and talking back. After a promising junior career, he signed for Charlton Athletic but was off-loaded after criticising the coach's training methods. A problematic relationship with authority became a recurring theme. He went to West Ham United.

A successful career (238 appearances and 10 goals) at centre-half was curtailed after he contracted tuberculosis in 1957 – part of a lung was removed. In the meantime, he became a mentor to, among others, Bobby Moore (cf p187-91) in the great West Ham team of the mid-60s.

Moving into coaching, he left Plymouth (after a row with the board, naturally) to join Manchester City. This is where he made his name, as the boisterous visionary coach alongside genial manager Joe Mercer. City were promoted to the First Division in 1966, won the league in 1968, the FA Cup in 1969 and became the first English team to win a domestic and European trophy (the League Cup and European Cup-Winners' Cup) in the same season in 1970.

As former City player and England international Mike Summerbee put it, 'He was probably the greatest coach this country will ever see… People are doing things today that Malcolm Allison was doing in 1965.' Although it is fair to say that most modern coaches would not hire a steeplejack to climb onto the roof of Old Trafford and lower the flag to half mast as City pipped United to the league title.

Allison introduced a new form of training, with the emphasis on fitness and diet. He brought in British Olympic athletes to race against the players, had the local university hospital keep tabs on their heart rate and height-to-weight ratio.

> 'I looked up to the man. It's not too strong to say I loved him.'

England captain Bobby Moore.

Tactically, he took his lead from Willy Meisl, the Austrian sports journalist who developed a theory called 'The Whirl'. It involved giving free expression to players and encouraging them to develop their own ideas. It worked.

Football was an abiding passion, but attractive women, cigars and champagne came a very close joint second. His women included Christine Keeler of Profumo scandal infamy, an entire warren of bunny girls (including the second Mrs Allison) and a Hungarian stripper who he met in Turin after being interviewed for the Juventus job, but who he left after getting tired of walking her chihuahua.

He once told a restaurant manager who had the effrontery to ask him to settle a £1,000 bill to 'F*ck off and don't come back until it's double that.'

At Crystal Palace, before being sacked – an invitation extended to and accepted by soft porn actress Fiona Richmond to get in the players' bath was a key factor in the termination of his contract – he changed the club nickname ('The Glaziers') to that of Benfica ('The Eagles') and the kit colours to those of Barcelona.

There was a precedent – at City he had changed the club's away colours to those of AC Milan, red and black stripes. He came back to Maine Road, his spiritual home, in 1979 after a typically peripatetic journey around the footballing world, sold the best players and almost bankrupted the club – his second period in charge is synonymous with the name Steve Daley, a British record signing from Wolves at just over £1.4 million sold less than two years later for £300,000.

He would not care about the money involved today – 'If it's there, spend it,' was his motto. 'If it's not there, spend it anyway,' was the postscript. At the time he was spending millions at City, he was simultaneously denied the use of a personal cheque book by his local bank. That was 'Big Mal'.

After leaving City for a second time he went on to win the double with Sporting Lisbon – the nine-year-old son of the assistant has subsequently called him 'my inspiration'. That was Jose Mourinho. Want to know where the 'I'm the Special One' brand of arrogance, ability and supreme confidence came from? Have a wild guess. BILL BORROWS

 AD NAUSEAM

Not strictly an advertisement as such but, as Crystal Palace manager, 'Big Mal' coached a team of bunny girls to play a team of 'Apes' – the film *Battle for the Planet of the Apes* was about to launch – in a charity fundraiser for the World Wildlife Fund in 1973.

HELL RAISING 9

SPORTING ACHIEVEMENTS 7

BEFORE HE WAS FAMOUS
After leaving West Ham, Allison had a brief period as a car salesman, another as a professional gambler and one more fronting a London nightclub where regular guests included the Kray twins.

 THE MOMENT HE BECAME A LEGEND
When he walked up to the Stretford End at Old Trafford and threw four fingers in the air to indicate how many goals City would score in the derby. City won 4-1.

Billy WRIGHT

BORN **6 FEBRUARY 1924** ■ DIED **3 SEPTEMBER 1994**

Rock-solid centre-half for Wolves and England who became the first footballer in the world ever to earn 100 international caps.

When Billy Wright retired in 1959, *The Times* noted: 'What he embroidered into the fabric of our lives were the values of loyalty and industry. Billy Wright, the man, is a human being of exemplary character. Billy Wright, the footballer, was a national treasure.'

Like the Industrial Revolution, William Ambrose Wright was forged in Ironbridge, Shropshire, 15 miles from Wolverhampton.

Aged 14, in 1938, he went to Molineux for a trial and was taken on as an apprentice. His early days at Wolves didn't mark him out as special and manager Major Frank Buckley broke the news to Billy that he was 'too small' to make it. A tearful Billy was then told that Buckley had changed his mind. It wasn't a decision the Major would ever regret.

'Snowy' (named for his ice-cream quiff of blond hair) redoubled his efforts to improve his game and was making good progress when World War II intervened. Billy spent the war guesting for Leicester City and serving as an Army PT instructor.

On the war's full-time whistle, Billy was ready for first team football and soon became captain, replacing Stan Cullis, who became the manager and architect of Wolves' glory years. He would remain a one-club man.

The effects of Cullis's management and Wright's on-field leadership were immediate. In 1949, Wright led Wolves

out for an FA Cup final meeting with Leicester, who were beaten 3-1. The following season, Portsmouth pipped Wolves on goal average to the League Championship.

But, under Cullis's regimental style of direct football, Wolves were not to be denied. They won the title in 1953-54 and then, with Wright converted from wing-half to centre-half, they repeated the feat in 1957-58 and 1958-59.

Wolves were top dogs in England and, after unforgettable 'friendly' victories in 1954-55 against Spartak Moscow and Honved under the new Molineux floodlights, the men in old gold were claiming they were 'Champions of the World'.

In the twilight of his playing career, Billy acquired a little glamour. Decades before Posh & Becks (cf p154-6), there was Billy & Joy. Enjoying chart success with the likes of 'I Saw Mommy Kissing Santa Claus', the Beverley Sisters were three sisters plucked from the street and launched into stardom. Had *Hello!* magazine been around in 1958, the showbiz-football wedding would have filled it cover-to-cover. The exclusivity clause might have been useful too, as, for all his celebrity, Wright was still nailed to the maximum wage of £20 a week.

As a centre-half who commanded the box despite standing only 5ft 8in, a fierce tackler and an astute reader of the game, he was a humble man who let others do the talking. His manager at international level, Walter Winterbottom, noted: 'Billy had a heart of oak and was the most reliable of men.'

In August 1959, noticing that he had been trailing behind younger

'I only had two things on my mind as a player… to win the ball and then to give the simplest pass I could to the nearest team-mate.'

Wright shows that football is a simple game.

BEFORE HE WAS FAMOUS
Cleaned boots and swept the terraces as a Molineux ground-staff boy. Strictly speaking, more 'Cinderella' than 'Snowy Wright'…

THE MOMENT HE BECAME A LEGEND
Skippering Wolverhampton Wanderers to their first ever League Championship in 1953-54.

38

A pioneer in the field of footballers' hairstyles, this one is called the 'Wave-breaker' and takes hours to get just right.

players in pre-season training, Wright announced his retirement. Although offered a job for life at Wolves, Wright opted for his other team – and took the post of England Youth manager.

Wright had made his England debut as a player in September 1946, in a 7-2 victory over Northern Ireland, making captain in 1948. He led England through three World Cup finals tournaments, skippering his country 90 times in his 105 caps.

Although he had designs on the England manager's job, Wright was unable to resist Arsenal's offer in 1962. After a decent start, little progress was made in his four seasons in the Highbury hot-seat and he was sacked in the summer of 1966.

He didn't work in football again, but was a familiar figure for many years as presenter and producer of ATV's *Star Soccer*. Wright was invited onto the Wolves board in 1990.

Billy Wright died in September 1994, aged 70. He lived long enough to see a stand dedicated to him at Molineux, but not the statue outside. His funeral brought Wolverhampton to a standstill and his ashes were scattered on the pitch. GS

AD NAUSEAM

'Patent Rubstuds' complied in every respect with FA Law 4 (Revised). They came with a personal recommendation from Billy – and a set of nails which were then hammered into your thick leather soles.

 HELL
3 RAISING

 **SPORTING**
8 ACHIEVEMENTS

Denis LAW

BORN **24 FEBRUARY 1940**

The Law of Natural Selection: well, would you ever leave the ultimate goalscoring machine out of the side?

As the man himself said, 'It was one of those goals that's invariably a goal.'

In just the same way that the greatest runners are perfectly built for speed and the finest fighters for power and resilience, so Denis Law was seemingly created with the sole aim of scoring goals. He played with a smile on his face, which endeared him yet more to the fans, as well as a fierce competitor and patriot; but it's a measure of his specialised skill that these characteristics are entirely secondary to goals, goals, goals.

As a pale, skinny scoring machine, Law was peculiarly efficient, a textbook case study in utilitarian design, performance and reward per effort.

Brought up on an Aberdonian diet of fat and fish, he turned out slight but agile and deceptively powerful.

When he made his Scotland debut, aged just 18, his economy of movement and sense of balance were naturally sublime, his anticipation already otherworldly, the source of that vital extra inch of speed from a standing start.

In 1958, when he was a kid at Huddersfield, the boss Bill Shankly (cf p177-81) called him 'The greatest thing on two feet'. Law's spatial awareness and lateral vision were those of a primal predator, a stalker in the quiet slow-motion of the killing zone, a ruthless finisher of his bobbling pigskin prey.

Translated on to the football field, these gifts meant that Law never received a ball without knowing precisely where the ball and his body were in relation to the goalposts and his team-mates.

Not such a rare skill, you might think; but this applied even when he received a hoofed cross from the wing, 20 yards from goal and seemingly facing the wrong way. Bang! A signature scissor-kick, in off the post. Time after time.

It was a law that applied when George Best (cf p192-6) raced diagonally across the area and shot the ball across the face of goal at 60mph, leaving The Lawman – who just happened to be arriving four feet out, unmarked, poised – to deflect the ball over the line.

It applied in cup finals, Scottish internationals, practice matches or whenever the ball came skidding, swerving or lobbing in to Law. Turn instantly, acrobatically, automatically, and shoot, the calculations already made subconsciously half a second before the ball arrived. Bang!

Only then did Law turn away from goal, the right arm and forefinger held aloft, the cuff of the shirt still held tight in his clenched fist to help guard against accusations of handball, even though the ball was now dead.

If you think you've read similar observations about other 'goal machine' players – Lineker (cf p42), say, or Greaves (cf p66-7) – this is where the utilitarian theory diverges from the norm, and gets proven beyond all doubt.

Witness a shocking revelation from Jimmy Hill. 'Denis could never be described as one of the world's great ball artists. I remember filming him for television when, because of the pressure and the excitement of the camera rolling, he had some difficulty just keeping the ball up on his feet.'

Only on reflection do you realise such fripperies are surplus to the goalscorer's strictest requirement. Why would Law ever want to juggle a ball when it's a skill that has never put a ball in a net? Far more efficient and useful to Law was the lightning glance with the head, the deadly single 'flick with the foot', as Hill described, 'with defenders wondering just where he had come from.'

After a £55,000 British record move from Huddersfield to do well at Manchester City, Law switched again to Torino for a record Anglo-Italian fee of £110,000. He failed to settle in Italy, but still kept up his tickover of a goal every two games. It was at Manchester United, bought by Matt Busby (cf p124-6) for a British record fee of £115,000, that our ultimate Darwinian goalscorer evolved into a legend.

'Denis would have been good value at twice the price,' Busby said. 'Denis was the sharpest striker I had ever seen, and he was also the most

'How long did the feeling last? How long ago was the game? The subject always crops up. It's always there and I am always remembered for it. That's a shame.'

Law recalls his notorious goal for City against United in 1974.

unselfish. He was seconds quicker than anyone else in thought and deed.'

He scored and played a blinder at Wembley in the 1963 FA Cup victory, then scored an English post-war record 46 goals in 1963-64, when he was crowned European Player of the Year. At United, they called him 'The King' – a title he retained even as George Best emerged – and he went on to score 237 times in 11 years, his share of goals naturally reduced by playing in a great forward line with Best and Charlton.

He went on to help United to two league titles, in 1964-65 and 1966-67, but missed out on the European Cup final of 1968 because of injury – an issue that was to become a greater problem for him, as opponents tried to kick him out of the game.

He scored in three successive years against England, leading the attack when Scotland humbled the world champions at Wembley in 1967 – Law's own favourite career moment, having claimed that he'd played golf rather than watch the Auld Enemy in the 1966 final.

Law moved back across Manchester, to City, and scored in his final league game. United were already doomed to relegation, but Law's cheeky back heel was the final straw: 'I was inconsolable. I didn't want it to happen... They were pals.'

He played his last-ever match at the 1974 World Cup and shares his country's record goal tally with Kenny Dalglish (cf p76-7), but reached 30 in just 55 appearances compared with Dalglish's 102. DH

AD NAUSEAM
Play better football in a Denis Law Umbro Soccer Set. Comprising Jersey, Shorts and Hose in leading 1st Division colours. Colour photo of Denis Law reproduced on lid. From 25/6 at Sports Outfitters and Leading Stores.
Umbro advert, 1964.

HELL RAISING 5

SPORTING ACHIEVEMENTS 9

Paula RADCLIFFE

BORN **17 DECEMBER 1973**

Hugely gifted, beanpole long-distance runner with the courage to bounce back from a series of setbacks...

For all Paula Radcliffe's rollercoaster ride of glorious achievements and frustrating injuries, the records and the medals, the successes and the failures, she is largely known for three moments: one heroic, one tragic and one comic...

Paula was the offspring of keen runners, and showed early promise joining the esteemed Bedford County Athletic Club. She first raced at national level in 1986 in the Schools Cross Country Championships and finished an underwhelming 299th out of 600; but there was rapid improvement when she came under the wing of coach Alex Stanton, and the following year she finished fourth in the same event.

Stanton said of his charge: 'Success certainly didn't happen overnight for Paula. She didn't win a major race until her late teens. But she knew exactly where she was going and she just worked incredibly hard.'

Paula made slow but steady progress, injuries and viruses permitting, before eventually winning a silver medal at the World Cross Country Championships in 1997 and another in the 10,000m at the World Championships in 1999. In 2002, the decision was made to run marathons, and she exploded onto the scene.

Her wiry frame and nodding action became a familiar sight that year: she retained her World Cross Country Championships title in Dublin, won the London Marathon (setting the second best ever time on her debut), struck 5,000m gold at the Commonwealth Games in Manchester, won another at the European Championships in Munich in the 10,000m and then topped all that off with victory in the Chicago Marathon, smashing the world record by 89 seconds.

She stopped running only long enough to accept an MBE and the BBC Sports Personality of the Year.

In 2003 Radcliffe won the London Marathon again, trimming yet more off the world record with a time of 2.15:25,

so when she travelled to Athens for the 2004 Olympics she was looked upon as a virtually guaranteed gold medal by the media and the public.

However, a couple of weeks before the games, she picked up a leg injury and had to take anti-inflammatory drugs. This was later pin-pointed as the reason she could not absorb food properly, as her Olympic dream turned into a nightmare.

'I have been doing a hundred and twenty miles a week, when normally I would do about a hundred and forty.'

Yeah, me too.

Radcliffe's style depended on setting a gruelling pace, but as she was overtaken by Mizuki Noguchi of Japan and then Kenya's Catherine Ndereba, it was clear that something was amiss.

At one stage she pulled up and appeared to be in an agony of indecision before continuing the race, but at the 36km sign, 6km short of the finish, she pulled up, sat on the kerb in a distraught state and sobbed. She had run out of steam.

There were more tears in the ensuing press conference where Paula dabbed her eyes with a tissue and said: 'I just feel like I have let everyone down.'

BEFORE SHE WAS FAMOUS
Paula Radcliffe learned how to cope with exercise-induced asthma from an early age.

THE MOMENT SHE BECAME A LEGEND
Sitting on an Athens pavement during the 2004 Olympic Marathon, sobbing in frustration and despair.

The queue for the ladies' toilet was always a nightmare, but Paula usually got there first.

An opportunity for a fairytale ending presented itself in the 10,000m less than a week later, and the chance of redemption was too much for Paula to resist. However, she pulled up and stepped off the track 20 minutes into the race, retiring with eight laps remaining and the public mood back home turned from sympathy to hostility.

A year after Athens, Radcliffe bounced back with a win in the London Marathon, but it was not the victory that was the main talking point in the media after the race.

It was the fact that Paula, leading with four miles to go, had an unscheduled pit-stop – squatting down in front of the TV cameras, pulling her running shorts to one side and relieving herself in a London gutter.

At first the media referred to it as a 'pee'. But there was no avoiding the truth, Paula admitted it had been a problem with stomach cramps and the grim reality was that it was something altogether more substantial. As they say, shit happens.

Never mind the world records and medals. There has never been more memorable proof of an athlete's absolute commitment to their sport. GS

 AD NAUSEAM

The 'I am a runner' advert for Nike where she has to pause her workout to lean over the pram and tickle her baby's ears. Andrex missed a trick.

 **HELL**
2 RAISING

 SPORTING
9 ACHIEVEMENTS

Geoff HURST

BORN **8 DECEMBER 1941**

World Cup final, blah blah… Hat-trick, blah blah blah… And the forgotten history of Geoff Hurst, arguably the most important striker of the modern era.

It's unlikely that any reader who's made it this far will be unfamiliar with Geoff Hurst's unique place in football history. Or could it be that his starring role in 1966 now blinds us to a contribution that cast a far longer shadow? Is there more to the celebrated West Ham and England striker than meets the eye?

First things first: for the record, Hurst scored the only World Cup final hat-trick in history, which simultaneously secured England's single moment in the sun as world champions. Of course, these achievements were of a stature that would totally eclipse other events and landmarks in any player's career – and that's even without the eternal, irresistible addition of two ironic footnotes to Hurst's weighty legacy.

That's right: Alf Ramsey (cf p104-05) started the tournament playing not Hurst up front, but Jimmy Greaves (cf p66-7), at that time England's greatest goalscorer, who was then injured in the group matches. But he was fit in time for the final. Alf loyally stuck with his winning team. So Hurst robbed Greaves of

Hurst's ability to levitate was considered an unfair advantage and eventually outlawed by FIFA.

talkSPORT
LEGENDS

his 'rightful' place in the team and football folklore.

And, of course, there's the endlessly ponderable third goal – Hurst's second – in off the crossbar, at least according to the 'Russian linesman' (who was actually from Azerbaijan): 'Was it a

feet but able to pick out a pass with his head or chest.

Although he wasn't built for speed, Hurst had the knack of finding the net, battling and shimmying and drawing defences out of shape before turning unexpectedly to slam the ball home

After winding down his career with Stoke and West Brom, Hurst teamed up with Ron Greenwood once again as England's assistant manager in 1977. He was then picked out by another great football thinker, Danny Blanchflower (cf p39), to join him

'As I was heading towards goal, Alan Ball was shouting: "Hursty, Hursty, give me the ball!" I said to myself, "Sod you, Bally, I'm on a hat-trick!"'

Hurst explains his strategy at the end of the World Cup final.

goal?' Hurst asked himself. 'Did the ball cross the line? Those two questions have haunted me for most of my adult life. They are the questions I am asked most often – and I don't know the answers.'

Trouble is, it's all too easy to write off Hurst as a one-game man, forgetting not only his cracking record of 24 goals in his 49 England games, but also his rightful place as arguably the most influential forward in the post-war game.

Lancashire-born but raised in Essex, Hurst was scouted by West Ham and made an early league debut for the Hammers aged just 18 in 1960. He actually played most of the 1961-62 season in midfield before new manager Ron Greenwood converted the tall and powerful player, expert in holding and shielding the ball, into a lone striker, or 'target man' – then an entirely new position in the English game.

Hurst ran free on to balls out of defence, making streams of intelligent runs that induced panic and confusion in opposition defences. He held the ball up and laid it off expertly, fast with his

with a rasping shot from either foot.

When West Ham won the 1964 FA Cup and the 1965 European Cup-Winners' Cup, other managers and forwards began to copy the pattern and play the forward game so familiar to us today. So that's why Ramsey stuck with Hurst in 1966: because his club team-mates, Moore and Peters, were familiar with his 'foreign' style, and simply to leverage the control, vision and goalpower of the forward runner.

Hurst didn't just end up with 249 goals in 501 games for West Ham between 1959 and 1972, he also created hundreds more. He wasn't just the first target man, he was the greatest.

at Chelsea where he subsequently enjoyed a short spell as boss, but Hurst wasn't fated to stay in the game at managerial level. DH

 AD NAUSEAM

Two things you can guarantee every World Cup year – England will disappoint and Geoff Hurst will be promoting something or other. He is a McDonald's 'ambassador' and Director of Football.

 HELL RAISING 2

 **SPORTING ACHIEVEMENTS** 9

THE MOMENT HE BECAME A LEGEND

Ken Wolstenholme summed up the moment perfectly: 'And here comes Hurst! Some people are on the pitch. They think it's all over. It is now.'

Jimmy JOHNSTONE

BORN **30 SEPTEMBER 1944** ▧ DIED **13 MARCH 2006**

Celtic's flame-haired wee winger who gave full-backs nightmares and won the European Cup with the Lisbon Lions...

An appointment with Jimmy Johnstone on top of his game was enough to give any full-back a reason to 'pull a hamstring' in the warm-up. Even for the best opposition, there seemed no answer to the frightening pace, perfect balance and low centre of gravity of the 5ft 2in winger.

Terry Cooper recalled the European Cup semi-final which saw Leeds lose to Celtic at Elland Road in 1970: 'I would love to have kicked Jinky [Johnstone's nickname], but I couldn't get near him. I still have nightmares. I had good anticipation, but I could do nothing to take the ball off him.'

England centre-half Emlyn Hughes was another tormented soul: 'Scotland beat us 2-0 one year, and I was embarrassed to come off the pitch. Jimmy absolutely crucified me.'

Born in Lanarkshire in 1944, Johnstone played games of street football from the moment he could run. Stanley Matthews (cf p130-32) was his hero and Johnstone improvised his own training exercises based on those he had read about in Matthews' autobiography.

He would dribble round rows of milk bottles to improve his control, walk along the top of fences for balance and wear heavy boots to strengthen his legs. It soon became clear that he was an outstanding prospect, and when Manchester United started to take an interest Celtic quickly signed him up.

Johnstone made his debut aged 19 in 1963, but this was not a happy era for Celtic – they hadn't won the title for almost a decade. But that would all change when Jock Stein (cf p106-07) took over as manager. The Bhoys won nine titles in a row under Stein and although Johnstone was his most potent weapon, he also gave him a few headaches with his fiery temper and fondness for a drink.

Johnstone was also petrified of flying. Playing at home in a European Cup first leg, Celtic were drawing 0-0 with Red Star Belgrade, when Stein whispered to Johnstone at half-time:

'If we win by four clear goals, Jinky, you can stay at home in two weeks' time.' An inspired Johnstone tore Red Star apart, scoring two goals and making another three as Celtic triumphed 5-1. Stein was as good as his word.

For all their domestic dominance over Rangers in the Stein era, Celtic's finest moment came in Lisbon, in 1967, when they became the first British club to lift the European Cup, with every member of the side born within 30 miles of Parkhead.

'There they were,' said Johnstone of European Cup final opponents Internazionale. 'Facchetti, Domenghini, Mazzola... all six-footers wi' Ambre Solaire suntans, Colgate smiles and slick-backed hair. And there's us lot – midgets. Ah've got nae teeth, Bobby Lennox hasnae any, and old Ronnie Simpson's got nae teeth top an' bottom.'

> 'Football was the greatest part of our lives, just like the boys from Brazil and Spain. They lived in poverty, like us, and that's where all the great players came from – the street.'

Johnstone extols the benefits of street football.

BEFORE HE WAS FAMOUS
Johnstone was a Parkhead ball boy at the age of 13 and an avid student of Stanley Matthews' skills.

THE MOMENT HE BECAME A LEGEND
The title-decider against Rangers in 1967 when he scored two goals at a muddy Ibrox.

The Italians are staring doon at us an' we're grinnin' back up at 'em wi' our great gumsy grins. We must have looked like something out o' the circus.'

But they didn't play like they were from the circus. Despite going a goal down to an early penalty, and having to get past an Italian side in full lock-down mode, the Lisbon Lions somehow found the two goals needed to overhaul their illustrious opponents and lift a trophy nearly as big as Jinky.

Stein wasn't the only manager to have problems with Johnstone, as Scotland boss Willie Ormond discovered in May 1974. Days before a meeting with England at Hampden, Johnstone and a few team-mates enjoyed a mammoth drinking session in Largs, Ayrshire. Jinky ended up in a rowing boat with no oars drifting out into the Atlantic, singing his head off. He was rescued by the coastguard. This didn't seem to harm him, as he helped Scotland beat the Auld Enemy 2-0 the following Saturday.

After 14 years, 515 games and 129 goals, Johnstone left Celtic for San Jose Earthquakes in 1975 and later briefly appeared for Sheffield United and Dundee.

In 2001, he was diagnosed with motor neurone disease that gradually saw him deteriorate, and he died aged 61 in 2006. In 2002 Jinky was voted 'Greatest Ever Celtic Player' in a supporters' poll. A bronze statue of him, poised and ready to beat a full-back, stands outside Celtic Park's main entrance. GS

Somehow, the mascot stayed on the pitch, scored one and laid on another two.

AD NAUSEAM
The Mitsubishi Lancer 'Birds And Bees' advert sees a small boy mentioning 'Jimmy Johnstone' from 'Scotland'.

 HELL RAISING 8

 SPORTING ACHIEVEMENTS 8

 talkSPORT LEGENDS

Barry SHEENE

BORN **11 SEPTEMBER 1950** ▪ DIED **10 MARCH 2003**

Live fast, die young – it was always the epitaph
most likely to apply to motorcycle racing's
Leader of the Pack...

Practising at Daytona, Florida, Barry
Sheene came out of a bend and
accelerated hard. He was travelling
at 175mph when his back wheel

locked. Thinking his engine might
have seized, he jerked at the clutch
to see if he could coast to safety.
No such luck.

The back of the bike tried to
overtake the front and was actually
travelling sideways before Sheene
went cartwheeling down the track. He
broke a femur, wrist, collarbone, two
vertebrae and several ribs... 'Apart
from that, I'm fine,' he joked, grinning
from beneath hospital sheets and
trying to cadge fags from the nurses.

If Sheene's life was presented as
fiction, it would surely receive a critical

Barry Sheene: a man with more scar tissue on his knees than Courtney Love.

panning for being over-cooked. The popstar looks and Cockney charm… the ultra-dangerous sport and that horrific crash… his relationship with a Playboy bunny girl… the time he jumped off his bike to apply life-saving first aid to fellow rider John Williams… and that bit when the Queen hands his MBE over and warns him: 'You be careful, young man.'

But this isn't fiction, this is, or rather was, Barry Sheene.

He wasn't just David Essex sitting on a motorbike – he was good. Very good. Born in Holborn, London, in 1950 with motor oil in his veins, his father Franco was a virtuoso bike-builder and tuner, and Uncle Arthur was a speedway star. Barry grew up in the race paddocks, zipping round on a Dad-built mini-bike by the age of five.

Riding Bultacos round Brands Hatch at 17, Sheene soon graduated to the 125cc British Championship, finishing as runner-up in his first season and winning the title the next. By 1971 he was on the world stage and had his first GP win in Belgium, two years later he won the Formula 750 World Championship for Suzuki. In 1974 he competed in the 500cc GP – the top of the game.

Now Sheene had begun to seep into the consciousness of the nation.

Unusually for someone in his sport, David Bailey had photographed him for *Vogue*, and *Tiger* magazine put him on a poster. But in 1975 his fame mushroomed with that spectacular crash at Daytona.

'I could feel the skin peeling off my back for two hundred yards.'

Sheene recalls the experience of that Daytona crash.

At the time, he was the subject of an hour-long Thames TV documentary, and though they unforgivably ran out of film just before the crash and failed to capture it, they did manage to get footage of him being shunted into the ambulance. Seven weeks later he was back on the bike.

Not only did Sheene recover for the 1976 season, he won five of the first seven races on his Suzuki RG500, and had his first Grand Prix title sewn up long before the end of the season. The fame and fortune moved up a gear.

Sheene bought a 14th-century mansion in Surrey and joined those other sporting legends Henry Cooper

(cf p161-4) and Kevin Keegan (cf p115-17) in flogging the 'Great Smell of Brut'.

Barry retained his title the following year, but now had a new breed of young rider coming up in his wing mirrors. American Kenny Roberts wrestled Barry's crown away in 1978 and kept it for a further two years that saw fierce competition between the two. Their classic showdown at Silverstone in 1979 saw them touching elbows at 160mph, but Sheene lost by inches.

He suffered his second major crash in 1982 at Silverstone, hitting debris on the track during practice. Surgeons battled to save his shattered legs and he ended up with more metal in him than the Bionic Man.

He never posed a title threat again and hung up his leathers in 1984. Suffering from chronic arthritis, Sheene took his wife (yes, he married Stephanie the bunny girl) and children to the warmer climes of Australia, before dying aged 52 in 2003.

If this were fiction Barry would have died at 175mph, but in the end he was taken by stomach cancer, because this was real life. And what a life. GS

BEFORE HE WAS FAMOUS
Second-hand car salesman and advertising agency courier. Never far away from a piston.

THE MOMENT HE BECAME A LEGEND
Flying through the air at Daytona before ending up in a hospital with his career in serious jeopardy.

 AD NAUSEAM
'Yeah but I wear it for a better reason – she likes it.'
Henry Cooper plays gooseberry as Barry gets changed and Steph rubs in the Brut.

 HELL RAISING 8    **SPORTING ACHIEVEMENTS** 7

Wayne ROONEY

BORN **24 OCTOBER 1985**

Scouse prodigy who was once a Blue but is now a Red and still has time to become England's greatest ever footballer.

'Wayne Rooney, remember the name!' was the sage advice from excitable TV commentator Clive Tyldesley when the prodigious scallywag became the Premier League's youngest scorer in 2002 – and it's been impossible to forget the striker ever since.

We've watched him emerge from being a teenage sensation with a short fuse into a world-class talisman with the hopes of a nation resting on his broad shoulders. Still in his mid-20s, the final chapter of Rooney's sporting life is still to be written, but this is the story so far…

Rooney comes from a working-class background, although his family have blue blood in their veins – not as aristocrats but as diehard Evertonians.

The walls of their small council house in Croxteth were already decorated with blue pennants and Duncan Ferguson posters when an Everton scout invited their son to sign for the club's youth team. And, for a nine-year-old boy who had

arrived at a Liverpool trial wearing an Everton shirt, Rooney didn't take much persuading.

As a teenager, the bullish man-child tore through the youth ranks and was soon playing with the big boys in the senior team.

Rooney was only 16 when he left a stain on Seaman's clean sheet with *that* goal against Arsenal. It gave Everton a 2-1 win that ended Arsenal's 30-game unbeaten run and stirred the normally reticent Wenger to claim Rooney was the greatest young talent he had ever seen.

England came calling a year later and Rooney was soon breaking more records as the then youngest player both to appear and then score for the national team. It wasn't a gamble of Theo Walcott proportions to take him to the 2004 European Championships – Rooney scored four goals before breaking a bone that sent him, and England's chances, out of the tournament.

With 'Roo-Mania' sweeping the country on his return, a move to a title-chasing club was inevitable. Everton were struggling and, to the anger of local graffiti artists, Manchester United signed him for £25.6 million.

Rooney hit a hat-trick on his debut for the club and continued to score more stunning goals while winning numerous titles, including three consecutive Premier Leagues and the Champions League in 2008. When Cristiano Ronaldo left for Real Madrid, he flourished – scoring 34 goals during the 2009-10 season to be named as both the PFA and Football Writers' Player of the Year.

'Nice to see your home fans boo you, that's loyal supporters.'

Delivered to camera with sarcastic intent as he left the pitch after England's dismal 0-0 draw with Algeria in the 2010 World Cup.

He is the last of a dying breed of player – a street footballer. His intense will to win comes straight from the Roy Keane school of volcanic temper – and sometimes leads to similar eruptions.

Rooney struggled to control his frustration during his formative years. He was the youngest player to be sent off in the Premier League and was frequently cautioned for reckless tackles or petulance.

This would come to cost him, especially while playing for England.

BEFORE HE WAS FAMOUS
Rooney comes from a family of boxers and aspired to being a fighter himself when he was young – naming Mike Tyson as one of his heroes.

THE MOMENT HE BECAME A LEGEND
Even Arsene Wenger didn't miss the incident that announced Rooney's arrival five days before his 17th birthday. Rooney escaped his marker before unleashing a 25-yard Exocet that screamed into the top left-hand corner.

The warning signs were there when he forced his own substitution after an ill-tempered display against Spain in 2004. And in 2005, he went ballistic at Beckham (cf p154-6) during an England qualifier, before being sent off for United in the Champions League after happy-clapping the referee.

But the worst came during the 2006 World Cup when a struggling Rooney was sent off during the quarter-finals against Portugal for stamping his authority…all over Ricardo Carvalho's testicles.

Whether Rooney will fulfil a prophecy to become the greatest player this country has ever produced, or fall into self-destruction like previous flawed geniuses, such as George Best (cf p192-6) and Paul Gascoigne (cf p169-72), still remains to be seen.

But he has survived various scandals to marry his childhood sweetheart and become a father. In the autumn of 2010, he asked to leave United, but emerged instead with a pay rise and eventually helped the Reds to a 19th league title by the end of the season, shaving the number 19 into his chest hair in celebration at beating Liverpool's record.

It might be ill-advised to predict there will be no further controversial incidents, but he seems to have calmed down his temperament without blunting his competitive edge.

England expects… RICHARD ARROWSMITH

The picture that inspired a £12,000 hair transplant.

AD NAUSEAM
The pre-World Cup 2010 advert saw an A-list of footballing talents fail to deliver. In Rooney's version, success would have seen him knighted and beat Roger Federer at table tennis while failure at the World Cup would leave him eating beans while living in a caravan. Hmmm…
Nike – Write The Future.

 HELL **8** RAISING

 SPORTING **8** ACHIEVEMENTS

Ronnie O'SULLIVAN

BORN **5 DECEMBER 1975**

Forget the three World Championship victories, he's undoubtedly the biggest draw in the game of snooker. Simple as…

Based on raw stats alone, there is no doubt that Ronnie O'Sullivan is the most naturally gifted player ever to pick up a cue.

Not that accolades sit well with 'The Rocket', who says he only wanted to become famous because he was a 'little f**ker at school'

and 'not very good at interacting with people'.

O'Sullivan grew up in Chigwell, Essex, and made his first century break aged ten, his first maximum at 15, turned professional at 16 and won the UK Championship at 17 – making him the youngest ever winner of a ranking title. At 19 he won his first Masters title (beating John Higgins 9-3 in the final).

Pictured 37 seconds before making a break of 113. In the next frame.

Three years later, in 1997, he made the fastest ever maximum break, needing a breath-taking 5 minutes 20 seconds to clear the table in the first round of the World Championships against Mick Price. It was captivating, like a man trying to finish his game with a taxi waiting outside.

In between winning three world titles in 2001, 2004 and 2008, all the other 20-plus ranking events, earning over £6 million in prize money and making ten maximum breaks under competition rules, O'Sullivan has struggled with addiction and depression. Not to mention the absence of his father – 'The centre of my universe,' as he has called him – who was convicted of a fatal stabbing and released in November 2010 after 18 years in jail.

'The Rocket' has been taken to task for everything from assaulting a tournament official to being tested positive for cannabis (for which he was stripped of his 1998 Irish Masters title) and playing left-handed against an opponent – which was taken as a sign of disrespect (he beat Alan Robidoux 10-3).

But he has always had a problematic relationship with the sport he was born to play. Broadsheet feature writers still seem almost compelled to call him 'complex' or 'troubled'. It might be true but it's lazy.

As Sigmund Freud might recognise, he is an amalgamation of emotions and exigency that have been rejected from awareness but still influence behaviour.

In the quarter-finals of the 2006 UK Championship, O'Sullivan got off to a slow start, going 4-1 down to arch-rival Stephen Hendry (cf p44). Despite

it being a best of 17, O'Sullivan quit, casually informing his stunned opponent, 'I've had enough of it, mate.' He subsequently apologised, but was fined for his behaviour.

> 'I've loved him since he was twelve. Total nutcase, but what a character.'

Snooker supremo Barry Hearn.

His contests with Hendry have often been intense. Surprisingly, when asked to pick his favourite career moment, he doesn't go for one of their most high-profile clashes, but chooses the untelevised European Open final of 2003 because 'there were hardly any mistakes throughout that match'.

Unpredictable and prone to baring his soul about anything and everything, O'Sullivan has almost single-handedly kept interest in the game of snooker alive since the turn of the century.

Whether he's simulating a sex act with a microphone in front of the local press in China or refusing the final black on a break of 140, O'Sullivan is, and always will be, box office gold.

But just try telling that to The Rocket. He smiles, shrugs and says, 'It's a job, innit.' Not really Ronald. It's a vocation and you were born to play. TB

 AD NAUSEAM
Has endorsed two-piece snooker cues (obviously), DVDs and Apps for the iPhone, iPad and iPod.

 HELL RAISING 8    **SPORTING ACHIEVEMENTS** 8

BEFORE HE WAS FAMOUS
Fourteen-year-old O'Sullivan, who was practising three hours a day during term time, paid a kid called Fasel Nadir a fiver to do his homework, warning him not to make it 'too clever'.

 THE MOMENT HE BECAME A LEGEND
Winning his first world title in 2001, earning £250,000 and the coveted No. 1 spot in the rankings for the first time.

Andrew FLINTOFF

BORN **6 DECEMBER 1977**

Big-hearted, injury-prone all-rounder and Ashes hero who loves a drink and an occasional go on a pedalo…

Sin when you're winning. That's the trick.

When Andrew Flintoff spent the day of the big Ashes Parade in September 2005 wandering round with a wide beam on his face, stumbling out of 10 Downing Street (after having a go on little Leo Blair's swing), and swaying and slurring his way through interviews, it only enhanced the Freddie legend.

'To be honest with you, David, I'm struggling. I've not been to bed yet and the eyes behind these glasses tell a thousand stories,' he admitted into David Gower's microphone in front of the thousands assembled in Trafalgar Square, who cheered him fit to wake Nelson atop his column.

The following morning Flintoff's sunset-pink eyes made the tabloid front pages under the headline: 'OFF HIS FRED!' amid speculation as to whether he had 'watered the plants' in the garden of No 10. But having just won the Ashes after one of the greatest Test series ever, no one dared to so much as tut at Fred's behaviour.

Eighteen months later, the Ashes had been meekly handed back to Australia – Flintoff skippering England to five straight defeats – and England had lost their first game of the 2007 World Cup to New Zealand.

After the game, Flintoff and several team-mates went out on the lash in St Lucia, ending up in Rumours nightclub. The party moved to the beach, Freddie ended up in a pedalo and then 'got into difficulties' and had to be rescued.

The England management took a dim view and Flintoff was stripped of his vice-captaincy, fined and dropped for the next game. The public and the tabloids weren't impressed by the 'Fredalo' incident either, and suddenly the drinking was no longer funny or clever.

But, like a puppy who had chewed your best trainers, it was difficult to stay mad at him for long. After all, Freddie, despite an injury-ravaged career, had given us so many great moments.

The 6ft 5in giant from Preston had known he was going to be a cricketer from a young age, which is why he abandoned his education, despite passing nine GCSEs. Once he found out you could make a living from cricket he didn't bother with 'A' levels and made his way through the ranks at Lancashire and England, premature predictions hailing him as the 'next Botham'.

His heavy frame put a lot of stress on his joints and he was plagued by back and ankle injuries from the early part of his career. By the age of 22, Flintoff seemed to have stalled. He wasn't fulfilling his promise for club or country and, devoted to beer and curry, he was carrying 19st around. Some harsh words from Lancashire coach Bob Simpson, and meeting his wife-to-be Rachael, woke up Flintoff.

Freddie finally 'arrived' in 2003. He scored a century and three fifties in the home Test series against South Africa, and continued his fine form in the West Indies, claiming five wickets in the Barbados Test while also scoring a century in Antigua.

Freddie had gone from being 'the Fat Lad' to one of *Wisden*'s Cricketers of the Year. The next year continued in the same vein, with Flintoff posting a half-century in each one of seven

'Mind the windows, Tino.'

Directed from the slips to West Indian batsman Tino Best, who promptly charged down the wicket aiming to knock the skin off the ball and was stumped by five yards.

BEFORE HE WAS FAMOUS
Young Flintoff was a school chess champion, representing Lancashire Schools and also beating the more famously cerebral Mike Atherton.

THE MOMENT HE BECAME A LEGEND
Hammering those nine sixes against Australia at Edgbaston in 2005 that had the crowd roaring.

victorious Tests against New Zealand and the West Indies.

Then came that glorious summer of 2005… England lost the first Test at Lord's. Subsequently, the Ashes, not held since 1989, seemed as far away as ever. But a huge contribution from Flintoff at Edgbaston, in what was dubbed 'Fred's Test', squared the series. Flintoff's total of 141 runs included nine sixes and he took seven Aussie wickets.

After a draw at Old Trafford, Flintoff struck a century at Trent Bridge, an England victory seeing them take a 2-1 lead with only the fifth Test at The Oval remaining. Freddie's 72 and five wickets in the first innings helped England to the draw they needed, sparking delirious scenes of celebration across a nation that had rediscovered its love of cricket.

Flintoff was named Man of the Series, and embarked on a heroic drinking session…

His last hurrah came in the 2009 Ashes series when he forced his body to make one last effort, bowling a match-winning spell at Lord's and then signing off from Test cricket with a direct-hit run out to dismiss Ricky Ponting at The Oval. GS

....

AD NAUSEAM
Scheming Aussies steal Flintoff's car, but he jumps in a pedalo to get to the Test match, with the aid of Sure for Men… somehow.

....

| HELL 9 RAISING | SPORTING 7 ACHIEVEMENTS |

'It's all right Brett, me old mate. It's not like we're going to win the Ashes again any time soon.'

Alf RAMSEY

BORN **22 JANUARY 1920** ■ DIED **28 APRIL 1999**

England full-back who went on to mastermind his country's only World Cup victory – without a second thought for the style critics.

When the great tactical revolutionary bossed Ipswich Town to the First Division championship in 1962, he caused a schism in British football that would come to a head in 1966, and continues to this day: should you play ugly and win? Or should you play pretty and lose?

When Alf Ramsey took over as Ipswich boss in 1955, the Division Three (South) club hadn't yet been 20 years in the Football League, but inside a decade they had progressed up the leagues to vanquish the historical giants and the rich, ball-playing teams without demur.

Ramsey's achievement on a shoestring budget, without star players, was arguably the greatest managerial achievement the British game has ever seen, although the manner of victory did not please many purists.

Ramsey had left behind the open, tactically naïve WM formation and replaced it with tight, defensive-minded 4-3-3. He built a fierce team spirit, insisting on 100 per cent effort, largely renouncing the use of orthodox wingers for a more direct style that employed not five men charging into attack, but often just a single striker.

'Now listen Stiles, unhand me or you'll lose the bottom set as well.'

talkSPORT
LEGENDS

If the story sounds familiar, that's because he then repeated the trick with England to lift the World Cup – to similarly mixed reviews. It wasn't just abroad that 1966 was written off by many observers as a victory for the defensive, utilitarian camp over prettier, skill-packed outfits.

Respected author and historian Frank McLynn called Ramsey 'A humourless boor… the epitome of negativity, and his legend far outstrips his actual achievement.' Nevertheless, he earned his place in this book as the first modern manager of the England side.

Capped 32 times as a right-back while collecting back-to-back Second Division and league championship medals with Spurs, Ramsey had first emerged in regimental football during the war – his nickname was 'The General'.

At Southampton, his first club, he was soon recognised for his supreme positional sense and reading of a game and was eventually bestowed with the England captaincy three times in his five-year international career between 1948 and 1953.

As a motivator and organiser he was first class, even if his obsession with tactics was out of synch with the free-thinking and running of his peers. And from the start Ramsey was seen as aloof, speaking in the clipped tones he had developed in the Army. He also had elocution lessons so as not to betray his humble working-class roots in Dagenham.

'We shall win the World Cup.'

Alf Ramsey, October 1963, upon his appointment as England manager.

Not a lot of fans today realise that the World Cup didn't just provide Ramsey with his crowning achievement, but also with his original motivation to rethink the game and revamp England's losing ways. He was actually in the team when England made their debut appearance on the world stage at the 1950 World Cup in Brazil.

Infamously, they lost to a team of gutsy US amateurs. FA bigwigs rode roughshod over the wishes of nominal team manager Walter Winterbottom when it came to selecting the team and even deciding on the tactics.

Sixteen years later, and as England set about the 1966 campaign, Ramsey was criticised for his tactics and team selection by everyone except his fiercely loyal group of players. Uncomfortable in the growing media glare, he came across as superior and snappy. Even when his decisions were ultimately justified, he betrayed no emotion.

At the final whistle against West Germany, his loyal assistant went ape in the dugout while Ramsey remained stone-faced, barking, 'Control yourself, Shepherdson!' in best Captain Mainwaring style.

In 1970, Ramsey's comments on Argentina four years before – 'We don't swap shirts with animals' – came back to bedevil a doomed campaign, and few mourned his eventual sacking after failure to qualify for the 1974 finals.

Put out to grass aged just 54, a powerless executive role at Birmingham City would sadly prove to be his last involvement with football. Ramsey lived out a reclusive life, suffering a stroke during the 1998 World Cup before dying almost a forgotten hero a year later. DH

 AD NAUSEAM
'What happens if foreign food gives our boys a belly ache? Don't worry, it's not a risk a team manager will take in a foreign country.'
Ad for Findus ready meals, pre 1970 World Cup.

BEFORE HE WAS FAMOUS
As a youngster in the East End, Alf harboured ambitions to become a grocer.

 THE MOMENT HE BECAME A LEGEND
After the final whistle in 1966, Nobby Stiles tried to hoist Alf up onto his team-mates' shoulders, but a stern-faced Ramsey pushed him away.

 HELL RAISING

SPORTING ACHIEVEMENTS

Jock STEIN

BORN **5 OCTOBER 1922** ■ DIED **10 SEPTEMBER 1985**

The gaffer who brought unprecedented success to Celtic, helping them to become the first British club to win the European Cup.

As it was passed around the victorious Celtic dressing room, each of the Lisbon Lions sipped champagne from the European Cup. Billy McNeill, their illustrious captain, handed it to Jock Stein, who declined the opportunity to imbibe.

It was 25 May 1967 and he'd just masterminded a 2-1 win over Italian giants Inter Milan, but as true to his teetotalism as he was to his side's attack, attack, attack philosophy, he rejected the offer.

John 'Jock' Stein was born in 1922 in the Lanarkshire village of Burnbank and, after leaving school at 16, worked as a labourer in a carpet factory before becoming a coal miner. He continued to work in that industry throughout his eight years with first club Albion Rovers.

He was made from hard stuff. While playing for junior club Blantyre Victoria in 1941, a year before signing with Rovers, the *Burnbank Gazette* reported: 'J. Stein of the Vics was suspended for 14 days for a field offence.' He was nothing other than committed.

However, it was a struggle for the team to find any sort of rhythm during his first years in football, with the Second World War meaning constant changes, although signs of the personality that would make him a legendary boss are referenced in the Jock Stein biography.

'Celtic jerseys are not for second best, they don't shrink to fit inferior players.'

Stein issues a mission statement.

Barracked by fans who were watching his team being given the run-around, he controlled the ball on the touchline and booted it into the crowd shouting: 'I'm a mug? You're the mugs for payin' to watch me.'

As a result of the drubbings the team suffered, Jock moved to Welsh side Llanelli in 1950, where he was paid £12 a week and, for

the first time, could call himself a professional footballer. However, his stay in Wales was short. His wife and daughter joined him shortly after his move, but within eight weeks their house in Scotland was burgled and homesickness kicked in.

They wanted a return home and in 1951 Celtic paid for his services. Much was made of his Protestant background and many of his close friends never spoke to him again, but nonetheless it was to be a masterstroke.

It wasn't long before he became Celtic captain and he played over

150 games in the heart of defence. However, injury meant he eventually enjoyed less match time than he should have, and in 1956 he played his last match before returning nine years later as manager, after spells in charge at Dunfermline and Hibernian.

Billy McNeill said of his appointment: 'When I heard that I got a tremendous lift. Everything was a joke at Parkhead. We did nothing you'd describe as proper planning or preparation. We thought all clubs did what we did. I knew right away times would be different.'

The following month he lifted the Scottish Cup, the club's first major trophy since 1957. It was the beginning of 12 years of dominance that included nine league titles in

BEFORE HE WAS FAMOUS
He worked in a carpet factory before becoming a miner. He was playing for Albion Rovers at the same time.

 THE MOMENT HE BECAME A LEGEND
Guiding the 'Lisbon Lions' to a first European Cup victory in 1967. He was Celtic's fourth manager and their first Protestant one.

talkSPORT LEGENDS

a row and a first European Cup – the players were all born within a 30-mile radius of Glasgow. It was the ultimate achievement.

His team were playing 'Total Football' years before Johan Cruyff and the Netherlands turned up.

After a serious car crash in 1975, his influence declined. However, his final record with Celtic was: played 421, lost 59.

The next job, with Scotland in 1978 – ignoring his 44-day spell in charge of Leeds – was to be his final one. He took them to Spain in 1982, but at the end of a World Cup qualifier with Wales at Ninian Park in 1985, he collapsed and died later in the medical room.

Although awarded a CBE for reaching the European Cup final again in 1970, Jock, unbelievably, was never given what Matt Busby (cf p124-6) and Alex Ferguson (cf p110-11), who was Stein's Scotland assistant, later received for winning the trophy: a knighthood.

Disgracefully, his name was removed from the New Year's Honours list after four of his players were sent off for brawling in the Intercontinental Cup game with Argentine champions Racing Club in 1967.

Hardly a fitting tribute to a great man. DM

The European Cup, post champagne but before being filled (and emptied of) Tennent's Super. Nobody remembers what the next player chose.

AD NAUSEAM

Jock Stein existed in an era before it was *de rigueur* for footballers advertise everything from Pizza Hut to Castrol. That said, the Celtic Supporters' Club will flog you a Jock Stein pinbadge for £2.99 – at least, they would if they hadn't already sold out.

 HELL RAISING 3

 **SPORTING ACHIEVEMENTS** 9

TORVILL & DEAN

BORN **7 OCTOBER 1957** and **27 JULY 1958**

Sporting perfection on thin ice.

The punters on the Clapham omnibus tended to agree: it wasn't really a sport if it involved a) music, b) frilly costumes, or c) a requirement to maintain a fixed smile with a series of alarming transgressions on counts of spangly tights and micro skirts (she) and velveteen trouser suits (he), shamelessly aggravated by a propensity to interpret badly amplified show tunes.

And so, the charge sheet looked ominous for would-be sportspersons Jayne Torvill and Christopher Dean.

They might well have been GB's best bet for Olympic gold in Sarajevo, but only in a sport that veered dangerously close to dancing – they were on thin ice you could say. Incorrectly.

Back in 1984, there were even distinctly unsporting tabloid assumptions of an eight-year-long romance between the Nottingham skaters, simply because they'd been together since winning their first skate-boogie trophy back in 1976. As Dean would say later, 'I never felt

pressure on us from the press to have a romantic relationship. It was all just part of the story. Everyone wants a happy ending, so we'd never have come out and said no.'

To top it all, there was even a worrisome celebrity involvement in the pair's preparation for the 1984 Winter Olympics, with Michael 'Ooh, Betty' Crawford emerging as the mentor who 'taught them how to act'.

True, the couple had done nothing but win British Figure Skating Championships, Europeans and Worlds since coming fourth at the 1980 Olympics, but everyone knows showbiz,

'Are you sure these sleeves work for me?'

'Winning at the 1984 Olympics was a really big thing. A friend of mine said to me the other day, "I don't think you realise that if you'd have done that today you'd be almost like Posh and Becks – you wouldn't be able to go anywhere."'

Jayne Torvill wonders what might have been. Shortly before weeping with relief.

celebrity and proper sport can never mix? Well, they thought they did then.

It must have come as something of a shock, therefore, when Jayne and Chris's compulsory routine inspired nothing less than awe in a transfixed nation of sports fans, hungry for gold.

No matter who you were – a sulky indie kid, a Conservative politician, a striking miner – or what you were doing, everything stopped for Torvill & Dean. Only a fool could have quibbled about their Paso Doble routine or whether it was technically suitable for an athlete to be flipped and twisted around like a bullfighter's cape in the pair's second superhuman display of power, control, timing and balance.

However, because Jayne and Chris were British, and because this was sport, there was also a pleasant frisson of potential *schadenfreude*, of an accident waiting to happen in the last round. Over 24 million people in the UK watched in breathless unison as the pair got down on their knees to start their final routine, to Ravel's *Bolero*.

Take a ten-year-old child and attempt to spin it up to shoulder height with no apparent effort and the grace of a swan. Now, just in

case you've met with success, try to do the same thing with an athletic young woman of 5ft 2in. Spin her around your torso and then hoist her upside-down so she can perform a full doughnut ring before flipping her into a crowd-pleasing cantilever.

Now try to do it while you're balancing on one leg. Standing on a 2mm-thick blade of tempered steel. Travelling at 30mph. On ice, naturally. Do it without missing a beat in a series of complex ballet moves, timed to last exactly four minutes, ten seconds – the maximum allowable by the rules. One extra second, and you're disqualified. Oh, and make it sexy.

The viewing public looked on open-mouthed in shock and awe at

the unsurpassable poise, power and precision of Torvill & Dean – the performance scored 12 perfect 6.0s and six 5.9s, including maximum artistic impression scores of 6.0 from every judge. Sheer perfection.

Turning professional after the Olympics, their spectacular ice shows ran before packed houses for 14 years. Upon retirement in 1998, Dean moved to the US with his wife and young family, while Torvill lived in Surrey with her husband and children.

In 2006 the pair were tempted out of retirement to act as coaches, choreographers and performers in ITV's *Dancing On Ice* and were still pulling in the viewers after more than 20 years. Some achievement. DH

 AD NAUSEAM

'Torvill & Dean will once again train a cast of celebrity novices to become skating superstars [on *Dancing on Ice*], with a number of surprises along the way…'
ITV press release.

HELL RAISING

SPORTING ACHIEVEMENTS

BEFORE THEY WERE FAMOUS
Back home in Nottingham, Chris was a policeman and Jayne an accounts clerk. Any suggestion that she played Mrs McClusky, the headmistress in *Grange Hill*, can officially be put down to the sporting fantasies of men of a certain age.

 THE MOMENT THEY BECAME LEGENDS
Sprawled out on the ice at the end of the *Bolero* routine. What followed was the highest ice-dancing score of all time.

Alex FERGUSON

BORN **31 DECEMBER 1941**

Red-faced, combative Scot who turned Aberdeen into one of the best sides in Europe before taking Manchester United to the top.

'I'd never been afraid of anyone,' remembered former East Stirlingshire FC forward Bobby McCulley when asked about his former manager. 'But he was a frightening bastard from the start.' Alex Ferguson was 32 and embarking upon his managerial career. 'Time didn't matter to him,' continued McCulley. 'He never wore a watch.' He does now, of course, to keep track of 'Fergie time' when so many United goals are scored.

Almost four decades later, Ferguson (or Sir Alex, as the famous socialist has been known since 1999) continues to show, week-on-glowering-week, that the fires still burn. And they are fires that, like so many great British managers, were forged and stoked in the industrial heart of working-class Scotland.

Indeed, Ferguson is perhaps the last true heir of a line that includes Matt Busby (cf p124-6), Bill Shankly (cf p177-81) and Jock Stein (cf p106-07) – to date he has won 36 trophies with United, during a reign that will span 25 years in November 2011. If he is not the greatest British football manager of all time, he is surely the most remorseless.

Born in Govan on New Year's Eve 1941, Ferguson was brought up against the backdrop of the Glasgow docks, using football as a means of escape from the tough post-war conditions. A rugged forward with an eye for goal, his playing career peaked in two

seasons with Rangers, but ended with his retirement in the summer of 1974.

He then moved into management. A brief but memorable spell with East Stirlingshire (as attested to by McCulley) led to four seasons at St Mirren, with whom he won promotion to the Scottish top flight.

Next came eight sensational years with Aberdeen (he famously told his squad to 'Eat your greens and enjoy sex'), during which Ferguson led a team in the shadows of the 'Old Firm' to a first Scottish league title since 1955, four Scottish Cups and the 1982-83 European Cup-Winners' Cup final win over Real Madrid. Aberdeen went on to win two further Scottish league titles before the manager's departure for England in late 1986.

His first foray into the English game, having previously spurned a move to Nottingham Forest because his wife did not want a move south of the border, was with Manchester United. The sleeping giant was a club struggling to rise from the ashes left at the end of the Matt Busby era and which had seen bitter rivals Liverpool dominate English football. He famously pledged to 'knock [Liverpool] off their f*cking perch.'

In 2011, he finally achieved this as the club recorded its 19th league title to overhaul Liverpool's record of 18. To think, when he arrived at Old Trafford, the score was 16-7 in favour of the Merseyside outfit.

Despite the slow start and a thoroughly humiliating 5-1 defeat at the hands of Manchester City that had the press saying he was on the brink of dismissal in the 1989-90 season, he was as good as his word. United won the FA Cup that year – after a replay against Crystal Palace. That's when it all started. It has yet to end.

'The euphoria evaporates almost immediately.'

The day after Manchester United won the Champions League in 2008.

BEFORE THEY WERE FAMOUS
Ferguson worked for American machine manufacturers Remington Rand for six years and led colleagues in a protest against the sacking of another member of staff.

THE MOMENT THEY BECAME A LEGEND
Aberdeen fans might disagree, but leading Manchester United to their first league title in 26 years might just surpass winning the European Cup-Winners' Cup with the Dons.

Ferguson has created not one but three or, arguably, four great United teams. He has nurtured the home-grown talent of Ryan Giggs (cf p60) and Paul Scholes, spent a fortune on players from Roy Keane to Cristiano Ronaldo and Wayne Rooney (cf p98-9) and never been afraid to sell star players (Mark Hughes, David Beckham (cf p154-6) *et al*) for the good of the club. Oh, and he also bought Eric Cantona from Leeds United for a fee that amounted to daylight robbery.

He is an empire builder and remains the most revered coach in the sport, an intimidating link to the great disciplinarians of the past but as innovative in his tactical approach as the modern masters Jose Mourinho and Josep 'Pep' Guardiola.

Since Ferguson joined United they have won 12 Premier League titles – the first of which, inspired by Cantona, came in 1993 – five FA Cups, four League Cups, one Cup-Winners' Cup and two Champions League titles. Three of those (the Champions League, Premier League title and the FA Cup) came in one season – 1999.

After Liverpool won their first European Cup in 1977, defender Tommy Smith asked, 'What the hell do we do for an encore? The treble? No way … we are the team of the century … and no side will ever get nearer. It can't be done.' Manchester United scored two goals in stoppage time 22 years later to beat Bayern Munich 2-1 in the 1999 Champions League final to prove him wrong.

Incredibly, as he prepares to enter his seventies, Ferguson's appetite appears undimmed. A huge influx of foreign players has posed no discernible

You Never Actually Own An Alex Ferguson [watch], You Merely Look After It For The Next Referee.

problem for his Glaswegian brogue, while he continues to effectively motivate men of unfathomable wealth despite being 40 or 50 years their senior.

Stories of Fergie's outbursts have persisted – Beckham was hit on the head by a flying boot Ferguson kicked across the dressing room – yet he inspires absolute loyalty from almost every individual he has ever managed, and is respected by rival managers.

Off the pitch, he has rarely failed to provoke and amuse. Who will ever forget Newcastle boss Kevin Keegan (cf p115-17) falling apart in front of the Sky cameras in the 1995-96 title run-in or, in fact, remember why

Fergie continues to refuse to speak to the BBC. Brace yourself, because the hairdryer's still plugged in. TH/JG

....

⊘ AD NAUSEAM
In the 1990s, United appeared in an advert for Pepsi. Losing 3-0 at half-time, Fergie gives a stirring team-talk while chucking cans to his players – hilariously, of course, Schmeichel drops his. Do you see what they've done there?

....

 HELL RAISING 7

 **SPORTING ACHIEVEMENTS** 10

James HUNT

BORN **29 AUGUST 1947** ■ DIED **15 JUNE 1993**

Dope-toking, Dom Perignon-downing, playboy hell-racer who arrived from nowhere — at 200mph — to win the World Championship.

Despite everything, the British public couldn't resist *liking* something about the brattish ex-public schoolboy with the wide hippy streak who drove a car without care, like a jet-propelled dodgem. Despite the uncontrollable temper and the playboy antics. Despite the dope smoking and the haughty disregard for authority. And finally *because* of all that, and more.

The suntan, the cheekbones and the long blond hair of a spoiled angel clearly helped drag half the population on to his side, but gradually we all came around to James Hunt. And, perhaps curiously for a mouthy posh boy on an apparent suicide mission, we came to accept him as 'one of us'.

That is to say, if we could have escaped the fetters of being a spotty kid or a slack-gutted dad hunched in front of the TV, then we too would have been more like Hunt. Out on the champers at four in the Monte Carlo morning, fending off pneumatic models. Rolling in to formal functions in jeans and a T-shirt and no shoes, flashing two fingers to the boss.

When Hunt punched his fellow drivers, slapped errant lap-timers and even attacked a steward trying to pull him from a smouldering wreck, we could somehow empathise: if we'd ever made 200mph only to find our bullet-like progress hampered by inefficient or overzealous people, then by crikey we'd probably have set about them too.

In the early days, you had to work hard to find ways to excuse the privileges and excesses of Hunt and his sponsor, Lord Hesketh. It helped enormously when everyone in the racing fraternity wrote off 1973's all-new DIY F1 team as a posh dreamer with money to burn, and a brash no-hoper liability still known as 'Hunt The Shunt' from his Formula 3 days.

In a stroke, the super-rich boss and his playboy hireling became glorious underdogs, without so much as a corporate sponsor. Little touches like the crash-helmeted teddy bear team mascot hinted at humour in a world of slickness, as did the patch on Hunt's overalls: SEX: THE BREAKFAST OF CHAMPIONS. Now it was us against them.

The unruly Hunt lined up initially with only a series of F3 crashes and a sacking from the F2 March team to his name. Hunt called Hesketh the 'Good Lord', but his budget was apparently being blown on a Rolls-Royce chauffeur service and high-rolling parties rather than the all-important car and painstaking preparation.

The approach seemed a throwback to Hunt's formative years behind the wheel when he had first decided to become a racing driver on the strength of seeing a Silverstone race flash by.

Without any support from his stockbroker dad, he'd then done odd jobs to finance the purchase of a Mini. He spent two years doing it up, fine tuning the car and his own performance behind the wheel, only to have the car fail scrutinising to race on an actual circuit.

In retrospect, it was near miraculous for Hunt to barrel and barge his way to five podiums in two years with the Hesketh team, and twice achieve eighth in the drivers' standings. In the following 1975 season, he beat Niki Lauda to win the Dutch Grand Prix and achieve fourth place in the drivers' standings.

But then came an upset to the script – Hesketh ran out of money and sounded a hasty retreat from F1. Just as Hunt's dream seemed shattered,

'My first priority is to finish above, rather than beneath, the ground.'

Hunt reveals a scintilla of responsibility.

Emerson Fittipaldi also chose to move on, leaving a hole in the Marlboro McLaren team for 1976, and precious few drivers still available.

Now it was time for the jeans-toting rebel to win the drivers' championship on behalf of all of us, a nation of eccentrics, wannabes and underdogs. But no one ever supposed it would go

talkSPORT LEGENDS

He was justifiably furious when he discovered that someone had stolen his Rizlas.

James HUNT

'Bloody Moët… What about a Krug 1926?'

smoothly, as James hit the headlines for dining out with his pet Alsatian, Oscar, at a posh Mayfair restaurant.

Out on the track, Hunt was disqualified after winning the Spanish Grand Prix in a car 1.8cm too wide. He won the British Grand Prix, but was later disqualified for cutting back through an access road to restart after the initial first-corner pile-up. In Italy, his fuel was ruled illegal and he had to start from the back of the grid.

And then his close friend and championship leader Niki Lauda almost died in a crash in Germany, allowing Hunt – reinstated in Spain, and the glorious winner of six other Grand Prix that season – to close to within three points of him with only Japan still to run.

In torrential rain, leader Hunt suffered a puncture, a delayed pitstop and botched pit signals – but his limping, bedraggled third place

was enough to give him the World Championship by a point. And a new definition of 'celebration' was reached that night.

Disappearing almost as fast as he'd arrived, James won only three more races before his retirement in 1979. And yet he continued to endear himself to the public as a candid and hugely knowledgeable BBC race commentator alongside Murray Walker. Sex symbol James Hunt died an impecunious budgie breeder, aged just 45 in 1993, just hours after proposing to what would have been his third wife, a beautiful blonde half his age. DH

 AD NAUSEAM

Morecambe: 'Good morrow, Jane.'
Hunt: 'James.'
Morecambe: 'It's the way you walk. I trust all is well?'
Hunt: 'It's no good chaps, she still doesn't sound a hundred per cent.'
Wise: 'Well Mr James, we've changed the engine, the suspension, the tyres and the transmission.'
Morecambe: 'Ya crawler.'
Wise: 'We've even changed the chassis.'
Morecambe (to camera): 'The chassis! Just a moment, what about the petrol?'
Wise/Hunt: 'The petrol?'
Morecambe: 'Would you like me to put some Texaco in it?'
Hunt: 'What's in it then?'
Morecambe: 'Only you at the moment, sunbeam…'
Texaco TV ad, 1977.

 BEFORE HE WAS FAMOUS
A keen budgie breeder in his youth, Hunt hoped it would enable him to 'retire at thirty, a millionaire'.

THE MOMENT HE BECAME A LEGEND
The traditional champagne squirting as World Champion took some beating; but Hunt's habit of asking bystanders for their ciggies during pit-lane interviews was just as winning.

 HELL RAISING 10

 **SPORTING ACHIEVEMENTS** 8

Kevin KEEGAN

24

BORN **14 FEBRUARY 1951**

Heart on sleeve. Tears in eyes. English football's most passionate performer admits the Kop's 'You'll Never Walk Alone' made him cry as he played.

Back in the 1970s, the received snug-bar wisdom on Kevin Keegan suggested that, despite his goalscoring and trophy-gathering record at Liverpool, he was somehow all effort and not enough natural class. His sin was simple – he had learned to become a great player, and even had to practise at it. He was no George Best (cf p192-6), no Johan Cruyff. Keegan was a trier.

As ever, there was a twisted truth underlying the barstool pundits' argument. The bustling striker's ball skills fell short of the genius benchmark, although to decry the value of coaching, learning and commitment in post-1960s football was to be blind to the changes under way in the game.

Incredibly perhaps, this lazy pocket study of England's most valuable player of the 1970s has survived into the cool light of the 21st century.

Let's set the record straight. In his years at Liverpool between 1971 and 1977, Keegan was the most consistent match-winner in British football, helping the Reds to three First Division titles, two UEFA Cups, one FA Cup and a European Cup. He may not have known six different ways to beat his man, but what could be more exciting on a football pitch than a player darting and muscling in a blurry, headlong rush for goal?

'Robbery with violence' was how Bill Shankly (cf p177-81) described the capture of midfielder Keegan from Fourth Division Scunthorpe United for £35,000. Unusually, Shanks threw the kid from Doncaster straight into the first team from the start of 1971-72, and immediately the freshly converted striker romped up his learning curve, quickly shifting through the gears from good to great.

Keegan was small and powerful, a ball of energy with electric pace. He hit it off instantly with 'Big' John Toshack, made his England Under-23 debut on 16 February 1972 and arrived on the full international scene nine months later, winning hearts and minds at every stage.

He would soon become a national talisman, a TV celebrity, a chartbound disco groover and even a columnist for a kids' comic – the biggest little thing in the game.

As he once said, somewhat enigmatically, 'I know what is around the corner – I just don't know where the corner is.'

Thanks to the sickly gin 'n' korma whiff of Brut 33, it was possible to smell just like him, and kids were invited to cross the road safely with KK ('Take it from me... be smart, be safe'). Beyond that there were cereal-pack toys and Goal! lollipops with a little plastic Keegan on the top of

BEFORE HE WAS FAMOUS
It was Keegan's childhood dream to play for Doncaster Rovers. He got the thumbs down from his hometown club – but not a lot of fans know that Jimmy Hill's Coventry City also rejected him for being 'too small'.

THE MOMENT HE BECAME A LEGEND
When he was needled into trading punches with big (5ft 5in) bully boy Billy Bremner in the Liverpool–Leeds United Charity Shield of 1974.

Kevin KEEGAN

the stick ('Paint it to look like your favourite football star').

That was all very well for the boys but young ladies, too, found 'Little Kev' charming and dashing, cuddly and unthreatening, peering out from beneath his trademark bubble-perm. So, why did everybody love Kevin Keegan in the 1970s? Men, women, boys, girls, Liverpool fans (obviously), non-Liverpool fans (not so obviously)?

It was because he always wore his heart on his sleeve with transparent enthusiasm and was unafraid to show his passion to win over the final doubters – as demonstrated after

Cup final against Newcastle almost single-handedly.

As the heart and soul of the 1976 team (First Division championship and UEFA Cup once more), it felt like a nail being hammered into the coffin of the English game – too slow, too dirty and too defensive even to retain the interest of its one true star – when Keegan announced his intention to leave for the Bundesliga and mid-table Hamburg a year later, again seeking to improve and hone his game.

But even the few outraged Kopite boo-boys buckled when he helped bring the European Cup to Anfield

'I would love it if we could beat them. Love it. [Alex Ferguson's] gone down in my estimation. Manchester United haven't won this yet, I'd love it if we beat them.'

His famous rant on Sky Sports as Newcastle manager in 1996.

he climbed back on his bike after a spectacular crash on BBC TV's *Superstars* programme in 1976.

In 1972-73, he was Liverpool's top scorer, dragging them to an unprecedented First Division championship and UEFA Cup double. In more recent times, only the teenage Michael Owen has had a similar impact in terms of sheer visual excitement, impossible for the lumbering cloggers to handle – some would argue that the latter never really fulfilled his potential. By contrast, in 1974 Keegan won the FA

as a parting gift, beating Borussia Moenchengladbach 3-1 in Rome. He scored in every round leading up to the final.

While 'Mighty Mouse' thrived in Germany, twice landing European Player of the Year as he led Hamburg to the championship, we had to make do with 'Head Over Heels In Love' on *Top of the Pops* (he released his single in the summer of 1979 – it peaked at 31) and *Match of the Day* just wasn't the same without his cavalier thrust.

At least that was until he returned to lowly Southampton to scoop the

PFA Player of the Year award in 1982, having previously picked up the FWA version in his Liverpool days. He then went on to lead Newcastle United out of the wilderness before retiring in 1984.

Many felt he was left out of the England set-up too early when Bobby Robson (cf p142-4) decided to rebuild the side when he took over following the 1982 World Cup finals. As it was, Keegan made just one fleeting substitute appearance on football's grandest stage, his best years coinciding with England's wilderness period.

And that is concentration etched upon his face, just between the pair of furry headphones he seems to be wearing.

Subsequently, he re-emerged as a manager in the 1990s with a series of teams – Newcastle (twice), Fulham, England (an appointment he quit with a typically honest valedictory assessment that he was 'not up to the job') and Manchester City. He carved each in his naïve, attacking, magnificently gutsy likeness. In that time, he took Newcastle to promotion, and then their highest league position in the last 80 years (runners-up in 1996 and 1997); he also won promotion at Fulham and at Manchester City. DH

 AD NAUSEAM
From the Green Cross Code to Sugar Puffs, Keegan has always been a one-man promotional tool but will be forever associated with Brut 33 – the smell of the 1970s. The idea behind the locker room badinage between Keegan and Henry Cooper was weirdly homoerotic but it still got men to 'Splash it all over'.

 HELL RAISING 4

 **SPORTING ACHIEVEMENTS** 8

Bobby CHARLTON

BORN **11 OCTOBER 1937**

Gentleman and masterly midfielder at the heart of English football's greatest triumphs. The quiet man with a thunderous shot…

With that trademark wisp of golden hair flailing mournfully above his head, Bobby Charlton was not exactly the most obvious icon for the swinging sixties. On the contrary, the Manchester United and England maestro seemed like a relic drawn from some prehistoric age.

Yet as a decade defined by unfettered sexual impulse and hallucinogenic drugs drew to a close, Charlton was among the most beloved players in world football. While London swayed to the rhythms of the Rolling Stones and 'Fifth Beatle' George Best (cf p192-6) illuminated Old Trafford, the fads and trends of the day served only to underline Charlton's timeless appeal.

'He was as near perfection – as man and player – as it is possible to be,' said long-term manager Matt Busby (cf p124-6).

Although stories of Charlton's professionalism and modesty are legion, it was his beautifully refined touch and finesse on the ball that won him admirers from every corner of the globe. It was said that everyone in the world knew at least two words of English: 'Bobby Charlton.'

One of the few players truly comfortable using either foot, his game knew no flaws. There were raked cross-field passes and searing shots of ferocious power, allied with a tireless application and unflappable composure. Even Best, a dribbler of incomparable genius, claimed that his colleague went past players more easily than anyone he had ever seen.

A sackful of medals and honours cements Charlton's place in the sporting canon. European Footballer of the Year in 1966, ahead of Eusebio and Beckenbauer, he won three league titles, an FA Cup, and along with United team-mate Nobby Stiles, is the only Englishman to have won both the World Cup and European Cup.

If the consistency and longevity of Charlton's perfection was astonishing, his emergence as a footballer of great potential was not. Born in Ashington, Northumberland, he was nephew to the legendary Newcastle United striker Jackie Milburn, and his family was littered with professional footballers.

Bobby and older brother Jack spent every available hour either honing their skills on the nearby green or avidly watching the professionals at Newcastle's St James' Park.

At 15, Manchester United won the race to sign Charlton, despite interest from almost every top club in the land. After scoring twice on his debut against Charlton Athletic in October 1956, he quickly became integral to Busby's plans.

United were heading for their third league title in as many years when disaster befell the young team on the way back from a European Cup tie.

'There was a bag of scampi in the fridge and I had the idea – it turned out to be a little optimistic – that I could make a decent meal out of it for George and me.'

Charlton shows George Best his idea of a good time.

BEFORE HE WAS FAMOUS
To please his mother Cissie, Charlton undertook an apprenticeship as an electrical engineer until his career as a professional was assured.

THE MOMENT HE BECAME A LEGEND
Teed up by Geoff Hurst in the midst of a tight, tactical World Cup semi-final battle against Portugal, Charlton's second in a 2-1 victory eased the nerves of a nation (see picture p120).

In Munich, their plane failed a third take-off attempt and eight players lost their lives, among them some of Charlton's dearest friends. He was knocked unconscious in the crash but survived largely unscathed, and was back playing for United within a month.

It was an event that would irrevocably alter his life. With the 'paradise' of those early years cruelly snatched away, a once buoyant, bright-eyed face was replaced with a furrowed brow and receding hairline.

Luckily for United and England, the only manner in which Charlton could deal with his loss was to return to football and play in a way that evoked the best memories of the departed.

United recovered slowly, but Charlton's individual progress was startling. He marked his England debut with a goal against Scotland and played a key role in United's 1963 FA Cup final victory over Leicester City.

The trophy marked United's return to eminence. Busby built a new team around Charlton, record signing Denis Law (cf p88-9) and the mercurial George Best. The trio hit upon a thrilling synergy and United won the league twice in three years.

In 1968 they faced Benfica in the European Cup final. Charlton opened the scoring with a deft header, before netting his second with a superbly arced shot. United ran out 4-1 winners,

'Tell you what Our Bobby, that ball's got more hair than you.'

Bobby CHARLTON 23

Charlton scores the second goal against Portugal in 1966 to provide 'England Win Semi-final Shock!' headlines all over the world.

completing a remarkable journey back from the horror of Munich.

The emotion was too much for Charlton. As the celebrations began, he retreated to his hotel room. Exhausted, he collapsed onto the bed, plagued by thoughts of his former friends.

England's World Cup victory of 1966 had affirmed his status as a national hero. He scored three goals in England's successful campaign, none more vital than a typical shot of fearsome power and precision to seal England's place in the 1966 World Cup final in their tie against Eusebio's Portugal.

Many believe that, but for Alf Ramsey's (cf p104-05) hasty substitution of Charlton in the 1970

quarter-final against West Germany, England may well have successfully defended their trophy.

As it is, he still holds the club record at United for most goals scored (249) and his 49 goals for England have yet to be equalled – remarkable achievements for someone who played much of his career either on the wing or in midfield.

Charlton was knighted in 1994 and continues to work as a loyal and dedicated ambassador for Manchester United. Yet it's hard to escape the sense that he almost transcends his close affiliations with club and country. There exists a universal acceptance that he represents all of football's very best qualities.

Fellow England player Alan Ball declared that he was nothing less than 'Our Pelé'. It's testament to Charlton's profound achievements and epic career that even the exalted Brazilian would be chuffed with that. JOE GANLEY

....

⊘ **AD NAUSEAM**
Charlton recently appeared in an advert for yoghurt-drink Actimel. Seen walking his dog in the park, Charlton amazes a group of youngsters with some CGI-assisted shooting.

....

 HELL RAISING  **SPORTING ACHIEVEMENTS**

Lester PIGGOTT

BORN **5 NOVEMBER 1935**

True, he's an old tax dodger with a weird voice. But he's also the greatest jockey of his generation who captured the imagination of racing fans in spectacular fashion…

He often felt a little horse.

'The housewives' choice,' they called him, but things were different back then. These days, Daniel Craig stepping out of the sea in a pair of tight-fitting trunks would be the choice of most housewives, but in the 1960s, a jockey who could give them a run for their money in the Derby was all they craved. Ah, a simpler age.

Piggott couldn't exactly rival Craig in the looks stakes. Although pictures of him early in his career show him surprisingly fresh-faced, it has to be remembered he started riding (and winning) at the age of 12.

Tall for a Flat jockey at 5ft 8in, he was nicknamed The Long Fellow, and years of starving his body to two stones less than its natural weight made him a curmudgeon. But Lester could ride horses like ringing a bell. He was untouchable. If he was involved in a close finish, he would invariably win, because he desired victory more than anything else in life.

Some criticised him for over-use of the whip, but to Piggott he was simply utilising the tools at his disposal. If a horse needed walloping to get it over the line, Piggott figured, he'd wallop it.

Mostly the finishes weren't that close, though, because he was a master tactician. He had, as racing aficionados say, 'A stopwatch in his head.' He knew exactly how fast his nag, and all the others in the race, were going – and just how much he needed to crank up the pace to beat them.

Piggott was born to ride. His grandfather had piloted his way to three Grand National wins and his father Keith had won the Champion Hurdle. When the young Lester took to the saddle in 1948, he won his first

Lester PIGGOTT

Piggott and Nijinsky on the way to the winner's enclosure after the 2,000 Guineas in 1970. So, the tax payable on that is…

race, and in his first ride in the Derby six years later, he won that too (aboard Never Say Die).

But it wasn't until the mid-1960s that his career went into the stratosphere. It was then that he began his partnership with genius Irish trainer Vincent O'Brien, who was to provide Piggott with four Derby winners – two of whom, Nijinsky and The Minstrel – go down as among the finest racehorses who ever entered the paddock.

O'Brien and Piggott were an odd pairing. Racing writer Brough Scott summed them up: 'They were one of the most exciting, if least communicative, partnerships in racing history… The fact that in public Lester said virtually nothing and Vincent very little, only added to their attraction.' Luckily, the horses did the talking for them.

Piggott was the best, and the best by a long way – and he knew it. His disdain for most of those around him led to plenty of suspensions from racing. On one occasion, having dropped his whip, he simply snatched one from a rival's hand. On another occasion he felt a horse was too close and so shoved it away with his hand. And, consequently, the winners kept coming: in all, 30 classics.

He also became rich. And that's when the taxman took an unhealthy interest in his affairs, quickly establishing that Piggott showed little regard for financial regulations.

'The best thing you can do is put a bit of lead in his right ear, to act as a counterbalance… with a shotgun.'

When asked what the best course of action was for a horse that kept drifting left.

In 1987, he was jailed for three years for tax evasion on more than £3 million of earnings dating back 15 years. He served a year ('I decided to keep my head down, keep my nose clean'), and although by then he had retired from riding to train, when he emerged from prison he found that the owners had taken their horses elsewhere.

Piggott eventually decided to revert to what he knew best: riding. Within ten days of his comeback in 1990, O'Brien put him aboard the promising Royal Academy in the prestigious Breeders' Cup Mile, held at Belmont Park, New York. Piggott, by then 54, gave him a stirring ride to victory.

It was an extraordinary swansong for the old team.

Incredibly, Piggott still had one classic left in him and guided Rodrigo de Triano home in the 1992 2,000 Guineas, before eventually, once and for all, hanging up his riding boots in 1994. He had ridden 4,493 winners and been champion jockey 11 times – a figure which would have been much higher had he not been so selective about his rides in later years.

He still lives in Newmarket and still doesn't say much. SC

 AD NAUSEAM
Along with the Duchess of York, Piggott was one of the faces of Bai Lin Tea, launched in this country by Peter Foster, who last made the newspapers as an adviser to Cherie Blair.

 HELL RAISING 4

 **SPORTING ACHIEVEMENTS** 9

 BEFORE HE WAS FAMOUS
He was born. Then he started to ride horses. Piggott rode his first winner, in his first race, at the age of 12. These days we call it child labour.

THE MOMENT HE BECAME A LEGEND
Winning the Triple Crown of 2,000 Guineas, Derby and St Leger in 1970 aboard Nijinsky (the last horse or jockey to do so).

Matt BUSBY

BORN **26 MAY 1909** ■ DIED **20 JANUARY 1994**

Visionary Manchester United manager whose pioneering spirit and awesome powers of inspiration twice rescued his club from the brink of destruction...

'That's the end,' thought Bill Shankly (cf p177-81), as he surveyed a ravaged Old Trafford in the days after the Blitz. 'There'll never be another football team here again.'

When Shankly's old pal Matt Busby arrived as the new Manchester United manager in 1945, the landscape was no less austere. Stands had been shelled, turf violently uprooted, and a lunar-sized crater lay smack in the centre of the field. His team was forced to play at Maine Road, the home of Manchester City and could not return to Old Trafford until 1949.

What followed was not mere restoration, but a revolution that shifted the very contours of British football. Despite the cruel destruction of a team and eight key players in the 1958 Munich air disaster, Busby led United to five league titles, two FA Cups and a landmark European Cup victory, in almost 25 years at the helm.

Busby's ideas were infectious and his philosophies brave. He fearlessly threw young players into the white-hot heat of top-flight competition and insisted on fast, positive football chock full of vibrancy and pizzazz.

Although his avuncular charm was famed for its ability to convince mothers that their sons should sign for United, Busby was no pushover. Star striker Denis Law (cf p88-9) was slapped on the transfer list after asking for an extra tenner a week, while stalwart defender Bill Foulkes

> 'The greatest thing for a manager is to trust the talent.'
>
> Matt Busby explains his boundless faith in youth and skill.

was blasted a 'tramp' in front of his team-mates. Beneath the priestly veneer was a ruthless man, as any who crossed him found out.

When the Football League instructed United to reject an invitation to take part in the European Cup in 1956, Busby ploughed on regardless. If his ideas were new and exciting, the Scotsman's conviction was as ancient and sure-footed as the Highlands. He had seen how Hungary destroyed England at Wembley in 1953 and knew that continental football would help his team improve.

Born in the tough mining village of Orbiston, Lanarkshire, Busby grew up 'football daft'. After his father was killed during the Great War and his mother remarried, he almost set sail for the States with his family. Fortunately, Manchester City soon offered the professional contract he craved.

Busby enjoyed a successful career at City, where he played in the victorious 1934 FA Cup final, and then Liverpool, where he captained with distinction until the onset of the Second World War curtailed his career. He made just one appearance for Scotland.

He agreed to take on the managerial position at United only when his demands to have complete control of all playing matters and selection were accepted by the board. Busby then enlisted the services of coach Jimmy Murphy, a jowly Welshman and his most important signing. Within three years, United had won the FA Cup – it was the club's first major trophy in 37 years.

The first 'tracksuit' manager, Busby introduced simple innovations

BEFORE HE WAS FAMOUS
As his family prepared to emigrate, Busby went to work in the coal mines while he looked for a professional club.

THE MOMENT HE BECAME A LEGEND
After United's 4-1 victory over Benfica in the 1968 European Cup final, a tearful Busby was mobbed by his adoring players. Ten years on from Munich, United's redemption was complete.

talkSPORT LEGENDS

And in the advanced class Busby is seen teaching his players how to kick a ball.

like using three balls in the warm-up, so players with differing roles could prepare properly for the match. Forwards were converted to defenders and vice versa, as Busby and Murphy's fierce football logic (and tight budgets) began to shape the club at senior and youth levels.

Behind the scenes, his scouts were swarming all over Britain and Ireland, hoovering up every last speck of young talent they could find. In 1956, the team that the press had christened the 'Busby Babes' won the league by an enormous margin of 11 points. The

side had an average age of just 22, but there was more. Such were the club's riches that when an England side turned up for a practice match, they were tanked 6-1 by United's reserves.

But when tragedy struck at Munich in Feburary 1958, as United flew home from their European Cup quarter-final tie against Red Star Belgrade, Busby's career looked doomed. He barely survived the crash, and with his Catholic faith shaken, he contemplated quitting football.

Memories of the players lost, heroes such as Duncan Edwards (cf p145-7)

and Tommy Taylor, would haunt Busby until his dying day. But for a second time, he found the energy to haul the club back from the abyss.

It took five years, but when United secured the FA Cup in 1963, a new golden era loomed. With freewheeling genius George Best (cf p192-6) alongside loyal prodigy Bobby Charlton (cf p118-20) and the predatory Law, United were twice champions and in 1968 became the first English team to win the European Cup.

Best, Charlton and Law were wonderful players – each one was

Matt BUSBY

21

With the manager's back turned, all the players bunked off.

crowned European Footballer of the Year during the 1960s. Yet it was the Busby aura that fuelled United. Players occasionally questioned his decisions, but they could not evade the reach of his mystical inspiration.

Wearied by his struggles, Busby eventually stepped down in 1969, although Alex Ferguson (cf p110-11) fondly recalled his pipe smoke wafting around Old Trafford. However, he cast such a huge shadow over the club that few managers could live up to the expectations he had created.

A cuddly paternal image has endured, but Busby was a great progressive and phenomenally resilient. The romantic Manchester United he envisaged has become legend, but his heroic retrieval of the club from the ashes of war-torn Manchester and the slush and ice of Munich marks Busby as British football's most remarkable manager.

JOE GANLEY

 AD NAUSEAM

When Busby stepped down as manager, he bartered for a cut-price deal on the club's souvenir shop. Paying only a modest lease on the place, Busby achieved a regular profit.

HELL 2 **RAISING**

SPORTING 10 **ACHIEVEMENTS**

talkSPORT LEGENDS

20

Alex HIGGINS

BORN **18 MARCH 1949** ■ DIED **24 JULY 2010**

Volatile Ulsterman with a massive talent for potting, getting potted and landing himself in trouble.

You should have seen the other fella. Not a mark on him.

Alex Higgins' turbulent life ended where it began – in Belfast. He was born in Sandy Row in 1949. A diminutive figure and a loner, he was always picked last for football matches. He acquired the nickname 'Shitty' and, as a kid, where do you go from there?

In this instance, it was the snooker club – a dubious establishment called The Jampot, a natural home for the feckless and local hard-cases. Young Alex was small enough to sneak through the front door and go about his business unnoticed. That business was snooker, scoring for the adults until he had enough tips for his own table time.

'Have I enjoyed [my life]? I haven't really had much to do with my life. All I've done is take part in it.'

Higgins provides his own epitaph.

'Sandy' – as he was more affectionately known to his family – was soon a fixture at the club. In his last year at school, he turned up on just 36 occasions. Not that Mrs Higgins minded, reasoning he was 'Better in [The Jampot] than in mischief'. The two were not necessarily mutually exclusive.

Higgins had two heroes: Muhammad Ali and Lester Piggott (cf p121-3). Although not averse to

Alex HIGGINS

a scrap, boxing was not for him, so aged 15 he travelled to Berkshire to train as a jockey in the 'high octane' world of Flat racing, but he never made it.

Higgins returned to Belfast and improved his game until he was making money taking on all-comers. Word began to spread that a special player was in their midst. This was confirmed in January 1968 when Higgins entered the Northern Ireland Amateur Championships and won it comfortably.

Buoyed by this success, he decided his future lay in England and moved to Blackburn – Lancashire being a hotbed of snooker at the time. Squatting in a row of condemned houses, he would return each night to find his 'home' demolished and be forced to move down one. Legend has it he had five addresses in one week.

He thrived at the table and in 1972 beat John Spencer 37 frames to 32 to claim the World Snooker Championship at his first attempt. Alex was now 'The Hurricane' (on account of his speed around the table rather than his activities off it) and would go on to create as much damage as a tropical cyclone to hotel receptions, clubs, snooker halls and himself.

When colour TV propelled snooker into the big time, Higgins became a household name – antagonising the purists by playing to the gallery and charming the public with his maverick style. Despite getting himself temporarily banned from the flagship *Pot Black* show (he considered it a 'second-rate affair'), the Hurricane was hot property.

Daughter Lauren: 'Please Mummy, I want to get down now.'

Higgins embraced a hedonistic whirl of groupies, gambling, drink and drugs – his friends included The Who drummer Keith Moon and the bibulous actor Oliver Reed. Throwing fame and fortune into the mix was like pouring petrol onto a barbecue.

This was sport at its most rock 'n' roll. Higgins was snooker's Elvis Presley. Or possibly even Sid Vicious. He defined and transcended the genre, making himself and the game all the more appealing to the general public.

At his best he was unstoppable, dancing round the table with manic grace but, unfortunately, his best was seen only in spells and he lacked the grinding consistency of Ray Reardon or, later, Steve Davis (cf p49-50). In 1973, he lost his world title to Reardon and spent the next nine years trying to get it back. While others practised, he lived.

Within the game, he clashed, often physically, with other players and referees, and was fined and banned countless times. But, determined to re-assert himself, he reclaimed the World Championship in 1982.

After a stunning comeback against Jimmy White (cf p21) in the semi-finals, which included the famous 69 break (a string of suicidal but brilliant pots), Higgins faced arch-rival Reardon for the world title at the Crucible in Sheffield.

An unbearably tense final was finely poised at 15-15 when Higgins took the final three frames, the last with a stunning break of 135. In floods of tears, Higgins accepted the £25,000 winner's cheque and the trophy, and beckoned his long-suffering wife Lynn forward with their child Lauren,

hugging them for the cameras in what remains the abiding image of his life.

If this was a Hollywood ending, then he would have banished his demons and lived happily ever after. In reality, as wife Lynn pointed out backstage that very evening: 'Here we go. This is where my problems really begin.' Understatement.

They split in 1983, and his one-man riots became more frequent. The police arrested him in his house for throwing a TV through the window, and he was banned from five tournaments after head-butting an official who had the temerity to ask for a urine sample. He also slept with Marianne Faithful, was stabbed by a prostitute and attempted suicide. Deeply troubled and out of control, Higgins' game and life inevitably went into steady decline.

Aged 40, he defeated Stephen Hendry (cf p 44) in the Irish Masters. It was to be the last hurrah and in 1997 he was diagnosed with throat cancer, fought it and beat it but the disease proved to be a very durable opponent. Like a wounded wild animal, he went home to die and his life ended just as it had started – hustling in Belfast, drinking and smoking.

His legacy, however, lives on in the enduring popularity of the game he almost single-handedly helped popularise and the careers of Jimmy White and Ronnie O'Sullivan (cf p100-01). Thousands lined the streets to pay their last respects and he is buried at Carnmoney cemetery, on the outskirts of North Belfast. GS

 AD NAUSEAM
Not really what you would call corporate gold, he did pose with Status Quo in a publicity shot for the pre-meditated murder of rock standard 'The Wanderer'.

 **HELL RAISING** 10 — **SPORTING ACHIEVEMENTS** 7

BEFORE HE WAS FAMOUS
Apart from his attempt to become a jockey, Higgins worked in a paper mill near London Bridge during his first stay in England.

 THE MOMENT HE BECAME A LEGEND
When he tearfully mouthed 'Bring me my baby' to his wife having just landed his second World Championship.

Stanley MATTHEWS

BORN **1 FEBRUARY 1915** ■ DIED **23 FEBRUARY 2000**

Baggy shorts, brisk morning walks and not a single booking in a 30-year playing career — it's a Corinthian thing.

Dig out a bog-standard, old-fashioned encyclopedia and he'll be in it, a few entries after Henri Matisse and a handful before Somerset Maugham. It usually reads something like this:

for his age after an international friendly against England at Wembley a year later, he replied: 'It doesn't matter. How old was Stanley Matthews when he retired?'

have much to show for it – an FA Cup winner's medal, two Second Division championships and 71 goals in 697 league matches for Stoke and Blackpool – but he stood for all that was great about the British game.

He was never, ever booked. As an outside-right, he was more a provider than a finisher and his dribbling skills were legendary. 'On his day he was unplayable,' recalled England team-mate Joe Mercer. 'He beat fellows so

'If my father had pushed me harder, I think I would have gone in for cricket or tennis. I played everything with a ball, but it was finding the time.'

Matthews gives cricket and tennis fans something to think about.

'Matthews, Sir Stanley (1915-2000). British Association footballer, who played for Stoke City (1931-47; 1961-65), Blackpool (1947-61) and England, for whom he played 54 times. A skilful winger, he played 886 first-class matches, his last at the age of 50.'

So what if Matisse could invent fauvism with boldly patterned and vibrantly coloured still lifes and nudes? We'd like to have seen the Frenchman make the ball disappear up the leg of one billowing short and reappear down the other three seconds later. Sir Stan could. Probably.

Matthews was English football's first international superstar, remembered with as much affection in the townships of South Africa as the suburbs of Stoke-on-Trent.

When Roger Milla, Cameroon's corner-flag dancing goal machine at the 1990 World Cup finals, was asked

To this day Africa retains a soft spot for the 'Wizard of Dribble' – following his retirement in 1965 he became a footballing missionary on the continent and was most recently celebrated by a generation of older black South Africans during the 2010 World Cup for his pioneering work with poor and underprivileged young footballers in Soweto.

Matthews made his league debut way back in 1932 and was still playing in the First Division in 1965. He didn't

easily, with such pace and balance, often taking on four or five at a time.'

For England, he made his debut in 1934, played (and scored from the edge of the penalty area) in the notorious 1938 game against Germany when the players had to give the Nazi salute, appeared in the 1950 and 1954 World Cups, and was still in the side in 1957.

His finest hour was undoubtedly the 1953 FA Cup final, when he inspired Blackpool, 3-1 down with 20 minutes left, to a 4-3 win over Bolton Wanderers,

BEFORE HE WAS FAMOUS
Joined Stoke City on his fifteenth birthday as an office boy, meeting his future wife Betty on his first day there.

THE MOMENT HE BECAME A LEGEND
Easy. Has Wembley ever witnessed a finer individual performance than his for Blackpool in the 1953 FA Cup final?

'Has anybody lost a small leather case? Contents include a small medal of some description.'

Stanley MATTHEWS ====== 19

A St John ambulanceman looks on as he prepares to apply a cold compress to yet another defender with a major headache.

but typically gave the credit to hat-trick hero Stan Mortensen.

Malcolm Barrass, who was part of the Bolton defence that day, takes up the story: 'Stanley had been on the losing Blackpool side in his previous two finals [1948 and 1951] and the whole country wanted to see if he could win it this time.

'You never think a match is won until it's over, especially an FA Cup final, but I must admit that when we were 3-1 up I thought we were close to it. But there you are. Blackpool came back with three goals and Stanley crossed for two of them.

'At one point in the game, I went to tackle [him] as he was going down the wing. He just swept away and centred the ball. The incident was caught on camera. I wouldn't have minded so much, but I went out shopping a little later and there was the picture. Stanley had a contract with a boot manufacturer and they were using the shot to advertise in my local Co-op!'

A dozen years later, around 35,000 attended Stan's testimonial match at the old Victoria Ground, when his British XI lost 6-4 to a European XI that included, among others, Lev Yashin, Ferenc Puskas and Alfredo Di Stefano. Matthews was carried shoulder-high off the pitch at the final whistle.

Having retired, he had a brief spell in charge at Port Vale, where he showed a Busbyesque faith in youth, fielding a forward line in one game where the oldest player was just 18.

He died in February 2000, three weeks after his 85th birthday, and his funeral was attended by the likes of Nat Lofthouse, Tom Finney and the Charlton brothers. Over 100,000 people lined the streets of Stoke to pay tribute.

Voted Footballer of the Year in 1948 and 1963, he remains the only man to be knighted for his services as a player (as opposed to a manager). The West Stand at Blackpool's Bloomfield Road is named in his honour, and he has statues outside Stoke City's Britannia Stadium and in the centre of Hanley, his home town.

The dedication on the former reads: 'His name is symbolic of the beauty of the game, his fame timeless and international, his sportsmanship and modesty universally acclaimed. A magical player, of the people, for the people.'

The last word goes to another admirer, Pelé: 'Stanley Matthews was the man who taught us the way football should be played.' It doesn't really get any better than that. DC

 AD NAUSEAM

The original poster boy endorsed 'Lighter, more flexible, speed-making soccer boots' in *Charles Buchan's Football Monthly*. 'You can bend them double!' was the slogan.

 HELL RAISING   SPORTING ACHIEVEMENTS

Nick FALDO

BORN **18 JULY 1957**

Born into a two-bed council house, the putative ballet dancer went on to become the greatest British golfer of the modern era: a man who collected almost as many wives as Majors…

Two golfers dominated the late 1980s and early 1990s. Of Greg Norman, it was said he won two Majors and many friends. Of Nick Faldo, it was said he won six Majors and many *admirers*.

Faldo was a conundrum – a great British sporting hero, at a time when there were not many of those, yet someone who utterly failed to make the public like him. He won three British Opens and three US Masters – no post-war British golfer has come close to that sort of achievement, yet he registered almost zero on the public affection scale, though he was voted BBC Sports Personality of the Year in 1989.

At least some of the home crowd at Muirfield in 1992 wanted Faldo to win.

Nick FALDO

Nicholas Alexander Faldo – his parents gave him a posh name in the hope he'd live up to it – was a gauche, clumsy, awkward sort of chap when he started out. He wanted the public to like him, but kept saying the wrong thing at the wrong time. And, on the golf course, he was so obsessed with winning that his relations with his fellow players were often strained.

'I'd like to thank the press from the heart of my bottom.'

Faldo famously thanked his 'close friends' the media in his 1992 Open victory speech.

His crowning glory came in 1996, by which time he was already assured of immortality with five Majors to his name. Going into the final round of that year's Masters, he trailed Norman by six shots, and few gave him a hope of winning.

But The Great White was as flaky as he was brilliant. His talent deserved many more wins than he actually achieved. And when he woke up on that fateful Sunday morning, the one person he didn't want staring at him in his rear view mirror was Faldo.

Unblinking. Focused. Driven. Ruthless. Relentless. Faldo.

By the end of the day, even British fans were wincing. Faldo had started brightly, and when Norman faltered, the Englishman caught the merest hint of cordite in his nostrils.

'The guy who coughed on your putt is over there Mr Faldo, the one in the pink pastel slacks.'

It was all he needed. Hole by hole he squeezed the life out of Norman, systematically, brutally, until his opponent was dead and buried. Faldo shot 67, Norman shot 78: an 11-shot swing when seven would have done. It was, effectively, the end of Norman's career.

At the end of the day, they embraced. 'Don't let the bastards get you down,' Faldo told his adversary, knowing the press would slaughter Norman for his collapse. From that moment the two men, never previously more than acquaintances, became firm friends.

Faldo came to golf relatively late. He was a talented cyclist of 13 when he watched Jack Nicklaus win the 1971 US Masters on TV in his Welwyn Garden City home, and from that moment decided he wanted to be a golfer.

But, unlike today, when talented youngsters are snapped up by US colleges, Faldo was snapped up by a local carpet firm on leaving school. The trainee carpet fitter still found time, however, to become one of the brightest amateur talents of the era – he won the English Amateur and British Youth Championships in 1974 and 1975 respectively, and turned

pro a year later. By 1977 he became the youngest-ever Ryder Cup player, having just turned 20.

Success on the European Tour came easily to Faldo, but he craved more: having been inspired by Nicklaus, he wanted to be him. And to be Jack, Faldo had to win big. He came close at the 1983 Open and the Masters the following year, but his methodical swing let him down when it mattered most. The press dubbed him Nick Foldo.

The criticism stung Faldo to the core. For someone allegedly so aloof, he was only too aware of the shortcomings of his game, and employed coach David Leadbetter to dismantle his swing from start to finish, and build a new one. It was an astonishing move. One of the brightest talents of his generation, not yet 30, had gone back to the drawing board. If this didn't work, he was finished.

At first, he struggled to master his new swing, but slowly it came together. And by 1987 he was ready. Finally he won his first Major, that year's Open, famously parring every hole in the final round. He won the Masters two years later, and in 1990 won both tournaments. He bagged his third Open in 1992 (see picture p133) before his final, crushing win in 1996.

Squeezed in the middle were runner's-up spots in both the US Open and US PGA too.

In the space of nine years, Faldo was king. Seve and Norman may have had more talent, but Faldo knew how to extract every last ounce from his game. He won just one fewer Major than those two put together.

In the Ryder Cup too, Faldo was a machine. The one-on-one format of matchplay suited him and he compiled one of the best records of all time. Sadly, he couldn't replicate that as captain in 2008, leading his team to humiliating defeat in the US (having selected, among others, DJ Spoony to be on his backroom team).

Off the course, Faldo proved to be human. He married Melanie at 21, but an affair with Gill led to divorce. He married Gill, but an affair with Brenna led to divorce. When he left Brenna, she smashed up his Porsche with a golf club. He then married Valerie, but the pair eventually divorced. Meanwhile, he spent 14 years with Fanny – but she was his caddy rather than a romantic interest and they parted in 2005.

Faldo is now a respected commentator on CBS and barely plays. He was knighted in 2009. SC

BEFORE HE WAS FAMOUS
Long-limbed, his parents hoped he would be a ballet dancer or a concert pianist. In the end, he took up golf aged 13, having watched Jack Nicklaus win the 1971 Masters.

THE MOMENT HE BECAME A LEGEND
The 1996 US Masters when he destroyed Greg Norman. It was his final Major but the one that endures.

 AD NAUSEAM
Did anyone ever do more for diamond-patterned sweaters? Faldo was the face of Pringle for most of his professional career.

 HELL
6 RAISING

 **SPORTING**
9 ACHIEVEMENTS

Geoffrey BOYCOTT

BORN **21 OCTOBER 1940**

The 'Yarksher' batsman who survived a near-death encounter with a mangle and established himself as one of England's most successful openers...

Boycott is the cartoon-style benchmark for the archetypal bloody-minded, stubborn and determined Yorkshireman.

Though adored by the Headingley crowd, many fellow players felt less warmly about him. Ian Botham (cf p173-6), for example, claimed he was 'totally, almost insanely, selfish' and jubilantly sang 'Bye-bye Boycott' from the England balcony on hearing that Boycott had been dropped from the national team.

Blunt as a sledgehammer, it isn't difficult to see why Boycott was unpopular among some of his contemporaries. He had the capacity for rubbing people up the wrong way: who else could get dropped from the England side after scoring 246 not out?

Boycott was born in the mining village of Fitzwilliam, West Yorkshire, in 1940. When he was eight years old, he fell off a fence and landed on an upturned mangle, impaling himself on the handle. His ruptured spleen had to be removed as doctors fought to save his life.

Two years later, in 1950, another accident befell the Boycott family when Geoffrey's father, Tom, was hit by a coal truck in the Hemsworth pit. He suffered severe spinal injuries from which he never fully recovered.

Times were hard for the family, and you can hear Boycott's insistent Yorkshire accent as he explains: 'There was none of this compensation rubbish or disability pay back then. They used to promise my mum a few dozen eggs and it was all nice words but there was no compensation – the bloody union was useless.'

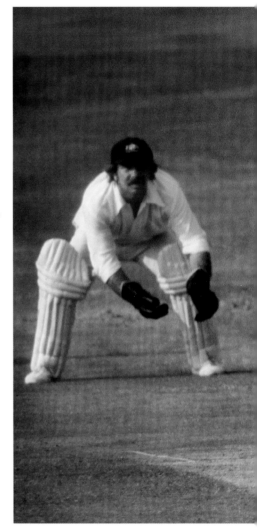

'Given the choice between Racquel Welch and a hundred at Lord's, I'd take the hundred every time.'

Boycott was never really offered the choice.

Then, after Boycott finished his 'O' levels, he no longer wanted to be a financial strain on his parents and took a job at the Ministry of Pensions & National Insurance in Barnsley.

Outside working hours, he was making a name for himself as an accomplished batsman for Barnsley in the Yorkshire League as well as a talented footballer. In the evenings, he would retire, exhausted, to the local picture house to watch his hero, John Wayne.

Unfortunately, the need to work forced him to choose between the two sports. He chose 'cree-kit', and worked Saturdays in the winter in order to build up enough time off to play in the summer.

He built his batting technique around a no-risk, highly defensive strategy – and was rewarded in June

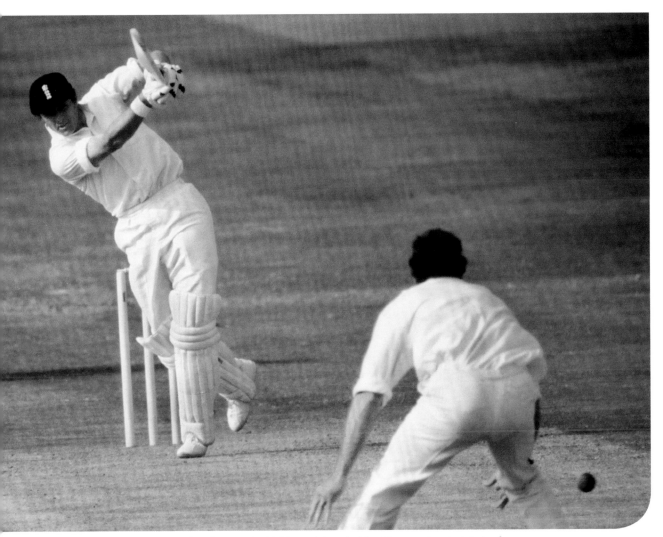

Boycott breaks the record for the number of consecutive birthdays celebrated while at the crease in a single innings[*].

1962 when he made his Yorkshire first team debut against the Pakistanis. So began a 24-year career at Yorkshire that would see Boycs play in 414 matches, reaping 32,570 runs at an average of 57.85, scoring 103 centuries and occupying the crease in the most stubborn manner imaginable.

In 1967, when his dad died of a heart attack, Boycott was in the middle of a match at The Oval: 'It was a Sunday morning in August. They asked me to stay and bat, then go home for the funeral… It was strength of character. I made seventy-odd.'

He captained Yorkshire between 1971 and 1978, but despite his own excellent batting stats, it was an unsuccessful and fractious time. Previously dominant, Yorkshire won

[*] Here he is completing his hundredth century, at Headingley in August 1977.

Geoffrey BOYCOTT

nothing under Boycott's captaincy and in 1973 they didn't win a single county championship game.

In September 1978, a few days after his mother had died of cancer, the committee relieved Boycott of his captaincy. He went on *Parkinson* and let them have both barrels: 'They are small-minded people who think they're always right… At least they could have postponed the meeting and allowed my mother to be buried in peace.'

His England career was scarcely less controversial. He clashed with team-mates over slow scoring rates and a perceived selfish attitude. Nevertheless, Boycott amassed 8,114 runs in 108 matches between 1964 and 1982 and, as opening batsman, laid the foundations for many victories with 22 centuries (no England batsman has scored more).

After his playing career ended, Boycott put his trenchant opinions to good use as a commentator, spitting out memorable lines such as 'I reckon even my mum could have caught that in her pinny'.

He has remained in the public eye since – although not always for the right reasons. In 1996, he was accused of assaulting a former lover at a swanky hotel in the South of France. Boycott strongly denied the claims, pleaded not guilty and lined up 13 witnesses in his defence. Despite this he was convicted, and perhaps understandably, was incandescent at what he saw as a 'farce'. Then, in 2002, he was diagnosed with – but successfully treated for – throat cancer.

Boycott continues to make a good living as a well-regarded commentator and it seems, just like John Wayne, Boycott will be the last man standing. GS

'A spade is NOT a garden implement with a flat iron blade adapted for pressing into the ground and an elongated handle… it is a spade.'

BEFORE HE WAS FAMOUS
Worked as a civil servant and also turned out for Leeds United Under-18s in the same side as Billy Bremner.

THE MOMENT HE BECAME A LEGEND
August 1977 when he scored 191 against Australia at a packed Headingley, claiming his 100th first-class century.

AD NAUSEAM
Made several appearances in the 'Roy of the Rovers' comic strip as chairman of Melchester Rovers.

 HELL RAISING 7

 **SPORTING ACHIEVEMENTS** 7

Roger BANNISTER

16

BORN **23 MARCH 1929**

Lung-busting, fast-legged medical student who made sporting history with one of the most famous runs in world history.

In 1954, everyone agreed it was impossible for a man to run a sub-four-minute mile. It wasn't just sensationalist newspapers pushing the fact, but also the assured voice of BBC radio.

Biological boffins, athletics experts and the runners themselves were all apparently of one mind, along with the massed crowds who at that time would pack 50,000-strong into athletics stadia: it just wasn't humanly possible.

But that wasn't enough to stop Roger Bannister trying.

For nine long years, the mile record had been stuck at 4 minutes, 1.4 seconds – the holder being the seemingly unbeatable Swede Gunder Hägg, whose tit-for-tat record-

'What do you mean your watch stopped?'

Roger BANNISTER

breaking duels with countryman Arne Andersson had robbed England's own Sydney Wooderson of his proud mile record set before the war.

But, as a 16-year-old schoolboy, Bannister had been fired with inspiration and ambition when Wooderson, 'The Mighty Atom', had come back in 1945 to run the Swedes close and set a new British record of 4:04.2.

Although born in Harrow and having attended London's University College School and Oxford University, Bannister's parents were from poor cotton-working Lancashire families. He enjoyed no privilege beyond intelligence and good health.

An athlete in the true Olympian tradition, Bannister was only ever a part-time runner. His training was arranged around his schoolwork and then the time permitted by his medical degree and gruelling rounds as a junior doctor.

Nevertheless, from the first time his name became known – after he ran the mile under 4:08 before the 1952 Olympics – Bannister received lukewarm press on account of his perceived aloofness.

At the Helsinki games, his lack of preparation time was exposed and he

A capacity crowd turned up for 'The Miracle Mile' at the 1954 Commonwealth Games just to see if Bannister actually was that pale.

was happily written off as yet another British failure. But the considerations of newspapermen never concerned the great individualist and idealist, who was quietly piecing together a holistic mental, cardiovascular and technical methodology in his training.

Bannister was perceived as 'The Thinking Man's Runner', combining the long stride born of his 35-inch inside leg with a phenomenal finishing kick. To that he added a future research neurologist's growing insights into the principles of cardiovascular exertion. This helped him combat fatigue and muscle failure.

As he subsequently explained, 'It's a question of spreading the available energy, aerobic and anaerobic, evenly over four minutes. If you run one part too fast, you pay a price. If you run

'I came from such a simple origin, without any great privilege, and I would say I also wanted to make a mark. It wasn't until I was about fifteen that I appeared in a race.'

Bannister takes stock of his achievements.

talkSPORT
LEGENDS

another part more slowly your overall time is slower.'

Incredibly, Bannister's part-time training increased his capacity for absorbing oxygen to nearly five litres per minute. At his peak, that was almost 50 per cent above normal.

In 1953 Bannister twice broke Wooderson's 1945 British record, running 4:02 using pacemakers, but elsewhere Australian John Landy and US Army man Wes Santee were also closing in on the magic four minutes, with miles completed in 4:02 and 4:02.4 respectively.

It was on 6 May 1954 at the traditional Oxford University versus the Amateur Athletic Association match at the Iffley Road track that Bannister chose to go for the record before a small 3,000 crowd. None of his old adversaries in the press was informed except the head of BBC Sport, who duly dispatched a camera crew.

It wasn't just spite on Bannister's part. For all his mastery of technique, he suffered a profound psychological block as he prepared to attempt the impossible, adding to his usual intense pre-race anxiety. 'When he goes out to run,' one of his colleagues commented, 'he looks like a man going to the electric chair.'

But logic, training and determination were to play their part in overriding the myth cooked up by sports journalists. 'Common sense and physiology,' Bannister later insisted, '[suggested] there was no physical reason why it could not be done.'

One potentially insurmountable problem that day was the weather. A wind was blowing that Bannister calculated could cost him a second per lap and ruin his run. But then the 25mph gusts suddenly dropped and his two key pacemakers, 'The two Chrises' – Chataway and Brasher – were briefed and confident… and they were off.

His three first quarter-mile times set the record within grasp. All he needed now was the greatest final lap in history. 'It was only then,' Bannister later said, 'that real pain overtook me. I felt like an exploded flashlight with no will to live. I just went on existing in the most passive physical state without being unconscious.'

At the track, the result was announced on the PA by former sprinter Norris McWhirter, soon to be author of the *Guinness Book of Records*. Drawing out the tension, he finally divulged the setting of a 'New English native, British national and British all-comers', European, British Empire and World record. The time is three…'

The crowd cheered before he could read out the exact time: 3 minutes 59.4 seconds.

The record was destined to be pipped the following month by Landy and the dramatic climax of the Bannister story came at the 1954 Commonwealth Games in Vancouver, where he re-established his superiority by taking the gold in 3:58.8, with Landy 0.8 seconds behind in 3:59.6. The press dubbed it 'The Miracle Mile' (see picture left).

With the pressures growing on athletes to train full-time, Bannister's achievements represented perhaps the final act of the true Olympian era.

Even before 'The Miracle Mile', Bannister had passed his final exams to qualify as a doctor – and at the end of 1954 he announced that he was quitting top-level running to become a neurologist. Eventually he would become co-author of the medical bible, *Brain and Bannister's Clinical Neurology*.

Cast-iron logic dictates that he considers his work in the field of medicine to be his 'Greatest achievement', but he knows how he will always be remembered.

He was 'The Man Who Broke The Four Minute Mile'. DH

 AD NAUSEAM
Strict amateur rules kept Bannister from receiving any prizes, endorsement or appearance fees.

 HELL RAISING    SPORTING ACHIEVEMENTS

BEFORE HE WAS FAMOUS
Bannister was a diligent medical student at Oxford University who would go on to specialise in neurology.

 THE MOMENT HE BECAME A LEGEND
Head tipped back, his face contorted with pain and gasping for breath as he powered over the line in 1954.

Bobby ROBSON

BORN **18 FEBRUARY 1933** ▪ DIED **31 JULY 2009**

From Suffolk and Tyneside to Holland, Portugal and Catalonia, the feeling for the former England boss is the same – much love.

November 1957. Bobby Robson could hardly believe it. Here he was, a promising inside-forward for West Bromwich Albion, emerging from the tunnel at Wembley flanked by the Manchester United trio of Tommy Taylor, Duncan Edwards (cf p145-7) and Roger Byrne.

'I was the proudest man in Britain,' he recalled. 'I'd been picked for England against France, my first cap. I wasn't to know then that my first international was to be the last for that great United trio [and] that three months later in the snow of Munich, fate would deprive England of their skills, their lives. But I shall never forget my training sessions with them before that game.'

England won 4-0 that day, with 24-year-old Robson twice getting on the scoresheet and going on to win another 19 caps and appear in the 1958 World Cup finals, missing out in 1962 through injury. He would, however, never win anything as a player.

Like many a great footballer from the North East, his progress was anything but straightforward. Born in the coal-mining village of Sacriston, County Durham, in 1933, he was spotted playing village football by Fulham, rather than his beloved Newcastle United.

The Cottagers offered him a trial and signed him in 1950 – on the same day, another youngster called Johnny

Haynes joined the club. Six years later, having scored 23 goals in his final season for Fulham, Robson was sold to West Brom for £25,000, a club record transfer fee at the time. He soon became Albion's skipper.

The maximum wage was lifted in 1961 and Haynes, his old pal at Craven Cottage, became the first £100 a week footballer. While in the middle of a dispute with Albion over his own pay increase, he was bought back by Fulham after the 1962 World Cup in Chile.

He stayed there for another five years before he was released and went to Vancouver to help pioneer the North American Soccer League. Eight months later, he was back in South-west London as Fulham manager. Eight months after that, he was fired.

'Here was the club that had introduced me to professional football as a teenager. They had moulded me, sold me and then bought me back. I felt I was part of the furniture, as

much a fixture there as the Cottage itself. After I stepped out of the board meeting, I went and stood on the centre-spot at Craven Cottage. The place was deserted except for a groundsman repairing a few divots. I just stood there and wept.'

After a short spell scouting for Chelsea boss Dave Sexton, he was appointed Ipswich Town boss in January 1969 in a move that was to change the course of history for both manager and club – and eventually the England national team.

It was at Portman Road that he learned his managerial craft, working miracles on a meagre budget and finessing his thrift and judgement in the transfer market. In a taste of things to come, he looked abroad for inspiration. 'I sold Brian Talbot to Arsenal for £450,000 and bought two better players, Arnold Muhren and Frans Thijssen, and put £100,000 change in the bank.'

Between 1973 and 1982 Ipswich finished in the top six on nine occasions. They won the FA Cup against Arsenal in 1978 and the UEFA Cup in 1981 after an aggregate win over Dutch team AZ67 Alkmaar. He must have been doing something right.

> 'Most managers want to do the job well, but the ones who succeed are the ones who don't despair. Only the strong survive.'

Robson in typical stirring and passionate mode.

talkSPORT
LEGENDS

In 1982 he was appointed England manager. Over the next eight years he would twice tender his resignation – after failing to qualify for the 1984 European Championships and in the aftermath of England's dismal showing at Euro 88 – but no other manager has come closer to emulating the World Cup triumph of 1966.

His England team reached the quarter-finals in 1986, losing to Diego Maradona's 'Hand of God', and went one better in 1990, with only penalties separating the side from eventual champions West Germany.

Following Italia 90, Bobby joined PSV Eindhoven and steered them to two successive Dutch titles. After a short spell with Sporting Lisbon – where he employed a young Jose Mourinho as his interpreter – he won two Portuguese championships with Porto before spending a year at Barcelona. Mourinho followed

A dejected Bobby Robson wonders if the FA will let him keep the suit after losing the 1990 World Cup semi-final on penalties.

Bobby ROBSON

15

him to Barcelona but stayed on after Robson left.

Newcastle finally came calling in 1999, and the prodigal son ensured the Magpies never finished outside the top five for his last three seasons there. At the end of August 2004, amazingly, he was dismissed after a poor start to the season. It was to be his last full-time managerial role, as a long and courageous battle with cancer ensued.

He was subsequently awarded the Honorary Freedom of the cities of Newcastle, Durham and Ipswich (where his statue now stands) and was knighted in 2002. In December 2007, Robson received the Lifetime Achievement Award at the BBC's Sports Personality of the Year show.

'There are all sorts of personalities who do well as managers,' he once said. 'But there are certain ingredients every successful manager does need. The players have got to understand that you won't accept failure, that you won't accept bad performances, and that you're simply not interested in players who are half-hearted about the game. All the great managers have had a burning desire to win.' Let that be his epitaph. DAVID COTTRELL

The West Brom skipper hears that the maximum wage has been abolished... shortly before leaving after a pay dispute with the club.

 AD NAUSEAM

Played Gary Lineker's guardian angel in one of those hellish Walker's Crisps commercials in 2004, with Terry Venables being the little devil. To steal or not to steal the crisps, you get the drift...

 HELL
2 RAISING

W SPORTING
8 ACHIEVEMENTS

 BEFORE HE WAS FAMOUS
Down the pit but as an electrician's apprentice for the National Coal Board at Langley Park Colliery. Don't look for it, it's not there anymore.

THE MOMENT HE BECAME A LEGEND
The dignified smile that said so much after England's glorious failure against West Germany in the 1990 World Cup semi-finals.

Duncan EDWARDS

BORN **1 OCTOBER 1936** ■ DIED **21 FEBRUARY 1958**

Fantastic young player with the world at his feet, robbed of his destiny by a plane crash in Munich…

It's easy to construct an imaginary, brilliant career-that-never-was, embroidered with optimism and gilded with artistic licence. But in the case of Duncan Edwards, you get the feeling that Manchester United, England and the world of football missed out on something very special.

'Duncan Edwards is the one person who, even today, I really felt inferior to. I've never known anybody so gifted and strong and powerful with the presence that he had.' Bobby Charlton (cf p118-20) said that.

And Matt Busby (cf p 124-6) said this: '[He is] the most complete footballer in Britain – possibly the world.'

Busby was the man who managed to whisk the Dudley-born Edwards away from under the noses of Wolves, and several other clubs who had kept a close eye on his impressive progress, which saw him playing for England Schoolboys at Wembley aged just 13.

Legend has it Busby knocked on the door of Gladstone and Sarah Ann Edwards just after midnight on their son's 16th birthday, so desperate was he to secure the talents of this prodigy. In actual fact, he had been signed by the club some four months earlier. Although Wolves were one of the country's top sides at the time, Edwards was keen to sign for United and they quickly discovered that he was even better than they had hoped.

By his mid-teens, Edwards already had the build of a grown man, with enormous thighs (he hitched up his shorts so opponents could see what they were dealing with), but for a hefty lad he was also fast, with an ability to change direction quickly. He also had a fierce and accurate shot, regardless of which foot he used, was as strong as an ox in the tackle and had great positional awareness.

United's coaching staff were scratching their heads as to how they could improve a player who already looked close to the finished article, and they had little choice but to stick him in the first team. On 4 April 1953 at

The memorial window to Duncan Edwards at St Francis Church in Dudley.

Duncan EDWARDS

Old Trafford Edwards made his league debut at the tender age of 16 years and 185 days against Cardiff.

The following season, Edwards turned out regularly for the first team, making 25 appearances, as Matt Busby implemented his plan to blood a young side, who were dubbed the 'Busby Babes'.

The 1954-55 season saw Edwards operating at wing-half, but looking comfortable all over the pitch, playing 36 games and scoring six goals. He was called up for his first England cap in April and made his debut – a 7-2 demolition of Scotland at Wembley – at the age of 18 years and 183 days, another record only broken by Michael Owen over 40 years later. He was an England regular from that point on.

Edwards played in all four of England's World Cup qualifiers, scoring two goals against Denmark in the home tie at Molineux, and it is certain that he would have had a major impact in England's 1958 World Cup campaign in Sweden.

For two years Duncan then became 23145376 Lance Corporal Edwards D, doing the majority of his National Service at the Nescliff Ammunition Depot in Shropshire. Fortunately for United, Edwards, along with his subordinate Charlton R, were allowed open-ended leave to play matches.

The arrangement must have worked, because United's young side won the League Championship in both 1955-56 and 1956-57. Edwards played in the 1957 FA Cup final against Villa, but United missed out on the Double when their keeper Ray Wood was crocked by Peter McParland early on and they had to play with ten men.

'And can you get me some spam, corned beef and a quarter of sherbet lemons.'

14

United's title wins opened up the chance to play competitively in Europe. Against the wishes of the Football League, they entered the new European Cup competition and stuffed Anderlecht 10-0 in their first home tie. United made it to the semi-final stage, but went out to the great Real Madrid side and a weak referee.

Edwards had time to send a telegram home: 'Flights cancelled, flying tomorrow. Duncan.'

Fifteen minutes later the plan changed again – Captain James Thain having calculated that a slower take-off would solve the problem – and the nervous passengers re-boarded in driving snow.

We'll never know what Edwards could have gone on to achieve in the game, but we don't think his contemporaries are exaggerating when they claim he was one of the game's true greats. GS

'What time is the kick-off against Wolves, Jimmy? I mustn't miss that match.'

Edwards to Manchester United assistant manager Jimmy Murphy from his hospital bed in Munich.

If this European campaign ended in controversy, the next was to bring scarcely believable tragedy.

United's 1956-57 title win gave them another crack at Europe, and when they beat Red Star Belgrade 2-1 at Old Trafford and drew the away leg 3-3, they were in the semi-finals again. As the United side flew home from Belgrade, BEA Flight 609 landed at Munich-Riem Airport to refuel.

Twice the plane attempted to take off to complete the journey to Manchester, and twice the pilot had to abort due to an engine problem. The passengers disembarked and

The plane reached the velocity beyond which they couldn't abort take-off, but then got held up in the build-up of slush. Instead of becoming airborne, it skidded off the end of the runway and hit a house, before smashing into a fuel store, which exploded.

Duncan Edwards was not one of the 20 people who lost their lives on the plane – though seven of his team-mates perished – but died 15 days later, aged 21, at Rechts der Isar Hospital in Munich. His body was returned to Dudley, where thousands lined the streets for his funeral.

 BEFORE HE WAS FAMOUS
Duncan's games master insisted that his 11-year-old pupil would one day play for England.

THE MOMENT HE BECAME A LEGEND
Making his debut for England in 1955, lining up alongside such greats as Nat Lofthouse, Stanley Matthews and Billy Wright.

HELL RAISING 1

SPORTING ACHIEVEMENTS 7

Phil 'The Power' TAYLOR

BORN **13 AUGUST 1960**

Darts god who rewrote the record books and drove the sport's popularity to unimagined heights.

It's not because of the 15 World Championship titles, the 11 World Matchplay crowns, the nine Grand Prix wins, the five Premier League trophies or the hundreds of other tournament victories. And it's not because of the record career earnings of millions of pounds. It's not even because of the nine televised nine-dart finishes in major competitions.

training than football (no half days for him), and is watched by a TV audience of millions. On top of that, Taylor's darts require more precision and hand-eye co-ordination than either of the Olympic sports of shooting or archery.

Taylor was raised in humble surroundings: the upstairs of his parents' house had been condemned,

Despite struggling under the weight of the pressure of being 'Bristow's boy', and having to put up with players like John Lowe questioning why on earth The Crafty Cockney had invested his money in him, Taylor slowly started to make an impact and amassed enough ranking points to qualify for the 1990 World Championship.

There, at the then undisputed home of arrows, Frimley Green, the rank outsider shocked the darting fraternity by storming through the field to reach the final, where his mentor awaited him. There was little room for sympathy or emotion – when Taylor was on the oche, there

'You've either got it or you haven't. It's not about practice. You can practise as much as you want, but you can't practise shitting yourself.'

Taylor goes 'off manual' and has clearly never had food poisoning.

Phil Taylor is one of Britain's greatest sportsmen because, with the possible exception of Don Bradman, no individual in the history of sport has so single-handedly dominated his chosen field and rewritten the record books to such an extent that it is an utter impossibility that they could ever be anything other than the finest exponent of their particular craft of all time.

One myth that needs to be debunked straight away is the sanctimonious notion that darts is not a sport, which would therefore nullify Taylor's claims to sporting legend status.

What he does is potentially more strenuous than cricket, requires more

while electricity was 'borrowed' from the neighbours. But, arguably the most impressive fact about the darts phenomenon was that he threw his first serious arrow at the age of 26, having been encouraged to get out of the house more by his wife Yvonne. Behind every man, and all that…

Two years later, when Eric Bristow (cf p40) decided to sponsor the promising Staffordshire thrower who had been performing well in the Burslem pubs and clubs – including Bristow's own, where the pair would play together for hours – he could never have imagined the impact his £9,000 would make on British sport.

never would be – and the pupil beat the master 6-1 to claim his first world crown.

Two years later, Taylor added a second world crown in arguably the greatest game ever played, as he defeated Mike Gregory in a sudden-death leg in the final set. In 2007, another extraordinary match would go the same distance, but this time Taylor was the vanquished, with his great Dutch rival Raymond van Barneveld prevailing.

In 1993, darts had become irrevocably split, with two rival organisations both staging world championships due to a row about sponsorship and promotion of

A few more tournament wins and he reckoned he'd be able to afford to get his tattoo finished.

the sport. Taylor was firmly in the WDC (later to become the Professional Darts Corporation or the PDC) camp and the Stoke thrower soon became known by his nickname 'The Power' – allegedly coined by Sky Sports TV executive Martin Turner.

As Taylor continued to sweep all before him and rack up title after title, there was little doubt among the true darting cognoscenti that here was not only the game's finest ever player, but also one of the country's outstanding sportsmen.

There was, however, still one test for 'The Power' in the shape of Van Barneveld, who was making waves in the rival BDO World Championship. In 1999, a one-off battle of the champions was set up, with the pair slugging it out for an hour live on ITV, but it wasn't much of a contest as Taylor underlined his authority with a whopping 21-10 success.

In later years, the rivals became friends and continued their rivalry when the Dutchman switched codes,

although Taylor's dominance was maintained – that epic 2007 final aside.

If anything, 'The Power' has actually improved with age. His most recent years have seen him perform better than at any stage of his career, as he rewrote the record books with a stupendous haul of televised, perfect nine-dart finishes. Such was Taylor's talent, he made the nine-darter seem far more achievable than it really should be, once claiming: 'I reckon I could throw two in a match. What would be the odds on that?'

Phil 'The Power' TAYLOR

It would have been hard to find a bookie who would have bothered to give a price on that, so preposterous a bet it would have been. But Taylor makes the impossible possible.

Having thrown seven perfect legs during his career, the Potteries legend jumped straight to nine one night at Wembley Arena in May 2010 on the way to beating James Wade and claiming another Premier League crown.

Just when everyone thought he couldn't surpass his previous achievements, he proved them wrong. That's what legends do. GERSHON PORTNOI

'The Power' didn't even remember entering *Celebrity Big Brother*, never mind winning it.

BEFORE HE WAS FAMOUS
Left school at 16 and worked in a factory making ceramic toilet-roll holders, earning £52 a week.

THE MOMENT HE BECAME A LEGEND
Weirdly, losing the PDC World Championship final in 1994 to Dennis Priestley, as that defeat spurred Taylor on to an unprecedented nine-year unbeaten World Championship run.

 AD NAUSEAM
Once appeared in a spoof ad for Whyte & Mackay whisky-flavoured aftershaves, mimicking a Posh & Becks photo-shoot for their DVB fragrance.

 HELL RAISING 3

 **SPORTING ACHIEVEMENTS** 10

12

Gareth EDWARDS

BORN **12 JULY 1947**

The miner's son who became Wales' greatest ever rugby player, youngest captain and scored the sport's greatest ever try – but not for his country.

The writing was on the wall for the fleet-footed kid from the Welsh valleys the moment the posh sorts at sport-orientated Millfield public school deemed him worthy of a scholarship – although even they couldn't have guessed just how great the young Edwards boy was to become.

Blessed with the upper-body strength and low centre of gravity common to so many great scrum-halves, Edwards also displayed a devastating turn of foot, assured passing off both sides and a gravitational pull towards the try-line that saw him awarded a first cap for Wales at the tender age of 19.

Almost by accident, some rugby broke out as the fighting continued, and Edwards went on to score one of the greatest solo tries ever seen at the Arms Park.

Gareth EDWARDS

The photographer sustained minor head trauma and a broken nose.

His selection, to face eventual winners France in the penultimate game of the 1967 Five Nations season, would be the first of a world record 53 consecutive international appearances – a staggering achievement by any player in any era, but particularly so by a scrum-half in an amateur period when opposing tackles were often meant to maim first and regain possession second. By the end of his career, he also held the record for most tries for Wales (20), and had been his country's youngest ever captain, at just 20.

Had that been the extent of Edwards' career CV, he might still have retired a happy man, justifiably proud of an 11-year run in one of rugby union's most iconic shirts.

As it was, however, Edwards just happened to be the prime mover behind the most successful period in the history of Welsh rugby, a sublime scrum-half and inspirational figure who, alongside Phil Bennett, Barry John (cf p22, who advised him 'You throw them and I'll catch them') and the mercurial J.P.R. Williams (cf p46), transformed how the sport was perceived. It moved from being seen as a slow-motion trudge through the mud enlivened by the occasional punch-up into a game of pace, flair and, wait for it, nuance.

The statistics speak for themselves. In those aforementioned 11 years as the Wales No. 9, Edwards was part of a side that won or at least shared seven Five Nations titles, including three Grand Slams and, between 1976 and 1978, the first Triple Crown three-timer in almost 100 years of Home Nations rugby.

But he wasn't just part of that Wales side, he was its essence: the sturdy but devilish sprite driving his lumbering forwards on, while encouraging and enabling the artists outside him to play with a freedom and expansiveness little seen in the game to that date.

And yet, for all the talent surrounding him in that period of sensational Welsh dominance, Edwards reigned supreme in fact

forward that ended with Edwards diving deep beyond the try-line to touch down for one of the sport's great individual tries (see picture p151).

That he rose with his face caked in the red mud of the dog track that used to surround the Arms Park pitch only adds to the legend – even if his mother, watching in the stands, thought he was bleeding profusely.

fellow Edwards… if the greatest writer of the written word had written that story, no one would have believed it.'

It was an appropriate memorial for a player who, as well as bestriding Welsh rugby and scoring what simply became known as *'That* Try', also starred for the British Lions on winning tours in New Zealand and South Africa.

'A supreme athlete with supreme skills, the complete package,' wrote Will Carling in 2007. 'He played in the 1970s, but if he played now he would still be the best. He was outstanding at running, passing, kicking and reading the game. He sits astride the whole of rugby as the ultimate athlete on the pitch.'

Edwards retired from international rugby after leading Wales to a Grand Slam – fittingly, against France at the Arms Park – in 1978. More than 30 years on, his legend endures. TONY HODSON

> 'There were two or three bloody ridiculous passages of movement before Phil Bennett did something completely different… Instinct and unpredictability, that's rugby at its best.'

Talking about '*That* Try' against the All Blacks.

as much as he does in myth – the Colossus of Gwaun-cae-Gurwen, they never called him, but they wouldn't have been far wide of the mark if they had.

Two moments stand out: both tries, one in the red of his beloved Wales and the other, more famously, in the black and white of those kings of the amateur era, the Barbarians.

The former, in a Five Nations game against Scotland at the old Cardiff Arms Park, was vintage Edwards. 'All I was looking for was a little snipe around the blind side,' he later said. It was nothing of the sort.

The 'little snipe', on the back of a stolen Scottish line-out just outside the Welsh 22, soon became a sprint beyond flailing blue arms – which in itself turned into a chip and chase

And if that try was all about the glorious talent of the individual, then the latter, for the Barbarians against the All Blacks in 1973, was the ultimate expression of the expansive game.

Beginning with some barely believable Phil Bennett footwork yards from their own line, the Barbarians launched a counter-attack of such flair and daring that, as Cliff Morgan said in the commentary box: 'Oh, that

 AD NAUSEAM
Worked to promote Welsh Water after privatisation.

 HELL RAISING SPORTING ACHIEVEMENTS
1 9

BEFORE HE WAS FAMOUS
Before rugby got hold of him, the 16-year-old Edwards signed schoolboy papers for Swansea City. What a Gazza he might have made…

 THE MOMENT HE BECAME A LEGEND
Crossing the line to score for the Barbarians in 1973 to round off an astonishing passage of play.

David BECKHAM

BORN **2 MAY 1975**

He's worth half a billion dollars, married to a pop star and has single-handedly made it OK for men to moisturise. Once vilified as England's public enemy No.1, he is now a national treasure.

In 1985, David Beckham, the son of a kitchen fitter from East London, was very much not a global brand. He was aged ten, rather skinny and – in his words – 'Not much of a scholar.' He would come away from school most afternoons with a football under his arm with one question on his mind: when would the next kick-about start?

Beckham soon fixed his sights on Manchester United, partly because he liked to watch Bryan Robson (cf p47) tear the opposition to shreds and partly because his dad supported them with a near fanaticism. He became a mascot for one game in 1986.

By the age of 12 his talents had been noted, and he got his first taste of life in the public eye when the local paper dubbed him the 'Chingford Football Sensation'. It wasn't entirely welcome and he later described it as 'a little bit cringe-making'. Although, coming from a man who once went out with his wife dressed in matching leather Gucci outfits (see picture p156), it's difficult to sympathise on that count.

The breakthrough, according to Beckham, came one afternoon in front of children's TV show *Blue Peter*. The Bobby Charlton Soccer Coaching School announced they would be running skills sessions across the country, and the regional winners would compete in the final at Old Trafford. Like a shot, Beckham was outside, practising his corners till it was too dark to see the ball and the dinner plates were drying on a rack.

Having won the competition with a record 1,106 points (despite being booed by some Spurs fans who objected to his Manchester United shirt), he ended up training with the Barcelona reserve youth team – but returned home halfway through the trip to play in Ridgeway's Waltham Forest Under-12 Cup final.

A trial with United followed – and a place on the youth team, part of the 'Class of 92' that also featured Ryan Giggs (cf p60) and Gary Neville among others. He made his first team debut for them aged 17.

In 1996, he became a household name by scoring from the halfway line against Wimbledon. The *Sunday Mirror* excitedly referred to it as the 'Goal of the Century!'. He was a photo- and telegenic working-class boy with the world at his feet, less than cerebral but truly gifted on the football pitch.

The tabloids loved him instantly, the broadsheets affected disdain at his burgeoning celebrity status, but he was becoming a fixture as much on the front pages as the back, especially when he met Victoria Adams, or 'Posh Spice' of the Spice Girls, in 1997, marrying her two years later.

He had a multi-million-pound film – *Bend It Like Beckham* – named after him in 2002 and also acquired a huge gay following, partly due to some underwear advertising.

During his time under Alex Ferguson (cf p110-11), 'Becks' (as he was now known to the wider world) won the Premier League six times, the FA Cup twice and the Champions League in 1999.

However, after a lacklustre performance against Arsenal early in 2003, the manager let loose with a flying boot, which happened to hit Beckham in the face – before the story then hit the tabloids. That was the beginning of the end at Old Trafford.

BEFORE HE WAS FAMOUS
He was a part-time glass collector at Walthamstow dog track.

THE MOMENT HE BECAME A LEGEND
That goal from inside his own half against Wimbledon as a 21-year-old. Did he mean it? Yes he did.

As Beckham was able to confirm subsequently, the Heskey choke-hold/lobe-chewing move was an uncomfortable business.

After leaving United, Beckham found time to win La Liga with Real Madrid in 2007. When they suggested Beckham find a new club, 'Golden Balls' (a nickname given him by his wife) chose to end his career surrounded by golden beaches at MLS team LA Galaxy in the States, a move that would earn him a reported £128 million. He twice went out on loan, in 2009 and 2010, to AC Milan in a bid to prove he could still justify a cherished place in the England set-up.

Indeed, it was in an England shirt that Beckham experienced his greatest highs – and lows. And when we say lows, the sight of several grown men burning an effigy of oneself outside a pub must have been rather disturbing. A week earlier, he had been red-carded for kicking Argentinean Diego Simeone (who later admitted he made the most of the incident) in the last 16 of the 1998 World Cup.

Beckham became public enemy No.1, and headlines such as 'Ten Heroic Lions, One Stupid Boy' served only to fuel the supporters' frustration. It was almost four years before he earned the chance to redeem himself, capping an all-action performance with a glorious stoppage-time free kick against Greece at Old Trafford to send England into the 2002 World Cup finals (see picture p155). As the commentator put it at the time, 'Give that man a knighthood.'

Despite having just recovered from a metatarsal injury and clearly not at peak fitness, as captain, he led England into the last eight. On the way, deliciously, he exacted revenge on Argentina by scoring the winning goal to knock them out – before England

David BECKHAM

11

No prizes for guessing whose idea this was. But she went along with it anyway.

'I have come to accept that if I have a new haircut it is front page news. But having a picture of my foot on the front page of a national newspaper is a bit exceptional.'

Beckham is astounded by the level of attention his metatarsal injury received in 2002.

themselves, predictably, were crushed by Brazil in the quarters.

Having relinquished the captaincy after the 2006 World Cup, Beckham was written off as an international on various occasions, but kept on coming back. He not only reached 100 caps, presented to him by Bobby Charlton (cf p118-20) amid an epic standing ovation, but went on to surpass Bobby Moore's (cf p187-91) outfield record of 108 caps in March 2009.

Sadly, a ruptured Achilles left him cheering the team on from the bench during the 2010 World Cup and it is unlikely he will add to his 115 caps. But never say never. He's not leaving your newspapers any time soon.

'Chingford's Footballing Sensation'? The boy done good. TB/DM

 **HELL
4 RAISING**

 **SPORTING
8 ACHIEVEMENTS**

RED RUM

BORN **3 MAY 1965** ■ DIED **18 OCTOBER 1995**

'Flamin' 'ell Edna, those bleedin' horses are jumping over the hedge again.'

RED RUM

Yes, he was a horse. But three Grand National wins mark him down as the most famous nag ever to race on these shores.

Red Rum may not have been the best horse and he certainly wasn't the fastest. But he was possibly the bravest and definitely the most famous. Even now, 34 years after he last won the Grand National and 16 years since he died, his name is forever linked with British horse racing.

It says as much about the National as it does about the horse that Rummy's three wins leave him among the immortals, while a nag like, say, Best Mate, who won the arguably more prestigious Cheltenham Gold Cup three times, is just remembered as a very good horse.

But then the National is the only race that encourages so many Brits to have a flutter that, traditionally, they would read out the result of the race at half-time at football matches. Cue general groaning and a few excited shouts.

A tremendous slog over four and a half miles, and peppered with some of the toughest jumps anywhere in racing (and they were much bigger in the 1970s than they are now), it requires a special sort of horse to win it. But Rummy made the race his own: he competed five times in total and in the two years he didn't win, he came second.

It was the way he did it. As each year came and went, he seemed to produce something more extraordinary, culminating in the 20-length win over Churchtown Boy to land his third National in 1977 (see picture p157).

Bred to be a Flat racer, Red Rum was born in 1965 and his first race, at Liverpool in 1967, was over the sprint distance of just five furlongs. He won it too, but 18 months later he was trying hurdles for the first time. His future lay in jumping.

But would he have a future at all? He suffered from a bone disease in his foot and although able to race, he became notoriously injury-prone. Different trainers tried to unlock the talent, but Anthony Gillam saw where Rummy's future lay when he entered him in the 1972 Scottish Grand National.

The horse finished a highly creditable fifth, but didn't seem to relish the run-in, hanging towards the rails and 'changing his legs' – not running a true finish. His owner at the time, Lurline 'Muffie' Brotherton, was exasperated and sent him to the Doncaster August sales in that year.

An interested observer of the Scottish National had been Donald 'Ginger' McCain, an extraordinary character relatively new to the racing world, having been granted his training licence as recently as 1969. Also a part-time car dealer and taxi driver (who claimed to have once chauffeured a lion from Liverpool to London), McCain wanted to find a decent horse he could train for owner Noel Le Mare.

McCain had asked the elderly Le Mare if he could work as a trainer for him and knew he was desperate to own a Grand National winner. In Red Rum, McCain could see the stars aligning.

He persuaded Le Mare to give him a war chest of 7,000 guineas with which to bid at auction. Ultimately, he got his nag for 6,000. Has a shrewder bit of horse-trading ever been undertaken?

At first, however, McCain feared he had been stitched up by Brotherton. Red Rum arrived in Liverpool and when the horse box doors opened, he appeared to be lame. McCain angrily ordered the horse into the sea at Southport, thinking the water would

'Respect this place, this hallowed ground,
A legend here his rest has found.
His feet would fly, our spirits soar,
He earned our love for evermore.'

Never one for actually speaking, Rummy's epitaph at Aintree will have to do.

10

either help his feet or drown him. Or so he said.

There must be something in the Irish Sea, though. Red Rum hobbled in, paddled around and then walked out, his legs and feet sound. From then on, McCain trained him only on the beach or in the sea (his pre-National dip eventually became something of a tourist attraction) and the horse, previously a difficult character, seemed to love every second.

That autumn, racing for McCain for the first time, Rummy paid back the faith that the eccentric taxi driver had shown in him. He won his first five races, all at three miles or more, and with Le Mare so keen to have a National winner carrying his colours, McCain knew that all roads pointed to Aintree.

The public had also seen that Red Rum had what it took to win the National and made him the 9-1 joint favourite. But when the giant Australian beast Crisp took what seemed an unassailable 20-length lead, hopes began to fade. But not inside Rummy's noble head.

Buoyed by the noise of the crowd, he pricked his ears and set off in pursuit under jockey Brian Fletcher, reeling in Crisp stride-by-stride, getting up alongside in the final furlong. If anyone had thought that Red Rum wasn't the genuine article in his younger days, he had now dispelled that notion. This was a brave, brave win. What was more, he set a new record time of 9:01.9 in crossing the line first.

The following season saw Red Rum at the height of his powers. He won a further four races before returning to Aintree to defend his title. This time

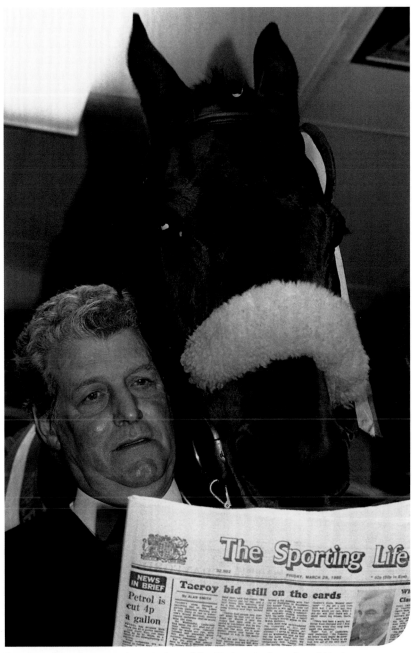

'Two down, "Most famous racehorse in the world"… blank, e, d… Second word, blank, u, m… Bed Bum?' 'Oh do be quiet.'

RED RUM

though, the handicapper gave him a stiffer task – forcing him to carry the top weight of 12st (one pound more than Cheltenham Gold Cup winner L'Escargot). Not a problem.

Honed to perfection on the Southport sands by McCain, Rummy lugged the weight around the course with a casual insouciance, careering away to win by seven lengths. Just three weeks later he won the Scottish National. It was clear to all by now that Red Rum was the horse of a generation.

But then came defeat. In 1975, Rummy was back at Aintree trying to become the first horse to win three Nationals, let alone in successive years. Forced to carry top weight once again, however, he had to give way to L'Escargot – his victim of the previous year. And the following year he was second again, this time behind the talented Rag Trade.

By now, Red Rum was a national institution. His two brave top weight-carrying second places had only endeared him more to the great British public, and concerns were expressed that McCain was over-racing his charge. There were calls for the horse to be retired.

Despite the 1976-77 season suggesting that the horse was past his best, McCain kept the faith. He was perhaps the only person in the country who did so – Rummy was looking lacklustre and uninterested. The trainer, however, knew his horse came alive at the National. He loved the crowds and the occasion and if he was to ever fall in love with racing again, it would be at Aintree – especially in Jubilee year.

Leading early under jockey Tommy Stack in the 1977 National, Red Rum was relentless. Churchtown Boy briefly threatened, but our hero took one scornful glance at him and powered away to win by a country mile, relishing the roar of the Aintree faithful as he crossed the line. Once again punters all over the country rejoiced.

He was entered in the 1978 race but fell lame the day before. A nation mourned. X-rays revealed he had a hairline fracture in his leg and Red Rum was retired at the age of 13. McCain insists that he would have gone on and won his fourth National if he had been fit.

Instead, he opened a plethora of supermarkets and rumours that he inspired the scene in Stanley Kubrick's 1980 horror flick *The Shining* when Danny, the boy in the film, goes into a trance while repeating the words 'red

rum' – 'murder' spelled backwards – remain unconfirmed.

For many years the horse returned to Aintree merely to run in front of the packed stands and soak up the adulation. When he died, aged 30, in 1995, he was buried under the winning post. sc

⊘ AD NAUSEAM
Red Rum lent his image, Princess 'Of Hearts' Diana-style, to any manner of plates, bags and general tat. But his favourite pastime was opening supermarkets.

 HELL RAISING

 **SPORTING ACHIEVEMENTS**

BEFORE HE WAS FAMOUS
Bred as a Flat horse, he once won a five-furlong sprint and was ridden by Lester Piggott.

THE MOMENT HE BECAME A LEGEND
In 1977, carrying an impossible 12st 11lb burden, Red Rum was cheered home by the whole nation as he landed his third Grand National. Not only did he win, he did so by 20 lengths.

Henry COOPER

BORN 3 MAY 1934 ▪ DIED **1 MAY 2011**

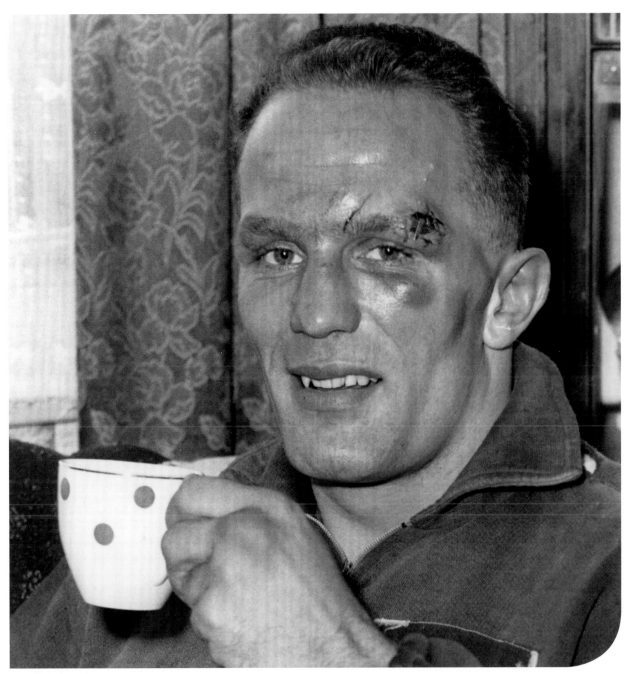

At first they weren't going to let him have three sugars, but he got his way in the end.

Henry COOPER

Affable, big-hearted sarf Londoner with an unlikely secret weapon up his sleeve: a pulverising left hook by the name of 'Enery's 'Ammer.

'Who's the bum now, Mr Clay?'

Ask anyone inside the game to name the greatest British boxer of all time, and they'll start making pound-for-pound comparisons, delving back in history to come up with a list that will certainly include all the fighters that appear elsewhere in our 100, as well as the likes of John Conteh, Lloyd Honeyghan and Naseem Hamed. They'll most likely inform you that Scottish lightweight Ken Buchanan won more fights than all of them, and so must stake a legitimate claim.

But the title-counting, point-scoring pundits are maybe too close to their sport to nominate the one boxer who won our hearts with his colossal courage toe-to-toe with true boxing giants, the boxer most likely to be nominated by any bloke in any pub in the country: '*Ladeez and gennulmen,* the *undefeated* heavyweight champion of British boxing... *Hennnry* Cooper.'

Now go ahead and ask that same boxing aficionado about the most famous fight in British ring history, and they'll tell you: Henry Cooper versus Cassius Clay, Wembley Stadium, March 1963.

This was the genesis of the Cooper legend, which enabled the personable Londoner – who had already been beaten eight times in his nine-year, 32-fight pro career – to transcend his sport. It's the most mythologised contest ever to feature a British boxer, and the most eulogised. And it's a fight that still inhabits that grey area in popular memory, where romance and partisanship can blur fact and fiction.

Today, it's unthinkable that a non-title fight could excite such passion; but remember this was back in British boxing's Golden Era.

For four years, Cooper had been holder of both the British and Commonwealth heavyweight titles, which he'd taken off Brian London.

'The British heavyweight title meant something back then,' Cooper recalled. 'If you stopped ten people in the street now and asked them to name the present British heavyweight champion, I bet you nine of them would have no idea. But in the fifties and sixties, because the BBC used to show all our fights on Wednesday's *Sportsnight*, they were all household names. British heavyweight title night was like the FA Cup final.'

There might have been no belt at stake, but it became a matter of immense pride – personal and national – that Cooper should beat Clay, the upstart Olympic champion, aged just 21, with his cocky, seemingly defenceless ring stance.

The wind-up started as soon as Clay got off the plane from the States and, in a hypercool display of jive-talking media savvy, casually referred to his opponent as 'a bum' as he predicted his downfall in five rounds. Now, Henry had almost certainly never been called 'a bum' before, and he didn't take kindly to it. Neither did the British public enjoy hearing their man belittled.

'This will be an annihilation,' the self-styled 'Louisville Lip' rapped at the weigh-in. 'If the bum don't fall in five, I won't come back to this nation.'

'I didn't hear it all, so I couldn't comment,' Henry replied, with a frankly magnificent show of British dignity. 'I only heard the last hour. Let him do all the talking – he does enough for both of us.'

In the Wembley Stadium ring, Cooper looked in great shape, long before the days of the pumped-up heavyweight muscleman. Tipping the scale at 185½lb, he'd be a cruiserweight today, even then giving away 21lb to his adversary. Clay entered wearing a gown that proclaimed him 'The Greatest', while it was down to Cooper's 35,000 fans to do their favourite's bidding: ''En-er-y, 'En-er-y, 'En-er-y, 'En-er-y…'

Cooper's big opening assault had Clay complaining to the ref about roughhouse tactics, as Henry looked to land his favourite left but, by the third, the American had more than weathered the storm and was cruising, looking to humiliate his opponent. That's when he cut Cooper over the eyebrow. He was known, in boxing parlance, to be a bleeder.

'He's almost treating Henry as a plaything,' commented Harry Carpenter at ringside. 'But that's the sort of chance you can take once too often… and if Henry nails him…'

Then a quick turn, Clay distracted; a fantastic left hook under the jaw, and the American was bouncing off the ropes on to the canvas courtesy of 'Enery's 'Ammer – only to be saved by the bell, when Cooper was a feather blow from victory.

'He still doesn't know where he is,' Carpenter gabbled as 'The Lip' walked like a zombie back to his corner. 'He's still half out, Clay.'

Cue trainer Angelo Dundee to illegally crack a phial of ammonia under Clay's nose – and the lights come flickering back on. Then worse: Dundee opened up a nick in his fighter's glove and pointed out the tear to the referee. Now we must leave behind verifiable fact for that otherworldly grey area. For nearly 50 years, Cooper told the story of the steward's race to find a replacement glove.

'By the time they brought a spare pair from the dressing-room – which at Wembley was a hundred and fifty yards away – Clay had two and a half minutes to recover. If it had been a straight fight,' Cooper remembered as if it were yesterday, 'I'd have beaten him that night, no question.'

Boxing mythology backs Cooper: it's widely believed spare gloves have been kept in every boxer's corner since this night. But real-time footage of the fight shows there was no replacement glove. The actual interval between rounds was not the prescribed minute, but 65 seconds.

Back on his feet, Clay furiously attacked Cooper's patched wound, opening up a wellstream of blood.

BEFORE HE WAS FAMOUS
Times were tough in the Cooper household, so young Henry earned extra money by collecting and selling golf balls at Beckenham Golf Club.

THE MOMENT HE BECAME A LEGEND
When Cassius Clay bounced off the ropes and hit the canvas, barely conscious – courtesy of 'Enery's 'Ammer.

Henry COOPER

And the fight was stopped in the fifth, just as he had predicted.

By the time the pair met again – in a world heavyweight title fight at Highbury in 1966 – Clay had changed his name to Muhammad Ali and he treated Henry with the utmost respect.

He put all his ring titles on the line in April 1971, when he took on the young naturalised Hungarian, Joe Bugner. The fight was a travesty, a tragic failure, yet succeeded in piling up yet more popular affection for Henry, as he was robbed of

'Henry Cooper has stolen the affection of the public for longer than any other sportsman,' observed boxing commentator Reg Gutteridge. 'He has indestructible dignity.'

The truth of those words was confirmed when Cooper died on 1 May 2011. His death began a period of near national mourning, and at his funeral were family, friends and stars from the world of sport and entertainment, all united in grief at the loss of someone about whom no one had a bad word to say – a fitting tribute to his life.

'En-er-y! 'En-er-y! 'En-er-y! DH

> 'Mr Cooper, have you looked in the mirror lately and seen the state of your nose?'
>
> 'Well, madam. Have you looked in the mirror and seen the state of your nose? Boxing's my excuse, what's yours?'

Cooper's swift response to boxing abolitionist Baroness Summerskill.

To his enormous credit, Cooper again had the better of the early exchanges, waiting for a chance to get in an 'Ammer Blow; but in the sixth the American landed an awkward angled punch which again saw blood cascade down the whole left of Cooper's body. 'It was the disappointment of my life,' admitted Henry with heartbreaking honesty.

Cooper's greatest ever win would come in 1970 when, at the age of 36, he overcame the fearsome Spaniard Jose Manuel Urtain, whose 34-1 record included 33 knockouts. It added the European heavyweight title to Henry's British and Commonwealth belts – not to mention the BBC Sports Personality of the Year award, which he became the first person to win twice (in 1967 and 1970).

all three titles by a 'controversial' – or some have claimed bent – referee's decision.

Disgusted and disheartened, Cooper would never fight again. But the British public refused to allow bad luck or bitter memories to bow their champ, and Henry soon proved a natural on TV's *A Question of Sport*, sundry lunkish adverts and, latterly, the A-list of after-dinner speakers. Henry Cooper was granted a knighthood in 2000.

On the 40th anniversary of that evening in 1963, Muhammad Ali, arguably the greatest sportsman of the 20th century, phoned his opponent to reminisce, generously later repeating the admission on TV that Cooper had, 'Hit me so hard that my ancestors in Africa felt it.'

AD NAUSEAM

Cooper's ad for Brut 33 spawned one of the most oft-repeated catchphrases of the 1970s: 'Splash it all ovah!'

 HELL RAISING 1

 **SPORTING ACHIEVEMENTS** 7

Daley THOMPSON

BORN **30 JULY 1958**

Selfish, uncomfortable with the public's adulation and hell-bent on victory: the double Olympic champion who mastered the most gruelling track event and has the records to prove it…

'I haven't been this happy since my grandmother caught her tit in a mangle' was Daley Thompson's response when asked if it was the happiest day of his life, as he left the press conference in the Los Angeles Coliseum in August 1984.

And who could blame him? Between 1978 and 1986, he won two Olympic gold medals, three Commonwealth golds and two European Championship golds. In 1983, when he took gold at the World Championships in Helsinki, he held all the major decathlon titles. He was, and still is, the greatest decathlete of all time.

As Sebastian Coe (cf p182-6) once opined: 'Daley is a Stalinist. It's not enough for him to win; he has to mentally destroy his opponent.'

It was an exceptional talent. Unfortunately, Thompson had another 'exceptional talent' – namely rubbing people up the wrong way. At his peak, he rarely seemed to miss an opportunity to make it plain that he couldn't give a tinker's cuss whether people loved or loathed him.

If being selfish was the only way to achieve total domination of his sport, Thompson was honest enough to face up to it. Consequently, the red tops took great pleasure in reporting an occasion

'Do you know the National Anthem?'
'You play it and I'll whistle it.'

he told young fans who had innocently asked for an autograph to 'Eff-off' ('I don't remember ever doing that'), not to mention printing lurid revelations under the headline 'Love Cheat'.

One such story in the *Mirror* claimed: 'They holidayed in Bali – in a room with a balcony.' The reply was the pure essence of Thompson's attitude: 'If only I'd hired a villa.'

Journalist Colin Hart refused to speak to him for two years, while another from *The Times* described Thompson as 'Objectionable, charmless and rude.'

And yet, in spite of all this, the British public voted him 1982's BBC Sports Personality of the Year – bumping 'People's Champion' Alex Higgins (cf p127-9) into second place. He could have accepted the public's heartfelt adulation gracefully, but that wasn't his style. Instead, he greeted the announcement by blurting out 'Oh shit!' live on air.

He wasn't in it to gain the public's approval. It was that simple. 'Oh shit!', however, was nothing compared to his antics in LA. After clinching his second Olympic gold, Thompson flounced into the room where the world's press had gathered, sporting a T-shirt bearing the slogan: 'Is the World's 2nd Greatest Athlete Gay?' And, as if that wasn't enough of a gift to the waiting hacks, he expressed a desire to 'give Princess Anne a baby'.

Thompson later claimed it was a joke, while the British Olympic Association pointed out that it was his way of telling the press to mind their own business. But by then, the horse had bolted.

The T-shirt was interpreted as a jibe directed at American sprinter Carl Lewis, who had denied rumours regarding his sexuality. And, as for the bit about Princess Anne, Thompson later backed it up and proclaimed that 'A woman only has to sit on a bed that I've slept in to get pregnant.'

Whatever his true intentions were, it's unlikely we'll ever be privvy to them. But then, Thompson has always taken comfort from the fact that nobody has managed to get inside his head – not his competitors, nor his long-term partners. 'Nobody knows me, except myself,' he once admitted.

Daley THOMPSON

But while he did not always have time for sentimentality, Thompson always had time for the stopwatch. The stopwatch never lied; the stopwatch was there to be worshipped. And, to this end, he put in double training sessions on Christmas day.

His success on the track would have come as no surprise to his mother. Even at the age of seven, when the young South Londoner was sent to a Sussex boarding school for troubled children, winning was everything: 'I just had to be first at everything, from catching the bus to finishing my lunch.'

Young Francis Ayodele, as he was known then, was good at football, but he was even better at athletics. And besides, Thompson was firmly of the belief that 'There was no team in I'. 'I like the winner-takes-all aspect. It's the only way.'

At the age of 12, a distressing phone call saw him return to the capital. His father Frank, who ran a mini-cab firm in Streatham, South London, had been shot by the husband of a woman he and his friend were dropping off. 'I guess you could say it was sudden,' he said later. 'As soon as the bullet hit him, he was shot.'

To his credit, Thompson had the maturity to extract a positive from the emotional wreckage and realised he did not want to finish life with a list of should-have-dones.

In 1974, he was introduced to the decathlon by his first serious coach, Bob Mortimer, after agreeing to train with him at the Essex Beagles running club. Despite his own reservations, he sampled the track and field event and competed for the first time at the

Welsh Open in Cwmbran in 1975. He won, of course.

'I'd never done six of the events before. But in Wales, at the end of the first day, I was thinking, I could be the best at this.' When his mates were heading off into the working world, he shunned it all. In order to continue training, he enrolled at Crawley College, studying biology and English literature. It meant he was eligible for a grant, which covered the relevant expenses needed to persist with his dream.

His qualification for the 1976 Olympic Games in Montreal indicated that he'd made the right choice. Thompson finished in 18th place, a considerable achievement for an 18-year-old who had not properly developed his technique. American Bruce Jenner, who took gold, was 26. Thompson had four years to eclipse him.

Gold at the 1978 Commonwealth Games was a sign that he was on the way and before he knew it, Thompson was in Moscow:

Day one: 100m run, long jump, high jump, shot-put, 400m run.

Day two: 110m hurdles, discus, pole vault, javelin, 1500m run.

A fine balance was needed. Too much emphasis on upper-body strength would hinder any chance of victory in running. Too much focus on sprinting and leg work would make it nigh-on impossible to throw any kind of competitive distance in the shot-put and javelin.

He was in devastating form and steamed to victory, beating Soviet counterpart Yuriy Kutsenko by 164 points to finish with a total of 8,495. He savoured his victory lap in Lenin Central Stadium, but there was no party to toast his achievement.

8

Caught in a torrential downpour at the World Championships in 1987, if he'd had to swim the 400m he would still have won.

Daley THOMPSON

'Another No.1 from Ocean'

DALEY THOMPSON'S DECATHLON

GO FOR GOLD!

Should have been called 'Daley Thompson's Have-You-Done-Your-Bloody-Homework-Yet? Decathlon'.

> 'I probably was occasionally a bit of a knob. Who isn't, when they're twenty-one?'

Thompson offers a rare glimpse of self-awareness.

Doping chiefs waiting for that all-important urine sample kept him on lock-down well into the early hours. Clearly, they had no idea who they were dealing with: Daley Thompson has never even drunk alcohol.

When he was finally allowed to wander off into the Moscow night, no one was around to celebrate. Instead, the newly crowned Olympic champion walked back to his room to let out a roar of delight.

Two years later, and Thompson was back doing what he did best: winning the decathlon and winding people up. Having been chosen to carry the British team's flag during the opening ceremony of Commonwealth Games in Brisbane, he declined. 'That ceremony would have taken six hours, in the heat. Then perform, three days later? I'm not a tourist.'

At the 1984 Los Angeles Olympics, the world's No. 1 decathlete was certainly feeling the heat – from dangerous German rival Jürgen Hingsen. Thompson opened with a sensational victory in the 100m sprint, clocking an emphatic 10.45 seconds, but by the start of the second day his lead was in jeopardy. In the discus, Thompson's first two throws fell 30ft short of those of Hingsen.

Facing defeat, Thompson knew he needed to throw further than he had ever done in his life…

'It's a better one! It's a better one! IT'S A BETTER ONE! He's dancing in the circle!'

Double Olympic champion or not, Thompson still managed to give the press something to talk about by whistling his way though the national anthem – a move that was considered disrespectful by some of his fans (see picture p165).

Before retiring, Thompson achieved immortality via an unlikely medium: the ZX Spectrum. Daley Thompson's Decathlon was the Guitar Hero of its day and brought unbridled 8-bit pleasure to over a million gamers, who were given three lives to get through a full decathlon.

Despite bestowing this gift upon the nation, Thompson is merely a CBE – scant recognition for his achievements. Perhaps it is because, to this day, he remains brutally honest, recently describing sprinter Dwain Chambers as a 'cheating bastard who shouldn't be allowed to compete'.

Or perhaps it is because when asked: 'Who do you think is the ultimate athlete of all time?' there is only ever one answer. He smiles and says: 'Me.'

DAMIAN MANNION

 AD NAUSEAM

In 1985 he appeared in an advert for Lucozade where he is seen refreshing himself with the drink while Iron Maiden blares out in the background.

 HELL RAISING 6

SPORTING ACHIEVEMENTS 10

BEFORE HE WAS FAMOUS
Had trials with Fulham and Chelsea while still at school in Sussex, but joined nearby athletics club Hayward's Heath.

THE MOMENT HE BECAME A LEGEND
Daley Thompson breaks the world record to amass 8,847 points to win his second successive Olympic gold medal at the 1984 LA games.

Paul GASCOIGNE

BORN **27 MAY 1967**

The tears. The booze. The plastic boobs.
The pranks. The heroics. The tragically
mis-timed tackle. The hair extensions.
The poignancy. The goals.

The year 1990 was the most momentous in English football since 1966. English clubs were banned from participating in European competitions – the game had gone backwards on the pitch, while violent yobs ran amok off it. Among the dying embers of the Thatcher government, there were poll tax riots and another one at Strangeways prison in Manchester. England, as a nation and a team, was a shambles.

Enter Paul 'Gazza' Gascoigne.

Under the paternal guidance of Bobby Robson (cf p142-4) it suddenly seemed possible that a daft lad with bad hair and fat cheeks could change English football forever and restore a nation's pride.

Gascoigne flew out to the 1990 World Cup as the subject of a police investigation. There had been reports in the tabloids of a brawl at a Newcastle nightspot. When asked if he intended to sue the papers, he is reported to have replied in broad Geordie, 'Nah. I whacked the c***, didnae!'

After a dismal start, England progressed from the group stages and Gazza turned from professional footballer to pop-star/pin-up. Pressure? The man/boy looked like he was on an 18-30, blasting out 'World In Motion' every morning and drinking beer round the pool. The fans adored him – he was one of them.

On the pitch, it was a different story. The fat lad proved to be a ballerina, weaving through four or five defenders with the ball pinging between his feet, playing with it like he owned it, threading exquisitely timed passes that didn't look feasible, and turning the opposition as if they were wearing concrete boots – and that was just on a bad day at the office.

As Bobby Robson remarked dryly, 'Every time we play him we need two balls – one for him and one for the team.' Here – at last – was England's Maradona.

Born in Gateshead, Gascoigne was the son of a hod-carrier. Short on qualifications, he dreamed – like most working-class kids on Tyneside – of playing professional football for Newcastle United. Once, during a geography lesson, his teacher caught him practising his autograph: 'D'you know only one in a million becomes a professional footballer, Paul?'

'Yeah sir. That's gonna be me.'

Gascoigne's childhood was blighted by the death of a young friend who ran in front of a car. It was a tragic accident, but Gascoigne felt partly to blame and was subsequently consumed by thoughts of death.

Football was a welcome distraction and he soon signed for Newcastle United as a schoolboy in 1980 and

made his first team debut five years later against QPR.

There were some off-the-pitch disciplinary problems (including driving a groundsman's tractor into the dressing-room wall), but his impact and progress on the pitch were impossible to ignore. Famously, he was photographed having his testicles squeezed by Vinnie Jones (cf p8 and 80-81) in a game against Wimbledon in February 1988.

With Newcastle either becalmed in mid-table or fighting relegation,

Gazzamania starring Paul Gascoigne, with the rest of the country in a supporting role.

Paul GASCOIGNE

Gazzamania 2: Back From The Wilderness, co-starring Colin Hendry as the hapless fall guy.

he became restless and other clubs came calling. In particular, Manchester United and Tottenham Hotspur. He chose the latter and went for a British record transfer fee of £2 million in 1988. Alex Ferguson (cf p110-11) later said that the biggest disappointment of his managerial career was 'Not getting Gazza'.

He thrived at Tottenham, and it was as a Spurs player that he

was transformed into a world-class international player. Two years later he went to Italia 90.

With the Group F stage behind them and a couple of tight games (extra-time wins against Belgium and Cameroon) out of the way, England faced West Germany in the semi-final.

You know what happened next: stuffy German goal (deflected off Paul Parker); late England equaliser to

get everybody's hopes up; extra time, penalties beckoning and then... an over-enthusiastic lunge, a German attempting a triple pike with salco and an officious referee.

Gascoigne received a yellow card that meant he would be suspended if England qualified for the final. Overwhelmed by the situation, he burst into tears as grown men in pubs all over England sniffed

7

He didn't know it then*, but his only World Cup was over. His life as the most famous footballer on the planet, however, had just begun.

He went back to Spurs, helping them to sixth in the league and scoring 19 goals, including a memorable free-kick in the 1991 FA Cup semi-final against Arsenal. But, minutes into the final at Wembley, and hopelessly over-excited, he went over the top on Nottingham Forest's Gary Charles, ruptured his cruciate ligaments and ended up watching Spurs win the FA Cup from his hospital bed. He was out for a year. He had just signed to Lazio for £8.5 million…

Months later, and Gazza was fit and ready to meet Lazio's fans, who welcomed him with a banner that read 'Gazza's Boys are here. Shag women and drink beer.'

Touched, he fell in love with Italy on the spot, but one Newcastle nightclub altercation later and his knee was busted again. Do not pass go, do not collect a £2 million signing-on fee.

Eventually, Gascoigne made his Italian debut in September 1992 (for a reduced fee of £5.5 million) and stayed for three seasons. It was business as usual: arguing with on/off girlfriend Sheryl Failes, hiding a dead snake in Roberto DiMatteo's pocket, punching an Italian reporter in the groin, belching into a live TV microphone and – *la pièce de résistance* – insulting Lazio owner Signor Cragnotti. 'I went

and claimed they had colds, while mums everywhere wanted to give him a cuddle.

As the camera focused upon the fragile and suddenly bereft midfield prodigy, Gary Lineker (cf p42) drifted into shot and indicated to the bench that something was amiss.

'Gazzamania' was born.

He dug deep, but the winner never came. As the players assembled in the centre circle for penalties, Bobby

Robson put his arm around his star player, who mumbled tearfully, 'I'm sorry.'

'Don't worry, son,' replied Robson. 'You've been absolutely magnificent. You've got your whole life ahead of you. This is your first…'

When Chris Waddle ballooned his penalty, Gazza sunk to his knees in despair. After hugging his team-mates, he walked to the England fans, kissed his shirt, turned, and walked away.

Paul GASCOIGNE

7

> 'I'm very pleased for Paul, but it's like watching your mother-in-law drive off a cliff in your new car.'

Spurs manager Terry Venables reflects upon Gazza joining Lazio.

up to him and said: "*Tua figla, grande tette.*" Your daughter, big tits.'

Despite winning the adoration of Lazio's fans, he scored just six goals in 46 starts, bought some ludicrous hair extensions, broke his leg in a training match and struggled with his weight.

So, it was *arrivederci* Lazio and och-aye Walter Smith's Rangers, signing for £4.3 million in July 1995. He made an immediate impact by running the length of the pitch and scoring a sublime goal. It was one of many emotional highs, but there were plenty of lows and Gascoigne fell into the habit of having a swig of brandy 15 minutes before a match.

Success at Glasgow Rangers earned him an England recall for Euro 96. Yet again, he made the tabloids – and yet again redeemed himself in spectacular style. This time it was against Scotland, chipping the ball over Colin Hendry with his left, before volleying it into the net with his right (see picture p170).

Without doubt one of the greatest England goals – and the celebration, a reference to his night on the razz in the 'Dentist's Chair' in Hong Kong, was

also pretty impressive. As the *Mirror* so delicately put it the next day: 'Gazza is no longer a fat, drunken imbecile. He is, in fact, a football genius.'

Despite the 'football genius' increasingly developing the shape of an average Sunday league pub team player, he signed for Middlesbrough in 1998 and helped them gain promotion to the Premier League. Then, in 2000, he rejoined Walter Smith at Everton but soon ended up at Burnley on loan.

Unprepared to face the end of a glittering career, Gascoigne pitched up as player/manager of Chinese no-hopers Gansu Tianma. It was a lonely period punctuated by depression and booze-fuelled blackouts. Eventually, he left for rehab in the States and never returned to China.

The offers and wage cheques dried up. In 2004, he briefly referred to himself as 'G8' (a combination of his initial and shirt number). 'G8 is right for us now,' he rambled. 'It sounds a bit like great. Paul's not right for us because it's too closely linked with the past.'

Despite being told to 'Give up drinking or you will die' by Venables, his futile attempts to escape the past continued. In August 2008, he briefly joined Iron Maiden's European tour,

arriving in Budapest wearing a pink shirt and trilby, struggling – with the help of a minder – to connect the flame of his lighter to the tip of the Embassy Regal in his mouth.

If this was how Gazza looked after £100,000 worth of rehab (paid for by friends), things did not look promising.

During 2008 he was sectioned three times under the Mental Health Act, and in 2010 pitched up wearing a dressing gown at the scene of murderer Raoul Moat's last stand. He claimed 'Moaty' was a mate, and had thoughtfully brought a fishing rod, a whole chicken and some cans of lager. It was a sad confirmation of what some had suspected since the death of his young friend three decades earlier – Gazza could love anyone but himself. TOM BAILEY

 AD NAUSEAM
His most memorable performance, of many endorsements, was the Walkers Crisps advert for 'Salt and Lineker' crisps. He tries to steal one from Lineker's pack and gets his hand crushed. He then cries. Geddit?

🔥 **HELL RAISING** 10   🏅 **SPORTING ACHIEVEMENTS** 7

BEFORE HE WAS FAMOUS
One of young Gascoigne's favourite scams was to return empty beer bottles to the pub and claim the deposit... before sneaking round the back, nicking the same bottles and returning them again. Repeat until thumped.

 THE MOMENT HE BECAME A LEGEND
That night in Turin when Gazza's tears changed the way so many people thought about football.

Ian BOTHAM

BORN **24 NOVEMBER 1955**

'Excuse me Sir, but you are not allowed to smoke indoors' is something they did not say in 1981. Particularly after 149 not out against the Australians.

Ian BOTHAM

The swashbuckling all-rounder who destroyed all-comers on the field, and partied hard off it. *Boy's Own* meets *Playboy*.

'Who writes your scripts?' asked Graham Gooch.

Ian Botham had just become the all-time leading wicket-taker in Test cricket, some feat in itself. But, in true Botham style, he had done it the unorthodox way.

He had been banned from the game, after admitting smoking marijuana, when just one wicket short of Dennis Lillee's record of 355, and some questioned whether he'd ever play for England again. He did so, against New Zealand, but as he trundled in to bowl, he looked a shadow – albeit a burly shadow – of the man who had terrorised batsmen for the last 15 years.

Surely he was no longer a Test cricketer. And then, as so often when Botham was around, an odd thing happened. Experienced Kiwi opener Bruce Edgar edged Botham's first ball into the hands of Gooch. Record equalled. Twelve balls later, Jeff Crowe fell LBW. Record broken.

Botham was perhaps the greatest all-rounder who ever lived. There will be plenty who argue that Garfield Sobers might claim that crown, but Botham was, for most of his career, playing in a poor England side. Much of what England achieved in that period was down to him. Unlike many all-rounders, there was little to choose between his ability with the bat and the ball.

A technically superb batsman, he could quite easily have been an opener, were it not for the enormous power he wielded coming in the middle order, mostly at No. 5 or 6. On his day – and on one very famous day in particular – he not only took the attack to the bowlers, he destroyed them. His record of 80 sixes in a season (1985) is unlikely ever to be beaten.

'Don't tell Kath'

The title of Botham's autobiography, referring to the long-suffering Mrs Botham.

With the ball, he was fast enough to open the bowling for England. A very canny swing bowler, he was a master at running through the lower order – Botham had a knack of working out a batsman's weakness immediately and exploiting it ruthlessly. And in the field, he was a remarkable slip catcher. Standing with hands on knees until after the ball had left the bat – almost impossible for mere mortals – he rarely put anything on the floor.

He was the perfect cricketer rolled into one. And yet, and yet.

Botham's career was mired in controversy to such an extent that it certainly seemed to affect his performance. In some cases it

enhanced it. In others it stopped him playing altogether.

By the age of 24, in 1980, he was England captain, a seemingly unstoppable force in the game who could do no wrong. In his 25 Tests until then he had taken five wickets in an innings 14 times and scored six centuries. But as England struggled against the formidable West Indies team, so too – for the first time in his life – did Botham. Looking distinctly out of shape and with his form in a mess, he was the victim of a concerted newspaper campaign to strip him of his captaincy, maybe even of his place in the team.

In the first two Tests of 1981 against Australia, Botham was captain. He scored a total of 34 runs in those four innings, including a pair at Lord's, and took a modest six wickets.

Eventually, the selectors took note and removed him from the captaincy with England 1-0 down in the series, replacing him with the experienced Mike Brearley, but they took a chance by keeping the out-of-form Botham in the team. And so began the greatest story ever told in English cricket. The series is now known simply as 'Botham's Ashes'.

Much has been written about the third Test, at Headingley. Certainly Bob Willis does not get the credit he deserves for a remarkable spell of sustained quick bowling (8-43) that dismissed Australia for 111 in the last innings to give England victory by 18 runs.

But it was Botham who swaggered in when England were about to switch off the life support machine. Indeed, so extraordinary was his performance

6

England react to another wicket during 'Botham's Ashes' with the restrained dignity you might expect.

Ian BOTHAM

that some actually blamed him for England's lack of success in later years, arguing that players felt they could win games through inspiration rather than perspiration. And only I.T.Botham could manage that.

His knock in the second innings gets most of the attention, and rightly so. But it's largely forgotten now that he took six wickets in the Australian first innings, and when England replied – slumping to 174 all out – it was only Botham's 50 that prevented abject humiliation. Australia enforced the follow-on and simply continued where they left off. By the time Botham came in, England were 105-5, still more than 120 behind.

You might argue the Aussies had switched off (though is that in their nature?). But Botham produced an innings of such majestic brutality that he dragged England back into the game. What made it more remarkable was that he was running out of partners. Geoff Boycott (cf p136-8) soon departed and was followed by wicket-keeper Bob Taylor. England were 135-7 by then and it was odds-on that Australia would win by an innings.

Somehow, Botham inspired Graham Dilley to give the performance of his life (a brave 56) and then nurse Chris Old along to a valuable 29. At the other end Botham, who wasn't wearing a helmet against the fearsome Dennis Lillee, was hooking, swatting, driving and cutting his way to 149 not out from 148 balls. By the time Willis was out, England had a lead of 129 and the rest is history.

Inspired, Botham owned the rest of the summer. At Edgbaston in the next Test, Australia were chasing just 150 in the fourth innings to win. Botham took 5-11, including one spell of five wickets for one run, to give England victory by 29 runs (see picture p175).

By now Australia were in a daze and the teams headed to Old Trafford. In the first innings, Botham went for a golden duck, but having taken 3-28 to help dismiss the Aussies for 130, he strode to the crease once again. His innings of 118 was, if anything, better than the 149 at Headingley – devastating yet chanceless, including 13 fours and six sixes.

The final Test of the series may have ended in a draw, but Botham still took ten wickets in the match. In the

space of four games he was a national hero. Inevitably, he was BBC Sports Personality of the Year.

His career afterwards may never have hit the same heights, but this was an era utterly dominated by the West Indies – the only team against which Botham never managed a century. Even so, his eventual Test record of 5,200 runs at 33.54 and 383 wickets at 28.40 remains a thing of beauty.

Off the pitch, his dabbling with drugs and enthusiastic partying made him constant fodder for the tabloids, and he fell out with fellow players and selectors – who he once labelled 'gin-slinging dodderers' – often.

He retired from cricket in 1993 after playing a couple of seasons for Durham and has gone on to raise millions of pounds for charity with a series of extreme charity walks for Leukaemia and Lymphoma Research. He has become one of the more thoughtful commentators on the game he bestrode, and was knighted in 2007.

SIMON CANEY

 AD NAUSEAM
'A herbaceous, minty Cabernet complemented by cedary oak'
That, apparently, was what you got in a bottle of Botham wine, launched in 2003. 'Anyone who knows me knows I'm a wine man,' he said.

BEFORE HE WAS FAMOUS
Botham was always destined to be a sportsman. Cricket was clearly his sport, but he was also offered terms by Crystal Palace (and later played professional football for Scunthorpe).

 ## THE MOMENT HE BECAME A LEGEND
When Botham went out to bat at Headingley in 1981, England were following on and 105-5 – heading for humiliating defeat. With the words 'Right, let's have a bit of fun,' Botham took the attack to the Aussies, smashing 149 not out and setting up a 500/1 win.

 HELL RAISING 10

 **SPORTING ACHIEVEMENTS** 9

Bill SHANKLY

BORN **2 SEPTEMBER 1913** DIED **29 SEPTEMBER 1981**

As he once said, 'If you're not sure what to do with the ball, just pop it in the net and we'll discuss your options afterwards.'

Bill SHANKLY

The football-crazy, eminently quotable Scot from Glenbuck who turned Liverpool FC into a hugely successful club.

Bill Shankly walked down the Wembley tunnel into the dressing rooms, and sat down for a cup of tea. He felt very tired. Outside, his Liverpool team, having just outplayed Newcastle in the 1974 FA Cup final, were parading the trophy around the stadium in front of their adoring fans, but Shanks had left them to it.

At the age of 60, after 40 years in the professional game, he had every right to feel exhausted and he made a decision that was to shake the game's foundations.

Kevin Keegan revealed in his *Shoot!* column that summer: 'I stepped off the plane at Manchester after a holiday in Spain and an agitated stranger dashed over to grab me by the arm. "Kev, have you heard? Bill Shankly has resigned!" I stopped in my tracks, my hand luggage containing family presents falling to the tarmac. I was stunned. When I arrived in Liverpool it was like visiting a city in mourning, I even saw people crying.'

The red half of Merseyside was in shock. What would they do without the man who had rebuilt Liverpool FC and turned them into the best side in the country? He had long since passed legend status, moved beyond sainthood and was fast becoming a religious icon. There were those who believed that Shanks could, if he wanted to, walk across the Mersey.

Gordon Milne, inside-right for Liverpool in the 1960s, revealed a glimpse of the boyish enthusiasm for the game that Bill Shankly never lost – and also the passion he shared with the followers of his beloved Reds. 'We'd played at Brighton and come back on the train to Euston to get the train to Liverpool,' Milne explained. 'It was about seven o'clock at night, there were a lot of Liverpool fans around and they'd found a deserted bit of platform to get an eight-a-side game going. Shanks joined in and there he was, tearing up and down with them for twenty minutes. You know, he didn't drink, so he couldn't just sit and have a beer, he couldn't stand still for long. So there he was playing football, and that sort of thing created a very strong bond between him and the fans.'

Shankly was born in the small mining village of Glenbuck, Ayrshire, in 1913. It was a primitive outpost (compared by Shankly to Outer Mongolia in terms of its remoteness) and as far as career choices went you could either go down the pit or starve. But there was a third way… football.

The village never had a population of more than a thousand, but it appears to have been a natural wellspring of football talent. In its half-century of existence, the Glenbuck Cherrypickers club turned out 49 players who went on to become professional footballers, including Bill and all his four older brothers.

Then the pit closed, the club was disbanded and the village was abandoned…

But see that patch of moorland fern,
Down there where sheep graze by
the burn,
Beneath that wilderness concealed,
You'll find a football field.

Go down and walk upon that land
For that was once a hallowed stand,
Out here they shaped the people's game,
A field of dreams, a place of fame.

They crawled in darkness underground
Until they heard the whistle sound,
Then left the danger and the dark
To run in sunlight on that park.

They played with style, they beat the rest,
Those Cherrypickers were the best,
Wealthy clubs came for the men
Who had the magic of the Glen.

Extract from *Remember Glenbuck* by Don Gillespie.

Shankly was swallowed by the black hole, working in the mine for two years, but he remained confident that he would make his living as a footballer and bided his time. Just after the pit closure in 1932, he left Scotland and the dole behind for Carlisle United, swiftly establishing himself in the first team – and after just 16 games he was snapped up by Preston North End for £500.

A right-half with endless reserves of energy, Shankly played a vital role in the Preston side that gained promotion to Division One in 1934, and lifted the

FA Cup in 1938. He also pulled on the navy blue shirt of Scotland for the first time in the same year but was then robbed of seven years of his playing career, and who knows how many caps, by the Second World War.

Shankly's understudy at that time at Preston was George Summerbee, father of Mike. They were rivals for the affection of the same girl, but it was the latter who won the race after Dulcie complained that Shankly was: 'So boring. He couldn't talk about anything else, only fitba' as he called it.'

as a professional footballer at Huddersfield, signing up the young Scot in February 1957. Then, in December 1959, he went to Anfield for a job interview – and neither the club nor the man would ever look back.

Having won the first post-war league title in 1947, Liverpool had gone into decline and were a struggling Second Division outfit when Shankly arrived. Anfield and the Melwood training ground were in poor shape.

Shankly and his backroom staff spent the first day of the new job

the training-ground staple. Ron Yeats and Ian St John were bought and Liverpool twice finished third, one place away from promotion.

Then, in April 1962, they won the Division Two title at a canter and, after seven years in the Second Division, the red half of the city rejoiced at returning to the top flight.

And if they were happy then, two years later they were ecstatic as the Reds beat Arsenal 5-0 at Anfield to seal the League Championship. Lawrence, Moran, Byrne, Milne, Yeats, Stevenson,

'It's fantastic. You look down at your dark blue shirt, and the wee lion looks up at you and says "Get out after those English bastards!"'

Shankly tended to play down his Scottish origins.

During the war, he served in the RAF and was a decent amateur boxer; he also helped Preston to a wartime double.

Shanks played for a couple of seasons when the league reconvened in 1946, but at 35 he realised his time was over when the club let him go and so he started the process of becoming a manager. However, even at 20, he had been volunteering to help set up a youth policy at Preston – it was clear to all who played with him that he knew his future lay in that direction.

He cut his teeth at various lower league northern clubs for a decade: Carlisle, Grimsby, Workington and Huddersfield, but was constantly frustrated by blinkered chairmen and sparse budgets. It did not stop him, however, from giving a teenage Denis Law (cf p88-9) his first opportunity

picking the stones and broken glass off the training pitches. For someone who proudly boasted he could shovel 20 tons of coal in a day it can't have been a strain.

Slowly but surely, things began to happen. The iron grip on the budget was gradually loosened. Twenty-four players were released from an overstocked squad – five-a-side games that encouraged swift passing became

Callaghan, Hunt, St John, Arrowsmith and Thompson – 'The Team That Shanks Built' – had conquered the summit of English football.

The following season Liverpool won the FA Cup for the first time ever, beating Leeds 2-1 at Wembley, but were robbed of a place in the European Cup final by some outrageous refereeing decisions in the away leg of the semi-final at Inter Milan.

BEFORE HE WAS FAMOUS
An 18-year-old Shankly would cycle 12 miles across Ayrshire to play for Cronberry Eglinton.

 THE MOMENT HE BECAME A LEGEND
Winning the league title in his fourth full season in charge at Anfield two years after gaining promotion.

Bill SHANKLY

Shankly stands on a deserted Kop. Alone but never alone in his place of worship.

A year on, Liverpool won the league title again with much the same side as two years before (with Lawler and Smith replacing Moran and Arrowsmith), confirming Shankly's status as a truly great manager. Through these heady days, however, Shanks' feet never left the ground. Although the village was no longer there, the man was still firmly rooted in Glenbuck.

Shankly's philosophy was of a grass-roots socialism, experienced in a close-knit and deprived community: 'The socialism I believe in isn't really politics. It's a way of living. It is humanity. I believe the only way to live and to be truly successful is by collective effort, with everyone working for each other, everyone helping each other and everyone having a share of the rewards at the end of the day.'

It was the same mantra he used to explain his success in the game: 'We devised a system of play which minimised the risk of injuries. The team played in sections of the field, like a relay. We didn't want players running the length of the field, stretching themselves unnecessarily, so our back men played in one area, and then passed on to the midfield men in their area, and so on to the front men. While there was always room for individuals within our system, the work was shared out.'

Shankly's press interviews underlined his legend. As football became a staple for mainstream TV, specifically including *Match of the Day* (which was first transmitted in August 1964), his quick-witted quotes, delivered in staccato tommy-gun style, delighted journalists and filled books.

People often recite the 'More important than life and death' quote but this has passed into cliché. This is more of the man: 'Of course I didn't take my wife to see Rochdale as an anniversary present… it was her birthday. Would I have got married in the football season? Anyway, it was Rochdale Reserves.'

This image of neat suits, hands in pockets pose and wisecracks also goes back to his Ayrshire days when young Bill and his father would walk the four miles to the nearest cinema in Muirkirk to see gangster movies starring Jimmy Cagney and Edward G. Robinson.

Shankly also owed his clean-living lifestyle to his father, who was an athlete and fitness enthusiast who never smoked or drank. 'When I go, son, I'm going to be the fittest man ever to die,' he told Emlyn Hughes.

And if Shankly ever made a miscalculation then it was based on his belief that his players were as fit and determined as he was. He thought his players could maintain their peak into their early 30s as he had, but his great side were getting tired, and faced new challenges from both Manchester clubs, Leeds and Arsenal.

There was no real decline – Liverpool never finished outside the top five – but there was no silverware either, for six years. A 1-0 defeat to Watford in the FA Cup in 1970 jolted Shanks into action and he began the painful task of weeding out some of the old guard and seeking younger men to take their place. Lawrence, St John, Hunt and Yeats made way for Clemence, Lloyd, Toshack, Keegan and Heighway.

In 1972-73 this wonderful side regained the League Championship and also claimed the UEFA Cup. Then, in 1974, they beat Newcastle at Wembley and lifted the FA Cup. Shanks had done it again and a new golden age had begun, but it would unfold without its architect. His faithful assistant Bob Paisley (cf p52) took the reins and soon eclipsed the old master as silverware rained down on Anfield for more than a decade.

Unbelievably almost, it was decided that Shanks was casting too long a shadow over the training ground on his frequent visits and he was told not to turn up at Melwood again. He spent the remaining eight years of his life, before a fatal heart attack in 1981, with his family, visiting Everton's training ground, where he was made welcome, and joining in kids' games on the park. GS

 AD NAUSEAM

Not so much an advertisement as an endorsement – of the Labour party. Shankly chose PM Harold Wilson to be the first guest on his Radio City chat show in 1975.

HELL RAISING 1   **SPORTING ACHIEVEMENTS** 9

Sebastian COE

BORN **29 SEPTEMBER 1956**

and Steve OVETT

BORN **9 OCTOBER 1955**

'Tough of the Track' versus 'Lord Snooty' in running shoes…?

Chariots of Fire, Hugh Hudson's 1981 classic film, reached back in history to the 1924 Olympic Games for its dramatic storyline of Eric Liddell running for the glory of God and Harold Abrahams bristling against anti-Semitism – though inspiration could equally have been taken from more contemporary events at the 1980 Moscow Olympics, as Sebastian Coe and Steve Ovett played out their fierce rivalry in front of a global audience…

Sebastian Newbold Coe was born in Chiswick, West London, in 1956, into a comfortable middle-class family – not quite the silver spoon heritage of popular perception, which seems to be based on little more than his sharing a Christian name with a *Brideshead Revisited* toff.

In fact Seb's father, Peter Coe, was born in Stepney in London's East End and took a further setback in life when he was jailed in Spain during the Second World War after jumping off a Nazi PoW camp train before making his way south from France.

Seb spent his childhood in Stratford-upon-Avon, which suited his RADA-trained mother Angela, until Peter became a production director of a cutlery firm, uprooted the family and moved them to Sheffield in 1967. Coe attended the local state schools and

joined the Hallamshire Harriers at the age of 12.

With enthusiastic coaching from his father, who applied his practical engineering skills to a specially designed fitness regime, it soon became clear that the younger Coe had a genuine talent for running middle-distance races.

The family home in Broomhill conveniently backed on to the university playing fields and Seb quickly became obsessed with athletics. At school, he was aided by a sympathetic teacher who would let him miss RE lessons to build up his miles.

After A-levels he attended Loughborough, the sportiest university in the country, where he juggled Economics and Social History, active participation in the Young Conservatives and running – coming under the wing of athletics director and renowned coach George Gandy.

With his natural talent and the guidance of both his father and Gandy, Coe started to post some serious times for 800m. Then he started to break UK records, and finally world records. In 1979, he set three in 41 days.

Despite having not trained to the usual high standard, due to the demands of his degree course, Coe was

Coe could never be accused of having a Messiah complex.

Sebastian COE and Steve OVETT

invited to the Bislett meeting in Oslo. On 5 July he beat the 800m record with a time of 1:42.33, later saying of the moment his time was announced: 'My world would never be the same again.'

'You find out a lot about yourself through athletics. If you're cut out to be a winner or a failure or a quitter, athletics will bring it out of you. You're always stripping yourself down to the bones of your personality.'

Steve Ovett.

Two weeks later, Coe was back in Norway for the Golden Mile. It was not his optimum distance, but he thought he had a chance. Deciding that he still felt fresh at the final-lap bell, Coe went for it, powered home 20 metres clear and shocked everyone by taking another world record with a time of 3:48.95.

On 15 August at the Weltklasse in Zurich, Coe became the first athlete to hold the 800m, 1,500m and mile world records simultaneously. Again, he ran a superb race and skimmed one-tenth of a second off Filbert Bayi's five-year-old record at 3:32.03.

With the Moscow Olympics a year away, Coe now had to deal with the huge expectation of Great British gold medal hopes... but he wasn't the only one.

Stephen Michael James Ovett was born in Brighton in 1955, the son of market traders. The driving force in Ovett's life was always his mother, Gay, just 16 years his senior. He attended Varndean Grammar School for Boys, where he discovered his talent for running, and joined Brighton & Hove Athletics Club, based at the Withdean Stadium.

Very soon it became clear that Ovett was an outstanding runner. At 13, he missed out on the 800m record for his age group by a tenth of a second. From 15 to 19, he set the record for his age every year (we're guessing that at 14 he was behind the bike sheds). His first big win came in the European Junior 800m in 1973, followed by a clutch of AAA and European titles in the mid- to late-1970s.

Ovett's ability took him to the 1976 Montreal Olympics aged just 20, where he made the semi-finals of the 1,500m and finished a respectable fifth in a fast 800m final. But soon the records tumbled and gold medals were won in the IAAF World Cup in Dusseldorf in 1977 and then in the 1,500m in the European Championships in Prague a year later.

It was in Prague that Ovett and Coe raced against each other for the first time at senior level in the 800m final. Ovett overtook Coe after the last bend with a powerful surge, but then East German Olaf Beyer came steaming past both of them to take gold, though subsequently secret police files were discovered that alleged he was one of many athletes from that country to be taking banned substances.

Dubious Iron Curtain performances aside, it was clear that Britain now had two of the best middle-distance runners in the world, this at a time when athletics enjoyed a far greater profile than today. Ovett won the viewer-voted BBC Sports Personality

BEFORE THEY WERE FAMOUS
Coe's epiphany came at school when he was 'led into a draughty hall to watch flickering black-and-white images of the Mexico games'. He says: 'I knew at that moment, this was what I wanted to do.'
Ovett became obsessed with athletics at school to the extent that he ran in a meet the day his grandfather died.

THE MOMENT THEY BECAME LEGENDS
When they nicked gold at each other's 'specialist' event to come away with the 800m and 1,500m medals at the 1980 Olympic Games.

4

Ovett always enjoyed having Coe behind him – never more than this moment, however.

of the Year in 1978, and was succeeded by Coe in 1979.

In the months leading up to the big showdown in Moscow, the British press had been busy ramping up the rivalry that existed between the two, and exaggerating their differences. Sebastian was the posh one, smooth on and off the track, and because he was accessible and charming with the press – the 'Goodie'.

Ovett was the working-class scrapper, spiky and evasive in interviews, on the rare occasions he granted them. He was arrogant, they said. Aloof. The media 'Baddie', but ultimately the athlete's athlete.

The nation was divided: Beatles or Stones, lager or bitter, Labour or Tory, North or South... you couldn't like both. But we all knew something for sure: GB was coming home from the USSR with middle-distance gold. The absence of many athletes because of an American-inspired boycott, following the Soviet Union's invasion of Afghanistan, did not change that fact.

Both runners eased their way into the 800m final – Ovett grabbing headlines along the way for writing 'ILY' in the air with his finger, a message home to his girlfriend – and on 26 July they lined up on the same track for only the second time at international level.

Ovett, in lane 2, was boxed in, while Coe, in lane 8, stayed out of trouble. East German Detlef Wagenknecht stumbled and almost fell after a dig from Ovett who was living up to his tough image, and he elbowed two more opponents aside as he moved up the field after 52 seconds. He fought his way through and made his move out of

Sebastian COE and Steve OVETT 4

the last bend, accelerating away from the pack, including the favourite Coe, who had left himself too much to do.

Ovett triumphantly crossed the finish line having won 'Coe's Event', while Seb himself looked shell-shocked at having run what he later described as 'the worst tactical race of my life'. His disgusted dad was even more to the point, telling his son: 'You ran like a c***.'

'World records are only borrowed.'

Sebastian Coe.

Coe's silver medal was no consolation, Clive James famously commenting, 'He looked like he had just been handed a turd.'

Coe had a week to get over his disappointment and focus on the 1,500m final. This was 'Ovett's Event' – he had gone three years unbeaten at the distance. But that was soon to change.

On the three-minute mark, Coe was second and Ovett third, poised where he liked to be, ready to strike. But it was Coe who kicked on for an incredible sprint finish, the run of his life. With a look of terror on his face, Coe looked over both shoulders like a gazelle awaiting the jaws of death.

But the bite never came. Coe crossed the line before collapsing to the ground, utterly spent. Ovett, unable to overhaul East German Jürgen Straub, didn't even come second (see picture p183).

Honours were even in Moscow, with both having won each other's event, and despite both claiming there was no animosity between them, there certainly seemed to be, and the media made the most of any opportunity to emphasise it.

Sadly, the sequel, in Los Angeles in 1984, had the drama but not the contest. Both made the 800m final, but Coe was still recovering from lymph gland problems and Ovett was having chronic breathing difficulties in the LA smog. Having scraped through to the final by diving across the finish line, Ovett had been advised by his doctor not to compete – advice he ignored, obviously.

Brazilian Joaquim Cruz, the favourite, won convincingly, with Coe picking up his second 800m Olympic silver and Ovett jogging in a distant last. Ovett was unable to leave the track under his own steam and was stretchered to an ambulance and on to hospital. The doctor had been right.

A week later, Ovett had recovered sufficiently to take his place in the 1,500m final. Joaquim Cruz was out of the picture, crying off with the sniffles, and the scene was set for another Coe v Ovett showdown for the romantics, if not the realists. At the bell, GB held second (Coe), third (Cram) and fourth (Ovett) places behind Spaniard José Manuel Abascal; but Ovett then left the track, bent over, struggling to catch his breath.

Coe powered home for gold with young Steve Cram just behind him for silver. The contrast between Coe and Ovett could not have been starker – Coe doing his lap of honour brandishing a Union Jack and beaming from ear to ear while

a distressed Ovett had an oxygen mask applied as he was loaded on to a stretcher for the second time in a week.

Work has begun on a BBC Films project portraying the Coe v Ovett rivalry, with infinitely more subject matter at hand than the 'Toff v Tough' images that led Ovett – from his Australian home of the past ten years – to refuse to co-operate with the film-makers.

Between them, the pair set 17 world records and won three Olympic golds, two silvers and a bronze. At one point in 1981, the world record for the mile changed hands between them three times in ten days.

There's enough material here to send *Chariots of Fire* running back up the beach. GS

- -

⊘ AD NAUSEAM

As a Conservative MP, peer and Chairman of the Organising Committee for the London Olympics, Sebastian Coe has spent his life adding the weight of his name to many campaigns and causes he considers suitable.

Steve Ovett, an intensely private man, once allowed his image to be used – for a statue erected in 1987 in a Brighton park. It was stolen in 2007 and never replaced.

- -

SEBASTIAN COE

HELL
2 RAISING

SPORTING
9 ACHIEVEMENTS

STEVE OVETT

HELL
4 RAISING

SPORTING
9 ACHIEVEMENTS

Bobby MOORE

BORN 12 APRIL 1941 ▪ DIED **24 FEBRUARY 1993**

Thinks: 'Is that it? The bedside light's bigger than that...'

Bobby MOORE

Barking boy who skippered West Ham to European glory and led England to their World Cup triumph in 1966…

As the decades pass, with decreasing hopes of England ever being able to repeat their solitary World Cup win, those images of 1966 grow ever more ethereal and distant, like a vision of Heaven.

Watching slow-motion footage of the post-match Wembley celebrations is like being absorbed into a stained-glass window, backlit by the setting sun. The shirts, unadorned but for the three lions, are impossibly red. The Jules Rimet trophy glitters like the Holy Grail. And the golden-haired captain Bobby Moore, beatific smile on his face, is held shoulder-high like a religious icon…

Robert Frederick Chelsea Moore was born in Barking in April 1941, a month before the Luftwaffe called off their bombing raids on London. Despite the deprivations of war, he grew into a chubby little lad, who was decent on the football field for Westbury School and South Park Boys, but not outstanding.

He was good enough to skipper Barking Primary Schools and represent Essex, and a scouting report that described him as 'useful' saw him invited along to Upton Park for twice-weekly coaching sessions with West Ham's youth academy.

Hammers' centre-half Malcolm Allison (cf p84-5) – yes, that Malcolm Allison – helped with training, and recognised something in Moore despite his limitations – a lack of pace and aerial prowess.

Allison helped the youngster work on his strengths: an ability to read the game and great awareness as to what was going on around him. He drummed into him Di Stefano's approach: 'Keep asking yourself, if I get the ball now, who will I give it to?' Moore later said of Allison, 'Every house needs a foundation and he gave me mine.'

When he turned 17, in April 1958, Bobby was offered professional terms at £12 per week. West Ham had just been promoted to Division One and he had no hesitation in signing.

Five months later, he was thrown in at the deep end, an injury crisis pushing him into the first team for the visit of Manchester United. Moore had a decent debut in a 3-2 victory, but any pride he felt in pulling on the claret and blue shirt was tempered by a cruel irony.

The previous season Moore's mentor, Malcolm Allison, had contracted tuberculosis. He had to have a lung removed, but trained relentlessly in an effort to return to the side, desperate to play a top flight game for the Hammers. It was a straight choice between Moore and Allison for the place, and manager Ted Fenton chose the younger man.

In his biography, Moore told Jeff Powell: 'For all the money in the world I wanted to play. For all the money in the world I wanted Malcolm to play, because he'd worked like a bastard for this one game in the First Division… I wanted to push the shirt at him and say "Go on Malcolm, it's yours. Have your game."'

Allison never got his First Division game. Bobby got four more that season and 12 in 1959-60. By the start of the 1960-61 season, aged 19, he was worthy of a permanent place in the first XI, a place he would keep for 14 seasons.

'Bobby Moore was the best defender in the history of the game.'

Franz Beckenbauer.

When Ron Greenwood arrived at Upton Park in 1961, he was already familiar with Moore, having called him up to the England Under-23 side. He'd seen enough to know Moore was worth building a side around and, despite his tender years, he made him captain.

Moore quickly progressed to the full England side, a late addition to the squad that travelled to Chile for the 1962 World Cup finals, and impressed enough in a warm-up game against Peru to keep his place through the tournament. By the time he earned his 12th cap in 1963, Moore was England's youngest-ever captain, in place of injured regular skipper Jimmy Armfield.

In 1964, Ron Greenwood's side landed the club's first-ever major

3

honour. A heroic 3-1 win in the semi-final against Manchester United on a Hillsborough mud-bath earned Moore and his team a date with Preston North End at Wembley. In a thrilling final, the Hammers twice came from behind to snatch a 3-2 victory with a 90th minute Ronnie Boyce headed goal.

A year after the Cup final triumph, West Ham returned to Wembley for the European Cup-Winners' Cup final, and one of the club's finest-ever performances saw them defeat 1860 Munich 2-0.

It seemed to the world that Bobby Moore had it all. Winners' medals with West Ham, captain of both club and country with the World Cup approaching, and Tina, his lovely young wife... But the world didn't know all the facts.

In the year between those Wembley appearances, there was a shadow over Bobby's seemingly perfect life. In November 1964 Tina insisted that her husband see a doctor about a persistent pain in his groin. Testicular cancer was instantly diagnosed and a testicle removed. In shock, the 23-year-old Moore went home to his wife, they sat on the floor in front of *Top of the Pops* and wept.

In those stoic times, they kept a stiff upper lip and shared the news with no one. After radiotherapy treatment the cancer appeared to have gone, but not the feeling that the Sword of Damocles was hanging over his head.

One way or another, it was fortunate that Moore appeared in the 1966 World Cup final tournament at all. Unable to agree a new contract with West Ham, and with one eye

'Can't a fella take his missus for a romantic stroll in the park while she's wearing nothing more than a football shirt and thigh-high boots without being disturbed?'

Bobby MOORE

Monday at school: 'So a half-naked Bobby Moore lifted up the FA Cup just for you as you looked inside the West Ham dressing room at Wembley? Yeah, of course he did.'

on a move to local rivals Tottenham Hotspur, Moore allowed his contract to expire.

As an unregistered player, he was not eligible to play in the World Cup finals. Greenwood was summoned to the team hotel on the eve of the tournament and Alf Ramsey (cf p104-05) ordered the two parties to thrash out a compromise.

Ramsey's side, after a cautious 0-0 opener v Uruguay, negotiated the Group stage with 2-0 victories over Mexico and France. Argentina were beaten 1-0 in an ill-tempered quarter-final, and Portugal offered a stern test in the semi. But two goals from Bobby Charlton (cf p118-20) ensured the hosts a World Cup final fixture against West Germany.

With Moore's West Ham team-mates, Geoff Hurst (cf p92-3) and Martin Peters, in the side there was a distinct Upton Park influence. The Germans took an early lead, but Moore's quick thinking soon led to an equaliser. After being fouled, Moore leapt to his feet and launched a quick free-kick upfield for Hurst to head home. It was a move straight off the West Ham training ground.

England took a 78th minute lead when a Hurst shot was blocked and Peters seized on the rebound, but the Germans' 89th minute equaliser took the game into extra time. Hurst's two goals, one controversial, one unstoppable, completed the 4-2 victory and Bobby led his triumphant team up the steps.

Thinking one step ahead, as usual, Moore wiped his muddy hands on the Royal Box's velvet drapes before shaking the white-gloved hand of the

Queen, who presented him with the Jules Rimet trophy.

This was as good as it got for Moore. His place in the nation's affections was sealed, but neither England nor West Ham could provide him with any more medals. The Hammers didn't live up to their mid-60s promise, becalmed in mid-table for season after season.

England travelled to Mexico for the 1970 World Cup (preposterously, he was falsely accused of stealing a necklace). They had high hopes of defending their world title, but no one could have beaten Brazil that year.

At their meeting in Guadalajara, England produced two moments which have a claim to be the greatest of their type. The 'Greatest Save', which saw Gordon Banks (cf p72-3) deny Pelé; and the 'Perfect Tackle', which saw Moore pick off the superb Jairzinho with the accuracy and timing of a sniper… and still England lost.

West Germany gained their revenge in the quarter-finals, England squandering a two-goal lead, and Moore and his team-mates flew home, probably not suspecting that England wouldn't make another World Cup until 1982.

In 1973, Moore had a poor game in a World Cup qualifier in Poland and was dropped for the disastrous return game at Wembley. The earth had shifted slightly on its axis. Moore was back in for his 108th, and final, cap in November 1973, a friendly defeat to Italy in which Fabio Capello scored the only goal of the game.

Moore's West Ham career was also at an end, with Fulham buying him for £25,000 in March 1974. Initially frustrated at not being able to join his old mentor Malcolm Allison at Palace, Moore went on to enjoy a four-season Indian Summer to his career at the Craven Cottage retirement-home, alongside team-mates Alan Mullery, Rodney Marsh and George Best (cf p192-6). They even made the FA Cup final in 1975, inevitably playing West Ham.

Moore retired aged 36, after a couple of spells in the States, with the intention of staying in the game. He was to discover that everybody loved Bobby, but no one wanted to employ him.

Bobby and Tina agonised over why it could be that nobody saw him as management material. His CV amounted to a couple of years at Oxford City and an unsuccessful

spell at Southend. Incredibly, neither England nor West Ham ever called upon him for any kind of role.

By the early 1990s, Moore was a commentator on Capital Radio. In February 1993, it was announced that he had colon cancer, news that Bobby had kept to himself for two years. He visited Wembley one more time, to commentate on England v San Marino, and died on 24 February 1993, aged 51.

The shock and grief emanated from Upton Park, where the floral tributes piled up, right across the world…

A 20ft statue was unveiled outside Wembley in 2007, but the last word belongs to Pelé: 'He was my friend as well as the greatest defender I ever played against. The world has lost one of its greatest football players and an honourable gentleman.' GARY SILKE

BEFORE HE WAS FAMOUS
Moore would sit in Cassetarri's Café listening to the 'West Ham Academy' of Allison, John Bond, Noel Cantwell, Frank O'Farrell and Dave Sexton (all successful future managers) discussing the game and soaking up their knowledge over the cuppas and bacon butties.

THE MOMENT HE BECAME A LEGEND
Holding the Jules Rimet trophy aloft at Wembley on 30 July 1966 as England's World Cup-winning captain.

AD NAUSEAM
Mr and Mrs Moore 'Look In At The Local' for a 1960s TV ad on behalf of the pub industry…

'Tina's not the best dart player in the world, but she enjoys a game while she's waiting for me. After a match we often meet our wives in the local: it's a nice friendly place.'

 HELL RAISING 6

SPORTING ACHIEVEMENTS 9

George BEST

BORN **22 MAY 1946** ■ DIED **25 NOVEMBER 2005**

Football and sex. Football and drugs. Football and rock 'n' roll.

'When I first started, I didn't mind the hard men too much because it gave me the chance to rubbish them with my skill. I'd go past them and they'd say, "Do that again and I'll break your f*cking leg." And next time I'd do 'em again and they'd say, "Right, I f*cking warned you." Next time I got the ball I'd stand on it and beckon them to me. I used to be like a bullfighter, taunting them, inviting them to charge me. They rarely got me. I was too quick. At moments like that, with the crowd cheering, I used to get the horn. Honestly, it used to arouse me, excite me…'

Georgie Best was pure rock 'n' roll. He was just 17 when he debuted for the Manchester United first team, a skinny Irish kid with a face like an angel and hair barely over his ears, but he hit the staid and dutiful team game of English football with the same impact of Elvis gyrating on TV in front of apoplectic America and its blushing daughters.

No player before him had ever been fast and free enough to float above team orders, playing the game on another plain, miles above such workaday considerations as tactics, team orders and passing.

Not that Best was a selfish player: on the contrary, he was like a streetfighter in pursuit of the ball, tracking back and tackling hard. But when the swivel-hipped kid was in possession, his magical dribbling control, imagination and acceleration made him practically unstoppable.

The crowd-pleasing nutmeg was his favourite trick, up there with the unerringly accurate 'wall pass' back off a defender's shins.

Manchester United manager Matt Busby (cf p124-6) called Best 'the perfect player', with more ways of beating a man than any other; with strength and courage, two good feet ('sometimes he seemed to have six') and the ability to score a goal out of nothing. Busby used to have fits when Best beat three opponents then lost the ball… 'But then he beat four men and scored the winner. What do you do about that?'

They called him the Fifth Beatle; but that was a cliché that diminishes Best's originality, his genius, and the brightness of the spotlight that fell on him. There were, after all, four Beatles. But, right from the start, George was out on his own. Almost instantly, he was bigger than his team-mates, bigger than Manchester United, as big as the rest of football put together.

As the first modern footballer, it fell on George Best's slender shoulders to invent new ways to deal with the media, which was growing as fast as football in the mid-60s.

Thinking on his feet, he was soon firing back at the massed notebooks a barrage of wonderful aphorisms, ready-made headlines for which he's scarcely ever been given credit. All too often he was viewed grudgingly as an idiot-savant Ringo Starr figure, rather than a wordy working-class hero with attitude, more akin to John Lennon.

'People say I shouldn't be burning the candle at both ends. Maybe they haven't got a big enough candle.'

'If I'd been born ugly, you'd never have heard of Pelé.'

'I spent a lot of money on booze, birds and fast cars. The rest I just squandered.'

Pictures of the fantastically photogenic beatnik youth sold newspapers and magazines, whether

'Would it have been different if I'd been different in temperament and nature? I'm sure it would, but it wouldn't have been such fun. I've had twelve incredible years where I've been right at the top and at the very bottom, and really I've enjoyed every moment of it. I don't think I'd want to change it at all.'

Best puts his life in perspective. After a fashion…

His attempt at a disguise to fool the waiting photographers was not a total success.

George BEST

he was sitting with a beauty-queen bird on the bonnet of his sports car or dancing through the mud around puffing stoppers with big white legs.

Yes, players of the 1950s had flogged Brylcreem for the leather-look hair of the day; but it was Best who had to deal with the first onslaught of modern marketing opportunities.

Best became the wholesome face of Irish sausages and Best crisps and even boiled eggs for breakfast. He floated through TV ads to promote Fore grooming aids, girls with ironed hair going weak at the knees. He put his name to Umbro football boots, became co-owner of two Manchester boutiques and a nightclub, the first footballer with the avowed intention of becoming a millionaire by the age of 30.

As football's first crossover superstar, perhaps unsurprisingly Best was an early adopter of the dreaded agent – an ex-table tennis hall baron who arranged for his model youth to appear in lilac slacks in the Great Universal Stores home-shopping catalogue. Before Best, only football teams had fan clubs; but George had 15,000 personally devoted members, attracting over 10,000 letters per week at his peak.

Best was the first footballer to achieve pin-up status not just in the media age, but in the new age of sexual freedom. He was the first footballer to discuss or evoke images of sex in relation to football. Schoolgirls, dolly birds and married women flung themselves at the sporty playboy, and George understood that it was rude to say no.

As football's first popstar, Best was of course asked to make a record: Busby quickly declined on his behalf.

Instead, he was invited to the *Top of the Pops* studio, where the elfin mod was filmed bopping in his Beatle boots. He later became the first footballer to become the subject of a BBC documentary, *The World of George Best*, whose title song by Don Fardon made him the first player with his own theme tune – 'Belfast Boy'.

You move like a downtown dancer
With your hair hung down like a mane
And your feet playing tricks like
a juggler
As you weave to the sound of
your name…

Cash. Sex. Fame. Fortune. Wit. Attitude. Beauty. Sex and booze and rock 'n' roll.

He may have been a natural football artist, but George just wanted to have fun. He wanted to get loaded. To have a good time. And so it was on day two of George Best's football career that the long process began of pegging back the upstart Irish kid – of cutting him down to size.

There was the opposition, of course, who would do anything to try to put him off his game. There were the finger-wagging referees, who never offered the longhair any protection from the burly cloggers.

Hundreds of times, Best would be carpeted by well-meaning Matt Busby, the man who made this beautiful Babe, but who couldn't constrain him; whose team, in turn, he made complete. There would be bookings and dismissals, mud-slinging FA hearings and meaningless fines. They would hound him, they would attack him and eventually leave Best in a bloody mess.

But still the knockers, the bullies, and the long, grinding victory of Great British *schadenfreude* could only have succeeded on the nod of one man. It would be George Best's own fatal flaw – a nagging lack of self-esteem, a self-destructive willingness to let himself down – that would see the genius slowly dismantled.

Trouble started when Best was left adrift without the close companionship of his newly married best mates, Manchester United's David Sadler and City's Mike Summerbee. 'By the time

BEFORE HE WAS FAMOUS
Signed up for Manchester United at 15, George lasted two days before homesickness carried him back to Belfast. His dad, a shipyard worker, packed him straight back to Manchester.

THE MOMENT HE BECAME A LEGEND
Up against Benfica away in the 1966 European Cup quarter-final, Busby's orders were to play a containing game. Within 12 minutes, Best had scored two – a header and a darting central run beating three players. United went on to win 5-1 and Best came home in a sombrero as El Beatle (see picture p193).

Ron 'Chopper' Harris arrives fashionably late, but not before Best can get his shot away.

I was twenty-five, I felt the team was in decline and alcohol was taking over,' he admitted. 'For three years I was out every night, and gambling became a drug, too.'

Early in his life and career, Best grew bored and frustrated, sensing that he would never fulfil his potential, despite inspiring United to league titles in 1965 and 1967, and becoming European Footballer of the Year in 1968, when they lifted the European Cup.

He always cited his inability to lift Northern Ireland on to the world stage as a personal millstone and yet when his country were just one win from 1970 World Cup qualification, Best staged one of his many no-shows and they fell 2-0 to the USSR.

Relationships with the women he loved were as destructive as those with the hundreds of scalphunters he simply screwed and forgot. In retrospect, many of Best's one-liners have a maudlin tone, tinged with bluster or denial.

'I used to go missing a lot: Miss Canada, Miss United Kingdom, Miss World.'

'In 1969, I gave up women and alcohol. It was the worst twenty minutes of my life.'

And the oft-repeated bell-boy story – Best in bed with a beauty queen, £20,000 cash and a bottle of champagne, the kid tut-tutting: 'Where did it all go wrong?'

Even in 1970, 'Belfast Boy' presaged Best's initial retirement/sacking at 26, picking up on the vibe of an accident waiting to happen as the great crowd-pleaser bowed to the pressure of always having to entertain – and to

George BEST

'He's lost his mind, Sarge. Keeps asking if we know who he is! He's clearly got some kind of amnesia.'

is largely wiped blank, there are, of course, a million photo-ops on file: waxwork Best; Best in sombrero; Best outside mod 'goldfish bowl' home; big, beardie Best and busty barmaid; and, in the video age, Best pissed and sweary on *Wogan*.

Nowadays, to piece together any meaningful image of Best the player, you need to seek out not just the brilliant old chestnuts – round the Benfica keeper to win the European Cup, kicking the ball out of Banks's hands, 'The Lob' against Spurs, the six against Northampton, the diagonal run and shot against Sheffield United, the Earthquakes wonder-goal – but also the ecstatic descriptions he teased out of stuffy contemporary sportswriters. Of course, they were the same writers who were first to voice the fears of all football fans when Best set about extinguishing his own precious spark. DEREK HAMMOND

Georgie, Georgie, they call you the Belfast Boy
Georgie, Georgie, they call you the Belfast Joy
And they say Georgie, Georgie, keep your feet on the ground.

the media circus that would always require one more performance.

Just play the way the ball bounces
And bounce the way the ball plays
Coz you won't have long in the limelight
No you won't have many days...

As the first crossover superstar of the media age, ironically little footage

of Best the footballer now exists. In the 1960s and '70s, only a handful of matches were recorded every week, and for every over-familiar run and shot and goal, there were a dozen others that were truly ethereal, of the moment. Unlike a star of the supposedly 'disposable' pop music industry, little of Best's classic product was destined to be fawned over 40 years after the event.

But while his footballing record

 AD NAUSEAM
'E for B and Georgie Best!' was the chant as Georgie set about flogging 'Eggs for Breakfast' for the Egg Marketing Board.

 HELL
RAISING 10

 **SPORTING**
ACHIEVEMENTS 9

Brian CLOUGH

BORN **21 MARCH 1935** ■ DIED **20 SEPTEMBER 2004**

And in the beginning was the word, and the word was 'Now'. The next three were 'Listen to me…'

Brian CLOUGH

Old Big 'Ead (OBE), goalscoring sensation, working-class hero, working-class anti-hero, icon, iconoclast, national treasure and infamously, the best manager England never had. A rebel with a cause… beautiful football.

ACT ONE: Brian Howard Clough is born as the sixth of nine children in a council house in Middlesbrough in an age of mass unemployment and extreme poverty just one year before the fabled Jarrow March to London.

Despite all that, he claims, 'If anyone should be grateful for their upbringing, for their mam and dad, I'm that person.' An intelligent and inquisitive boy, he fails his 11-plus but is also a gifted footballer. And very cocky. He joins his hometown club. This will be the escape route.

ACT TWO: In 1955 he makes his debut for Second Division Middlesbrough against Barnsley after the intervention of reserve team keeper Peter Taylor, who tells anybody who will listen about his talent – this ability to spot potential will serve both Taylor and Clough for the rest of their careers. Clough is a prolific goalscorer, as direct in front of goal as he is in person. He scores 204 goals in 222 games – an astonishing scoring rate of almost one per game.

He wins just two England caps, both in 1959, against Wales and Sweden. Sunderland, chasing promotion back to the top tier and looking for a man who can find the back of the net with almost

monotonous regularity, come calling two years later and pay a club-record £48,000. Len Ashurst, eventually to become the Sunderland player with the second-most appearances for the Mackems (with four goals to show for 409 appearances), will remember it thus:

'Brian Clough could be a plausible sort, but he had a huge ego and an antagonistic attitude towards those he could not abide. He justified his ego with his reputation as a goalscorer, which he made sure went before him. He was tolerated within the Sunderland dressing-room as he was going to be our bread ticket. The theory was, Clough would score goals and win us matches.'

Ashurst remembers correctly. Clough scores 54 goals in 61 games – an almost disappointing return compared to the one at Ayresome Park, but one that any other striker, including even Jimmy Greaves (cf p66-7), might envy.

Boxing Day 1962. The 'Big Freeze' descends. Sunderland are playing Bury. Ashurst hits a long ball towards Clough. As keeper Chris Harker rushes out, the striker thinks he can make it there first. He can't. They collide.

Clough sustains cruciate ligament damage and, bar three more appearances for Sunderland, at the age of 27, his football career is over. As a player.

ACT THREE: This is the big one. It is improbable enough to be almost impossible. It also requires a change of tense because this is when Brian Clough became a manager at the age of 30 – the youngest in the Football League – and *the* No. 1 talkSPORT post-war British sporting legend and why people will be talking about and quoting him when everybody reading this book, yes, you included, will be pushing up the daisies.

In October 1965 Hartlepools United became the first club to become acquainted with Clough's unique managerial style. Peter Taylor arrived as his assistant. They went to every pub and club in the area to raise money for the club but, inevitably, there was trouble with the board and then a coup that saw the chairman ousted.

With drive, and perhaps even thwarted ambition, urging him forward, Clough (and Taylor) then went to Second Division Derby County a month before *Sgt. Pepper* hit the charts in the summer of 1967. If John Lennon thought the Beatles were 'More popular than Jesus' – and he did – Clough thought he, rather than Lennon, was at least the equal of the 'Son of God'. As he put it many years later, 'The River Trent is lovely, I know because I have walked on it for eighteen years.'

A step up in terms of profile, but a club in need of some tender loving care, Clough turned an ailing provincial club into a genuine First

1

'What chance do you think I've got of winning this again next year?'
Hmmm… better than average.

He was building Derby County and an empire in his own image.

Astute signings such as Roy McFarland and Archie Gemmill (cf p41) arrived and Derby County became Division Two champions in 1969, Division One champions three years later and then European Cup semi-finalists in 1973. And that's Derby County we are talking about. His trademark was signing has-beens and misfits and turning them into world-beaters.

The defeat in the 1973 European Cup semi-final remains (in)famous for his outburst, when the Italian press demanded a reaction to the 3-1 defeat in the first leg. They got this: 'I will not talk to any cheating bastards!'

He had a valid point as indiscriminate bookings had ensured that key players were ineligible for the second leg. Portuguese referee Francisco Lobo reported that he had been offered a bribe by the Italians ahead of the second leg, which he officiated in.

The inevitable fall-out with Longson, and subsequent acceptance of his resignation, prompted the flares be-decked men and women of Derby to take to the streets demanding his reinstatement and the sacking of the board.

Brian Clough had made his mark. His particular brand of acerbic wit and sarcasm endeared him to most who had endured enough of the artificial and clipped tones of Alf Ramsey (cf p104-05) and the rest of the football establishment. In fact, make that 'The Establishment' *in toto*.

He even appeared on *Parkinson* – the most popular Saturday night chat

Division powerhouse. On the way, of course, he antagonised the board – and his relationship with chairman Sam Longson was fractious, to say the least. Clough broke the club transfer record twice (signing Terry Hennessey for £100,000 and then Colin Todd for £175,000), but smashed the record attendance at the Baseball Ground (41,826 against Spurs in September 1969).

It is often said, with apocryphal uncertainty, that he had two tea ladies sacked after a poor defeat at home. Apparently, he heard them laughing about an inconsequential football-unrelated matter. The club secretary and a groundsman definitely went.

Brian CLOUGH

The referee, his Middlesbrough team-mates, the opposing players and crowd wait for Clough to finish his shooting practice.
But then he did average almost a goal a game between 1955 and 1961.

show of the time – to advance his case. Clough was, in almost every regard, miles ahead of his time. A casual conversation in a club car park with a local journalist might be how other managers operated, Clough commanded prime-time national television coverage. It was 'The Big Time'. And everybody knew it. Especially Brian Clough.

He fell out with everyone on the way but cared not a jot. And then there was Brighton and Hove Albion and Leeds (the details of his 44 days at the latter have been detailed, controversially his family and others might say, in the film and book *The Damned United*). He was energetically dispatched from Elland Road in 1974 after it became apparent that the players under his command resented his presence.

This was chiefly because he had been their most vocal critic when the manager he replaced, Don Revie (a

man born less than half a mile from Clough), had led Leeds to promotion, two League Championships, the FA Cup and a couple of Inter-Cities Fairs Cups between 1965 and 1974.

On his first day in charge, Clough is reported to have told the players 'You can all throw your medals in the bin because they were not won fairly.' Although there may also have been a couple of expletives in there, you can almost hear him say it. Player pressure and one win in six games for the reigning champions ensured that Clough's position was untenable. He resigned.

After a period outside the day-to-day managing of a football club, the man the tabloids were now calling 'Cloughie' accepted the invitation to rescue another ailing East Midlands team – Second Division Nottingham Forest. It was winter 1975.

Eighteen months later he coaxed Peter Taylor (who had stayed on at

BEFORE HE WAS FAMOUS
Clough worked at ICI and then undertook his National Service in the RAF between 1953 and 1955 but, unbelievably, never made the national RAF team. '[The RAF] couldn't see the talent under their noses, much like the FA in later years,' he noted.

THE MOMENT HE BECAME A LEGEND
When Muhammad Ali objected to Clough's fast mouth: 'There's some fella in London, England, named Brian Clough, he's a soccer player or something... I heard all the way in Indonesia that this fella talks too much, they say he's another Muhammad Ali, there's only one Muhammad Ali. I'm the talker... now, Clough, I've had enough. Stop it!'

'Well, are you going to stop it?' asked *Big Match* presenter Brian Moore.

'No, I'm going to fight him,' replied Clough.

That's when you know you've made it. When the best boxer the world has ever seen takes time out to chastise you for stealing his thunder.

Brian CLOUGH

Brighton after Clough left for Leeds) to join him and they re-coined their familiar currency – elevating from the reserves, bringing in good young players and others who could be trusted before adding to the mix with veterans and journeymen. And then getting the best out of the entire ensemble. Taylor scouted, Clough sculpted.

Peter Shilton, Gemmill (once more), Viv Anderson and Kenny Burns among many others were all beneficiaries. In a counter-intuitive move, and he had been a TV pundit for the World Cup in 1974, he scaled down his media presence. He had a feeling that this might be his last chance to achieve some kind of destiny – to finally eclipse Don Revie, among other ambitions. Forest won the title, League Cup and Charity Shield in 1978.

Trevor Francis arrived at the club in February 1979 – arguably, the first £1 million player in British history (Clough said the fee was £999,999 plus taxes) and, almost certainly, the first to be part of a press conference accompanied by the man who had bought him with racquet in hand and dressed ready for a game of squash.

Francis subsequently scored the winner in the 1979 European Cup final against Malmo in Munich, a diving header from a John Robertson cross. As Clough shrugged, 'It wasn't a great game, but they were a boring team, Malmo. In fact the Swedes are quite a boring nation. But we still won, so who cares?'

They didn't have to qualify for the European Cup the next year. But, with a typical Cloughian flourish, won it anyway – 1-0 against Hamburg and

Kevin Keegan (cf p115-17). So, that amounts to back-to-back European Cups in an era when winning the European Cup was much harder than claiming the Champions League might be now. There were no group stages then. No margin for error.

In his 18 years at the club he won 11 trophies, with a peculiar predilection for the League Cup in its various guises. Only the FA Cup eluded him.

Clough brought results quicker to clubs than any other manager in the game – his time at Leeds can be considered to be a blip but, then, he hardly had a chance to show what he could do. Alex Ferguson (cf p110-11) took more than 12 years to win the European Cup at Manchester United, Clough took just over four years at Forest. As he put it himself, 'They say that Rome wasn't built in a day, [but] I wasn't on that particular job.'

How did he do it? Well, he did it by being Brian Clough. That's how he did it. By being Brian [and apologies for the industrial language about to be employed] 'Fucking' [Sorry, again] Clough. It was a phrase he employed on the many occasions he was asked, 'Who the fuck do you think you are?'

Frank Sinatra was his favourite singer and regrets – well, he had a few. This is the one he confessed to: 'Telling the entire world and his dog how good a manager I was. I knew I was the best, but I should have said nowt and kept the pressure off 'cos they'd have worked it out for themselves.'

EPILOGUE: There were concerns about his drinking. And as football entered the Premier League era, the

workload and media pressure grew more intense. As a younger man, he would have laughed it off, thrived on it even, but his age and the battle with the bottle took its toll and he resigned at Forest in 1993.

Forest were at the wrong end of a relegation season and grown men openly wept at the City Ground. Not because of the relegation but because He (capital 'H' intended) was going and they owed him all the success and entertainment they had enjoyed for 18 years.

Some of them now sit on seats in the Brian Clough Stand. Those that do not will have walked past the statue of him in Nottingham town centre. There are also statues in his home town of Middlesbrough and (fittingly, with Peter Taylor) at Pride Park in Derby.

'I want no epitaphs of profound history and all that type of thing,' he said. 'I contributed – I would hope they would say that, and I would hope somebody liked me.' You were wrong, young man. We loved you. BILL BORROWS

⌀ **AD NAUSEAM**

'I am going to get a hundred per cent out of you, but I won't get a hundred per cent out if you don't think a hundred per cent,' Clough tells a hapless team of lower league losers. He then presents the goalkeeper with a box of Shredded Wheat. As the team run onto the pitch, Peter Shilton appears instead. 'Hey,' says Clough, 'I told you not to eat three. Get off.'

HELL
RAISING 7

SPORTING
ACHIEVEMENTS 10

1 'I wouldn't say I was the best manager in the business. But I was in the top one.'

In a nutshell, Brian Clough on himself.

Britain's Greatest Sporting Legend communes with his flock before leaving the City Ground for the final time as manager.

Contributors

Richard ARROWSMITH (RA)

Freelance sports writer for *MirrorFootball*, the *News of the World* website,*Who Ate All The Pies* and *talkSPORT* magazine.

LEGEND ■ **GEORGE BEST** 2

Dave Cottrell (DC)

Worked on *90 Minutes* magazine before editing *Goal* in the 1990s. After a spell as contributing editor at *FourFourTwo*, he edited official programmes for Liverpool FC, several FA Cup finals and England international games.

LEGEND ■ **KENNY DALGLISH** 43

Tom Bailey (TB)

Writer for the *Sunday Mirror*, *Sunday Times*, *Mail on Sunday*, *Men's Health* and *ShortList*. Has interviewed celebrity football fans ranging from Elton John to Noel Gallagher.

LEGEND ■ **ALEX HIGGINS** 20

Tom Ellen (TE)

Staff writer at *talkSPORT* magazine between 2008 and 2010 and contributor to the *talkSPORT Book of World Cup Banter*. He has also written for *Time Out*, *ShortList* and *Viz* comic.

LEGEND ■ **PAUL GASCOIGNE** 7

Bill Borrows (BB)

Writer for newspapers including *Sunday Times*, *Guardian* and *Mail on Sunday*. Contributed columns for the *Sunday Telegraph* and *Daily Mirror*. Contributing sports editor at *Esquire* magazine and author of the bestselling Alex Higgins biography, *The Hurricane*.

LEGEND ■ **MALCOLM ALLISON** 39

Joseph Ganley (JG)

Football writer for a variety of publications including the *Independent*, *United Review*, *Football365* and *Sabotage Times*. Contributed to *The Rough Guide to Cult Football*. Columnist for *United We Stand* fanzine.

LEGEND ■ **GEORGE BEST** 2

Simon Caney (SC)

Editor-in-chief of *Sport* magazine, and previously editor of *Golf Weekly* and *Match* magazines, as well as helping to launch *Zoo* magazine in Australia.

LEGEND ■ **DAVID GOWER** 82

Derek Hammond (DH)

Co-author of *Got, Not Got: The A-Z of Lost Football Culture, Treasures & Pleasures* (Pitch, 2011). He has written for the *NME*, *Maxim*, *FourFourTwo*, BBC Radio, talkSPORT, *Time Out* and *MirrorFootball*.

LEGEND ■ **JIMMY GREAVES** 48

Tony Hodson (TH)

Deputy editor of *Sport* magazine since May 2009, formerly chief sub-editor of the same publication since launch in 2006. He has interviewed British, foreign and maybe even future 'Legends', such as Jonny Wilkinson, Fernando Torres, Gareth Bale and Luke Donald.

LEGEND ■ **DESERT ORCHID** 53

Damian Mannion (DM)

Senior writer at talkSPORT, contributor to *Sport* magazine and *Front* magazine. He has interviewed several 'Legends', including Kenny Dalglish, Sir Alex Ferguson, Ryan Giggs, Glenn Hoddle, Phil 'The Power' Taylor and Jonny Wilkinson.

LEGEND ■ **JONNY WILKINSON** 50

Chris Mendes (CM)

Writer for talkSPORT since 2008. He has interviewed, among others, Peter Crouch and Floyd Mayweather, and 'Legends' including Sir Ian Botham, Linford Christie, Sir Henry Cooper, Sir Alex Ferguson and Paul Gascoigne.

LEGEND ■ **BRIAN CLOUGH** 1

Gershon Portnoi (GP)

Author of *The Story of talkSPORT* and *Why Are You So Fat? The talkSPORT Book of Cricket's Best Ever Sledges.* Deputy editor of *ShortList* and has written for *Observer Sport Monthly*, *Nuts* and *F1 Racing*.

LEGEND ■ **PHIL 'THE POWER' TAYLOR** 13

Gary Silke (GS)

Editor of the *The Fox* fanzine and co-author of *Got, Not Got: The A-Z of Lost Football Culture, Treasures & Pleasures* (Pitch, 2011). He has contributed to *FourFourTwo*, *When Saturday Comes* and *MirrorFootball*.

LEGEND ■ **BILL SHANKLY** 5

Jeremy Stubbings (JS)

Freelance writer who has written for MTV and various London travel guides. He writes a football blog and is working on a book about the impact of international players in the English game.

LEGEND ■ **JOHN BARNES** 63

Richard Winton (RW)

Assistant sports editor of the *Herald* in Glasgow, having previously worked as a sportswriter with the *Sunday Herald* and freelance contributor for *FourFourTwo* and PA among others.

LEGEND ■ **KENNY DALGLISH** 43

Appendices

Star signs

Aquarius	13
Pisces	7
Aries	10
Taurus	8
Gemini	7
Cancer	6
Leo	7
Virgo	9
Libra	3
Scorpio	5
Sagittarius	10
Capricorn	8

Arise

Sir Roger **BANNISTER**
Sir Ian **BOTHAM**
Sir Matt **BUSBY**
Sir Bobby **CHARLTON**
Baron Sebastian **COE**, KBE
Sir Henry **COOPER**
Sir Nick **FALDO**
Sir Alex **FERGUSON**
Sir Tom **FINNEY**
Sir Geoff **HURST**
Sir Stanley **MATTHEWS**
Sir Stirling **MOSS**
Dame Mary **PETERS**
Sir Steve **REDGRAVE**
Sir Alf **RAMSEY**
Sir Bobby **ROBSON**
Sir Clive **WOODWARD**

Top XI middle names

1 **Wipper** (Allan **WELLS**)
2 **Morgan Ayodélé** (Daley **THOMPSON**)
3 **Claudius** (Lennox **LEWIS**)
4 **Newbold** (Sebastian **COE**)
5 **Chelsea** (Bobby **MOORE**)
6 **Antonio** (Ronnie **O'SULLIVAN**)
7 **Ivon** (David **GOWER**)
8 **Craufurd** (Stirling **MOSS**)
9 **Ambrose** (Billy **WRIGHT**)
10 **Sewards** (Fred **TRUEMAN**)
11 **Chapman** (Alex **FERGUSON**)

Sub **Winston** (Gary **LINEKER**)

Home internationals

The Legends by place of birth*

England	74
Scotland	13
Wales	6
Northern Ireland	6

* Andrew Strauss was born in South Africa represented England; Linford Christie and John Barnes were born in Jamaica and did the same (Christie also competed for Great Britain at international level); while Barry McGuigan was born in the Republic of Ireland but fought for Northern Ireland in the 1978 Commonwealth Games.

Giving up the day job

The majority of post-war Legends were either child prodigies who were spotted early and never knew a life outside sport before they hit the heights or were rescued from a life of crime by their abilities, usually at track and field, on the baize or in the ring. The remainder began their working lives in the real world (either as an apprentice or in a full-time role).

Among the rest of the illustrious list are:

Seven labourers (including Pat Jennings and Geoff Capes); six plasterers/electricians/joiners and plumbers (from Eddie 'The Eagle Edwards' to Kenny Dalglish); six miners (Freddie Trueman to Jock Stein); seven from a university background (J.P.R.Williams to Roger Bannister); six members of the armed forces, including National Service (Nigel Benn to Will Carling); five with administrative jobs (Jayne Torvill and Mary Peters); and three from the world of commerce (Bobb Nudd to Barry Sheene).

More unusually, Tony Jacklin was involved in the steel industry, Joe Calzaghe worked in a cake factory and Christopher Dean was a policeman.

PICTURE CREDITS

The publishers would like to thank the following for providing the photographs included in this book:

Angling Times page 33; Associated Newspapers/Solo Syndication pages 50 and 197; BBC page 20; Colorsport pages 41, 95, 136-7, 157, 170-1, 190, 200-01; Corbis Images page 51; Egmont UK page 57; Getty Images pages 14, 16, 17, 21, 24, 25, 26, 27, 29, 30, 35, 36, 37, 39, 40, 42, 43, 44, 45, 46, 47, 48, 52, 53, 54, 55, 56, 58, 59, 60, 61, 67, 71, 72, 75, 76, 79, 80, 83, 91, 92, 99, 100, 103, 104, 108, 111, 113, 114, 116-7, 120, 121, 126, 128, 131, 132, 138, 139, 140, 143, 145, 146, 149, 150, 152, 155, 161, 162, 165, 166-7, 169, 173, 175, 182-3, 185, 178, 185, 187, 189, 195, 196 and 199; Leo Mason pages 13 and 68; Mirrorpix pages 8, 11, 87, 88, 151, 178 and 193; PA Photos pages 10, 15, 18, 19, 23, 31, 32, 34, 38, 49, 63, 64, 84, 107, 115, 119, 122, 125, 127, 144, 156, 159, 177, and 203; Rex Features page 96; Phil Sheldon Golf Picture Library pages 133 and 134; The World Rugby Museum, Twickenham page 22.

While every effort has been made to trace and acknowledge all the copyright holders, the publishers would like to apologise should there have been any errors or omissions. If notified, the publishers will be pleased to rectify these at the earliest opportunity.